JAMES L. HUTTER
POLITICAL SCIENCE DEPT.
IOWA STATE UNIVERSITY
AMES, IA 50011-1204
jhutter@iastate.edu

The Permanent Campaign
and Its Future

The Permanent Campaign and Its Future

Norman J. Ornstein
Thomas E. Mann
Editors

American Enterprise Institute
and
The Brookings Institution

WASHINGTON, D.C.

2000

Available in the United States from the AEI Press, c/o Publisher Resources Inc., 1224 Heil Quaker Blvd., P.O. Box 7001, La Vergne, TN 37086-7001. To order, call 1-800-937-5557. Distributed outside the United States by arrangement with Eurospan, 3 Henrietta Street, London WC2E 8LU, England.

Library of Congress Cataloging-in-Publication Data

The permanent campaign and its future / Norman J. Ornstein, Thomas E. Mann, editors.
    p. c.
    Includes bibliographical references and index.
    ISBN 0-8447-4133-7 (cloth: alk. paper)—ISBN 0-8447-4134-5
      (pbk.: alk. paper)
      1. Political campaigns—United States. 2. Democracy—United States.
      I. Ornstein, Norman J. II. Mann, Thomas E.

JK2281.P395 2000
324.7N0973—c21

                                         00-058657

ISBN 0-8447-4133-7 (cloth: alk. paper)
ISBN 0-8447-4134-5 (pbk.: alk. paper)

3 5 7 9 10 8 6 4 2

American Enterprise Institute
1150 Seventeenth Street, N.W.
Washington, D.C. 20036

The Brookings Institution
1775 Massachusetts Avenue, N.W.
Washington, D.C. 20036

Printed in the United States of America

Contents

Preface

The "permanent campaign" has become a prominent feature of American politics since the publication of Sidney Blumenthal's book with that name two decades ago, or by some accounts since Pat Caddell coined the term in a transition memo to president-elect Jimmy Carter in 1976. For years it was shorthand in the political community for the use of governing as an instrument to build and sustain popular support. Presidents and members of Congress were seen to exploit the resources and opportunities of their offices, with increasing energy and sophistication, to advance their reelection prospects.

But this conception of the permanent campaign has proven much too limited to capture the growing importance of campaign strategies, tactics, and resources in all aspects of American public life. Candidates for the presidency and Congress now are in a perpetual campaign mode. Political consultants and pollsters occupy prominent staff positions with public officials. Fund-raising trumps all competitors in the struggle for the attention and energy of politicians and their aides. Interest groups launch sophisticated advertising campaigns to shape important public policy debates. Journalists employ campaign metaphors to frame their coverage of governing. The line between campaigning and governing has all but disappeared, with campaigning increasingly dominant.

This volume aims to make sense of this new meaning of the permanent campaign, to understand how and why it has evolved, to weigh its consequences for our ability to govern ourselves effectively, and to consider whether steps might be taken to ameliorate its more damaging effects. In publishing these essays, we seek to make a substantive contribution to understanding a critically important feature of contemporary American politics. The larger effort of which it is a part, however, the Transition to Governing Project, which is generously funded by the Pew Charitable Trusts, aspires to improve the conditions for governing by shaping the way in which campaigns are waged and covered by the press. By raising questions about governance during the 2000 campaign—about transition planning, agenda setting, dealing with Congress, coping with the permanent campaign, building domestic support for foreign policy and political reform—the project hopes to plant seeds that might blossom into genuine improvements in the American way of politics and governing.

As codirectors of the Transition to Governing Project, we would like to offer special thanks to the Pew Charitable Trusts, whose president, Rebecca Rimel, has championed efforts to improve the quality of campaigning and governing. Paul Light, former director of public policy programs at Pew and now director of governmental studies at the Brookings Institution, was instrumental in conceiving and launching the project. Michael Delli Carpini, the current director of public policy programs at Pew, offered his support and wisdom. Elaine Casey, also with Pew, monitored our progress and shepherded us through day-to-day difficulties.

John Fortier, the project administrator, has been absolutely crucial to the successful completion of this volume and to the conduct of the larger effort of which it is a part. The presidents of our respective research organizations, Christopher DeMuth of the American Enterprise Institute and Michael Armacost of Brookings, trumpeted the message of our project to the Washington policy community and provided crucial institutional support. Monty Brown, director of the AEI Press, moved the book swiftly through the editing and production process.

The views expressed in this volume are those of the editors and authors and should not be ascribed to the organizations listed above or to the trustees, officers, or other staff members of the American Enterprise Institute or the Brookings Institution.

Norman J. Ornstein
Resident Scholar
American Enterprise Institute

Thomas E. Mann
Senior Fellow
The Brookings Institution

The Permanent Campaign and Its Future

1

Campaigning and Governing: A Conspectus
Hugh Heclo

This chapter addresses two questions in an attempt to provide a background for the studies that follow. Should anyone really care whether such a thing as "the permanent campaign" exists? Does it make any sense to invent yet another term to characterize our public affairs?

First, some very good reasons, indeed, exist to pay attention to the relationship—and the distinction—between campaigning and governing. If campaigning and governing are merging into one indiscriminate mass, we would do well to ask whether that means that something important is happening. The chapter goes on to consider a series of interrelated features of modern American politics. No one of them may be entirely new, but the pieces fit together to produce a new syndrome. No one planned such an emergent pattern in the general management of our public affairs, yet it now seems to lie at the heart of the way Americans do politics—or more accurately—the way politics is done to Americans at the beginning of the twenty-first century. Second, to speak of a permanent campaign seems as good a way as any other to identify that state of affairs.

Prologue to the Endless Campaign

The term *permanent campaign* was first widely publicized early in the Reagan presidency by Sidney Blumenthal, a journalist who went on to work in the Clinton White House—and then was caught up in the semipermanent campaign to impeach the president. Calling it "the political ideology of our age," Blumenthal described the permanent campaign as a combination of image making and strategic calculation that turns governing into a perpetual campaign and "remakes government into an instrument designed to sustain an elected official's popularity."[1]

Others made similar observations, without using that exact term, before and after 1982. As the 1960 election approached, Samuel Grafton wrote in the *New York Times* about the troubling and growing reliance of politicians on the new public opinion polls. Grafton cited a worrisome curiosity: an "Eastern Senator [who] regularly has the voters in his state quizzed on a list of ten different public issues to find out which they react to most warmly. The Senator then becomes 'hot' about the issues he finds produce a temperature in the voters." Grafton went on to point out the ominous similarity between that kind of so-called leadership and the way television was selecting its shows.[2] Simultaneously, Richard E. Neustadt published his landmark book *Presidential Power*.[3] Although more nuanced than most readers noticed, Neustadt's study upset political science traditionalists, received widespread press attention for having John F. Kennedy's ear, and taught several generations of students the message that "the power of the president is the power to persuade."

Academic attention to the phenomenon of apparently endless campaigning gathered momentum in 1974 with the publication of David Mayhew's influential study, *Congress: The Electoral Connection*. Mayhew argued that the key to Congress lay in understanding congressmen's unremitting drive for reelection.[4] In retrospect, it is interesting that Mayhew's study drew heavy criticism from other congressional experts for interpreting congressional behavior as little more than a collection of 435 individual permanent campaigns for reelection. The 1980s and 1990s brought new accounts of a "plebiscitary presidency" that depended on immediate public approval and a growing tendency for presidents to lead by "going public" with direct appeals to mass opinion.[5] By the end of the twentieth century, accounts by outsiders and insiders had become dismal, indeed. In 1997 British political scientist Anthony King sought to figure out *Why America's Politicians Campaign Too Much and Govern Too Little*.[6] The following year, veteran Washington journalist Elizabeth Drew described *The Corruption of American Politics* in terms of the declining quality of politicians who operate in a debauched money culture of ruthless partisanship. Drew portrayed twenty-five years of change between the two impeachment trials of Nixon and Clinton:

> The full time campaign at the presidential level—the elected President does not stop running, even as Clinton has demonstrated, after he has been reelected to a second term—has now been taken up by senators and representatives. . . . People tend to think that the politicians in Washington are "out of touch" with their constituents, but if they were any more in touch, their ears would never leave the ground. The politicians of today are, on the whole, a highly reactive breed . . . reflect[ing] the momentary mood of the public.[7]

Reflecting on that history, one senses that many elements of the permanent campaign began crystallizing amid the political career of Richard Nixon. The young congressman's election first to the House in 1946 and then to the Senate in 1950 offended many political observers, including old-line Republicans, with his campaigns' ruthless competitiveness and public relations mentality. But that was just the beginning. With Nixon's political resurrection in the latter 1960s, something like harmonic convergence seemed to occur: a sophisticated public relations onslaught to sell "the new Nixon"—unprecedented White House use of public opinion polling, political consultants and comprehensive media strategies, predatory fund-raising, and eventually a campaign against "enemies," whom Nixon had always perceived to be no less endlessly campaigning against him.[8] Nixon the man was only a prodrome, however. Perhaps more than his ideas or personality, it was the contrived quality of Nixon's political appeal, his crafted ingratiating with Middle America that had long set teeth on edge in certain circles. To those who became known as Nixon haters, the man's whole political existence seemed a shabby and conniving permanent campaign.

Those brief observations imply one preliminary, important fact. Developments relevant to the permanent campaign are not limited to a single political feature, institution, or presidential term. Indeed, we may not yet have experienced the full-blown phenomenon. Examining the Clinton presidency, political scientist Charles O. Jones suggests that the campaign style of governing by President Clinton, far from being a culmination, may represent just another step toward the abolition of any distinction between campaigning for election and governing in office. The very idea of a transition period between the two may be obsolete.[9]

A reasonable person may ask, So what if there is nothing to transition between? Should campaigning and governing not be two sides of the same coin and link electoral promises to government performance? Does this talk about a permanent campaign really matter?

Should Campaigning and Governing Differ?

In one sense—a promissory sense—it seems clear that campaigning and governing should have much in common. Any democratic political system is based on the idea that what happens in government is related to people's electoral choices. Elections and their attendant campaigns are not a thing apart from, but integral to, the larger scheme of democratic government, both in guiding responses to the past election and in anticipating reactions to the next. In the long run, without good-faith promise making in elections and promise keeping in government, representative democracy is unaccountable and eventually unsustainable.

Although the two necessarily relate to each other, good reasons exist to think that campaigning and governing ought not to be merged into one category. Common sense tells us that two different terms are necessary, because we know that promise making is not promise keeping, any more than effective courtship is the same thing as well-working marriage. A closer examination of the essential ideas behind campaigning and governing will show why our common-sense distinction makes very good sense in political affairs.

The modern concept of campaigning for public office is only a few centuries old and has a shady lineage at that. Anyone recalling the drunken brawls depicted in eighteenth-century Hogarth prints will appreciate the low view of "vote canvassing" held by Anglo-American elites as representative democracy was being born. For educated gentlemen, overtly seeking popular support was not only unbecoming, it was thoroughly suspect. That disparaging view of what was later called "campaigning" expressed more than gentlemanly snobbery and moral self-righteousness. It dealt with what a classical education revealed to be literally a matter of life and death for any self-governing political community.

To be an educated person of the time was to be steeped in ancient Greek and Roman history and the timeless lessons about government that such history taught. Rhetoric was the classic art of persuasion, but it could be used for good or ill. Here, then, was the vital question posed by history and philosophy from the time of Plato onward: Was persuasion directed to the good of the political community—the operational definition of *virtue*—or to the personal benefit of the speaker who flattered his audience?[10] To that question history offered an answer. The telltale clue for deciding was self-seeking ambition—the restless virus that could spread the fatal disorder and set in motion the death cycle of republican self-government. Ambition inclined the self-seeker to tell the people what they wanted to hear—an act that nourished the people's own selfish inclinations and produced more suitors for more short-sighted public favor. That led to mounting factional strife and loss of common purpose. From there, it was a short step to the eventual resolution of chaos by turning to dictatorship and tyranny.

Educated persons of the day knew that such a death cycle was the fate of all previous republics. If popular self-government was to have any chance of surviving, citizens had a vital obligation to recognize and desire true virtue in would-be leaders and to discern and defeat its counterfeit. On that score the differences between eighteenth-century "democrats" and their conservative opponents were not so great as imagined. The former invoked a natural aristocracy without regard to conditions of wealth, birth, or other accidental circumstances, and the latter defended the existing structure of rule by the rich, the well-born, and the able. For both, however, the point was that notables "stood" for office; they did not "run" after public favor but dutifully allowed their names to be put forward.[11]

Both sides took seriously Francis Bacon's warning that "nothing doth more hurt in a state than that cunning men pass for wise." Thus, on that deeper ground were archrivals Jefferson and Hamilton united in their hostility and contempt for a man like Aaron Burr, who in founding Tammany Hall discerned the future far better than they.

Actual practice, of course, often fell well short of that republican ideal, especially in frontier regions where social hierarchies were flattened and would-be "notables" were the butt of jokes. Seeking election to the first Congress in 1788—having been frozen out of a Senate seat by Patrick Henry's maneuverings—even James Madison had to drop his aloofness and quietly help marshal electoral support. But the fiction of the unambitious man of prominence who stood, rather than the flatterer who ran, was not mere cant, and it was influential for many years in America.[12] Fictions endure because they are signs pointing to what people regard as significant truths, markers not so much of description as of cultural aspiration. For a long time, respectable opinion remained distainful of the idea of a politician's strenuously seeking to persuade people to vote for him. Would someone whose character was not already known and who had to sell himself really be fit for public office? Should one entrust power to someone who courted public favor?

Scruples against campaigning died a lingering death during the nineteenth century, but they did die. The legitimization of campaigning depended heavily on legitimizing the idea of a loyal opposition. That meant understanding that there could be competitors for public office whose attempt to replace existing officeholders did not constitute seditious ambition—much less treason against the state. In the United States, the crucial election for establishing the legitimacy of such opposition and of related campaigning was the 1800 election that pitted Adams and the Federalists against the Jefferson and the Democratic Republicans.[13] From then on, the idea of nominating people to *campaign* for public office went hand in hand with the nineteenth-century growth of mass political parties to organize and profit from that process. Not coincidentally, *campaign* as a political term seems to have originated in nineteenth-century American party circles. Once the idea of opposition had been housebroken, so to speak, it became safe to adopt imagery of warfare and to speak of parties' campaigns or of candidates' campaigning for office. The military analogy was apt. By the French term *campagne,* or open countryside and fields, seventeenth- and eighteenth-century writers on war meant the sustained series of operations an army would conduct when it left winter quarters and "took to the field" during the favorable summer weather. With the onset of winter, armies returned to quarters and waited to resume war during the next campaign season of active operations. So, too, political parties reposed in government office or in opposition; then, at election time, they "fielded" their candidates and undertook a series of engagements across the countryside in a campaign against the enemy. With the election battles decided, the parties returned to winter camp to wait to resume their war with the onset of the next campaign season.

While the designers of the U.S. Constitution had little use for parties and popular electioneering, the campaign analogy was not threatening in the nineteenth century, precisely because popular appeals had to be shaped to the constitutional system the framers had designed. On the one hand, it was a system brimming with elections—eventually hundreds for the federal House of Representatives, dozens in state legislatures for the Senate, and dozens more for the presidency (through the state electors), not to mention the thousands of elections for the state governments of the federal system. On the other hand, no one election or combination of elections was decisive. No election could trump any other as the one true voice of the people. The people, through elections shaped to the multiplex constitutional structure, were held at arm's length. Governing was what had to happen inside the intricately crafted structure of the Constitution. Every part of that structure derived its authority from—and was ultimately dependent on—the people. But the people never all spoke at the same time, and they never had residence in any one part or in the whole of the government quarters. Inside those quarters institutions were separated, and powers were shared, so that there would be a lot going on inside—a rich internal life to governing, a place of mutual accommodation and deliberation—if only because no one could do anything on his own, although each could defend his own turf. The people were out-side—in the open countryside to which their governors would have to come to give account of their stewardship.

The nineteenth century added the idea of parties' doing battle in the public countryside during the campaign season. That had not been part of the framers' vision, but it could not break their consti-tutional grip. Their whole constitutional system for representing people was nonsense unless one presupposed the distinction between campaigning and governing. For that distinction to break down and confound the Founding Fathers, something more than the introduction of mass political parties would have to occur. That "something more" has happened in our own time. But we should not get ahead of ourselves.

The point of this historical sketch is to recover notions of funda-mental purpose, foundations that are easily forgotten, the farther we get from our political roots. Amid all the confusions and intellectual embellishments surrounding any subject, it can be clarifying to ask the childlike (but not childish) question, What is this for? With the growth of democratic politics over the past two hundred years, many theories have been spun out recommending what political campaigns should do. During the nineteenth century they some-times held the vision of a moral crusade for the soul of the nation. Early in the twentieth century, Progressive reformers said a cleaned-up election process should bring forth the voice of informed citizens to produce efficient, good government—a marketplace of ideas where competing claims to truth would be tested. By the middle of the twentieth century, political scientists argued that campaigns should clarify choice and enforce accountability by responsible parties. "Issueless" politics with "me too" parties, it was said, should give way to electoral competition with sharp partisan differences among parties that could be held to account for their programs.

All those are perhaps valuable things for campaigns to do, but they are secondary purposes. The results an activity *might achieve* are not the same as what that activity is for. For example, however much a person might appreciate the tax advantages that come with buying a house, it would be a mistake to confuse tax advantages with the primary purpose for having housing—to provide comfortable and secure shelter. Or to take another example, the reason auto-makers produce cars is not to provide transportation. The purpose of making a car is to sell it. Transportation—having something to take one where he wants to go—is the main purpose for buying and driving a car. As Adam Smith pointed out in *The Wealth of Nations,* it is very beneficial that the purpose of the seller should mesh with the purpose of the buyer. Both parties then get what they want, and the larger society benefits as well. By definition, the purposes are not the same, and it takes thoughtful consideration to create an institutional framework that can facilitate their meshing. This focus on purpose should remind us of the central fact that campaigns are for persuading people to do something, usually to vote for X and not for Y. That, in essence, is what is happening when campaigning happens. In comparison with that purpose, everything else is inci-dental and secondary.

Similarly, we can think about governing in the light of essential purpose. Many things may or may not be happening when govern-ment happens. Multiple objectives always exist, and reasonable people will often disagree about how well any specific objective is being achieved. But not many reasonable observers would think that rule—which is to say political power institutionalized in gov-ernment—should occur for only one particular objective, much less for its own sake. Then, for the sake of what is governing happen-ing? The common-sense answer is that, behind all the many partic-ular objectives, the essential purpose of governing is to get on with the business of the group being governed.[14] The ancient Greeks expressed that basic idea very well with their word for governing: *kybernan,* meaning "to steer." That term for steering was then Latinized (*gubernare*) to give us the word govern, and in our own time the original word was readopted to designate the modern sci-ence of communication and control—cybernetics.

While references to the "ship of state" may seem a bit outdated, to think of governing in terms of the art of steering does make a good deal of sense. It does so because steering—the "cybernetic" combination of control and communication—is exactly what one generally expects to happen when governing is happening. In other words, governing is all about the interaction of information and power exercised on behalf of some group of people as a going concern. The idea of steering encompasses as necessary properties both power—in the sense of controlling something—and of communication—in the sense of continuing exchanges of information. With communication but no power of control, there is no steering, but only a directionless exchange of information about one's drift. But neither is power alone sufficient for steering: The unidirectional message "full speed ahead" can hardly be called steering. Power without communication is the mindless directionality of pure will, oblivious to circumstances. To see governing as the art of steering is to summarize a wide variety of activities that it seems reasonable to expect should occur in the day-to-day governing of anything. People with governing authority are like a steersman in that they are normally expected to be guided not only by destinations on the future horizon but also by knowledge of past performance and present position. They should know about the condition and capabilities of the ship. They are expected to be aware of the surrounding features of the environment and alert to the portents that might be discerned from that environment. And they are expected to be around for the long haul. Nongoverning members of the group do not have their many hands on the wheel, but they are the paying passengers and ultimately they, not the steersman, are the ones best able to evaluate their conditions on the journey and to determine whether it is taking them where they want to go—hence, a powerful rationale for periodic elections and their accompanying campaigns.

All that discussion is a more elaborate way of repeating the initial idea that the essential purpose of governing is to get on with the business of the group being governed. One does not need to have the classical education or elite predispositions of the Founding Fathers to realize that to campaign and to govern are inherently different things. Of course, governing also has to do with persuading—"public information" officers were appearing in most federal departments by the 1950s[15]—but that is supposed to be in the service of getting the appropriate steering done. Likewise, campaigning also has to do with steering—or else there would not be so many high-paid campaign strategists and consultants—but that is in the service of getting the persuading done.

It is plausible, therefore, to think that a vital and irreducible difference exists between campaigning and governing, because their purposes have an inherent difference. In the nature of things, warriors and navigators do not have the same ends in view. It might become clearer why campaigning and governing should differ if we conclude this section by thinking about some generic points of contrast between the two. In at least three important ways campaigning and governing point in different directions—that is to say, not always in opposite but in sufficiently divergent directions to matter.

First, campaigning is geared to one unambiguous decision point in time. In other words, campaigning must necessarily focus on affecting a single decision that is itself the outcome, the event determining who wins and who loses. Governing, by contrast, has many interconnected points of outcome through time—the line decision, so to speak, of the "going concern." Governing in that sense lacks singularity. Anyone who has worked in a political campaign will probably recall the initial enthusiasms of launching the campaign, the accelerating pace and growing intensity, the crashing climax of election day, and the eerie stillness of cleaning out the campaign offices in the period immediately following. Governing is different. It is a long persistence with no beginning or final decision point, something like a combination of digging a garden in hard ground and the labors of Sisyphus. The time scale for campaigning has historically been short and discontinuous, while that for governing stretches beyond the horizon.

Second, within its fixed time horizon, campaigning is necessarily adversarial. Nineteenth-century political writers borrowed the military metaphor precisely because it captures the essential idea of a contest to defeat one's enemy. The competition is for a prize that cannot be shared, a zero-sum game. In comparison with a campaign, governing is predominantly collaborative rather than adversarial. While campaigning would willingly drown out its opponent to maximize persuasion, genuine governing wishes an orderly hearing of many sides, lest the steersman miss something important. In that sense, campaigning is self-centered, and governing is group-centered.

To be sure, governing is not without its competition and oppositions. As noted earlier, political parties have their historic roots in a process of give-and-take that eventually legitimized the contest between the government and its loyal opposition. In a parliamentary democracy like Britain's, that tradition has been particularly strong, and in Washington's ideologically charged atmosphere of recent years, the partisan divisions between Democrats and Republicans in "government" and "opposition" have sharpened. Nonetheless, the governing process itself (and here we are speaking only of democracies) is necessarily collaborative in nature because no steersman has full power of controlling the enterprise. Since power and sure knowledge are rarely commensurate with steering responsibility, governing is a continuing invitation to consult, bargain, compromise, and renegotiate. Steering is not seeking a prize won against adversaries. It is puzzling out the course of action for a going concern, with everyone in the same boat.

In the third place, campaigning is inherently an exercise in persuasion. The point of it all is to create those impressions that will yield a favorable response for one's cause. In contrast, governing places its greatest weight on values of deliberation. While good campaigning often persuades by its assurance and assertions, good governing typically depends on a deeper and more mature consideration. This is so since whatever conclusions governing comes to will be backed by the fearsome power of the state. Taking counsel over what to do and how to do it lies at the heart of the governing process. Of course, it has to be acknowledged that *deliberation* may sound too genteel a term for the knife fights that are often associated with governing, especially along the banks of the Potomac. Nevertheless, the men and women governing public policy do make up a going concern as they bargain and seek to persuade each other inside the constitutional structure. The deliberation in view here means nothing more profound or high-minded than that.

Drawing such a contrast between persuasion and deliberation seems to stack the deck against campaigning as something undesirable. That would be a false impression. Campaigning has a legitimate place in democracy, but it is important to see that place for what it is. Crass as it may sound, campaigning is a matter of skill in making oneself attractive to others in such a way that they will yield. It is a sales job. The results may or may not be informative, but the skillful campaigner need not explore the truth of things. Within the confines of a campaign setting, what is true is what pleases the audience.

Campaigns are not necessarily insincere. In fact, since sincerity is usually very hard to fake, successful campaigners are often the ones who most truly do believe in their causes. That is precisely the point, however: campaigns exist to prosecute a cause, not to deliberate courses of action. As Burdett Loomis puts it later in this volume, "A campaign is nothing if not a series of seductions" (p. 162). Good seducers believe in themselves.

Obviously "issues" and "debates" exist in modern political campaigns, but the overarching concern is to get oneself chosen by the hearers rather than to engage in a genuine give-and-take discussion. Campaigning is about talking to win, not to learn or to teach. Thus, campaign experts rightly tell their candidates to "stay on message"— that is, essentially to keep giving the same speech—rather than to engage with what an opponent might be saying. Likewise, in the contest for public approval, it is more effective to "frame" issues than to inform the audience about anything in detail. It is more persuasive to project self-assurance than to admit ignorance or uncertainty about devilishly complex issues. It is wiser to counterattack and switch the subject than to struggle with tough questions. Those and many other techniques of effective campaigning are essentially antideliberative.

One might object that, if not exactly deliberative, at least an argumentative quality is inherent in campaigning. Often, one draws a parallel between competitive elections and the clash of legal adversaries in a courtroom, with the voters as jury deciding the outcome. That analogy quickly breaks down, however, once we recall that the adversarial contest in court occurs under strict rules that are explicitly intended to maximize reasoned deliberation and to minimize "irrelevant" information or appeals to emotion. Hence, the outcomes of legal proceedings are termed judgments and verdicts, not preferences or vote results. The truer metaphor for campaigning is not the courtroom contest but a commercial sales campaign between competing companies. The participants are bidders for support, not adversaries in an argument deliberately regulated to get at the truth. Hence, it is not surprising that the experts in modern campaigning emerged not from the legal fraternity but from the marketing and advertising professions of American business.

The foregoing comments should not be construed to say that campaigns are necessarily deceptive. If deception occurs, it is incidental to purpose, and no less incidental is any truth that may emerge from the same process. This is the reason that borrowing the military campaign metaphor in the nineteenth century was apposite. The essential purpose behind "taking to the field" is not necessarily to fight deceptively or honorably. It is not to weigh the relative merits of soldiers or strength of armies, or even to fight at all. The purpose is to defeat the enemy, and if that can occur without a fight, so much the better. What winning is to military campaigning, persuading is to political campaigning, namely, the essence of the purposive behavior by which one names the activity.

For the same reason, it is a mistake to conflate electoral campaigning with the classic image of a free marketplace of ideas. The notion of democracy embodying a science-like experimental method was popularized by John Dewey in the first half of the twentieth century and drew from a venerable argument for "the open society" that goes back at least 350 years to John Milton and the English Civil War.[16] According to that view, in a democratic society tolerant of diversity, truth claims are tested and error discovered through open debate. But when that expectation confronts actual election campaigns, the inevitable result is disillusionment. Political campaigning is certainly one part of the open society, but it is not so much the truth-testing marketplace of ideas as the alley where the most fervent rug salesmen compete for customers. Deliberation is what high-minded people hope will occur in the voters' minds, but it is not what campaigns themselves try or expect to produce. The aim of campaigning is for the voter to make a psychological purchase. That purchase should not insult one's reason, if reason were to be consulted, but the modern campaign's real aim is to engage the consumer's feelings in a preferred direction—in other words, not to win debates but to win the audience. Raymond Price summed up the essence of the difference between campaigning and deliberation in a landmark strategy memorandum written for the 1967–1968 Nixon campaign. Pointing out that "the natural human use of reason is to support prejudices, not to arrive at opinions," Price went on to describe credal facts of modern campaigning:

> Let's leave realities aside—because what we have to deal with now is not the facts of history, but an image of history. . . . *We have to be very clear on this point: that the response is to the image, not to the man,* since 99 percent of the voters have no contact with the man. It's not what's there that counts, it's what's projected—and, carrying it one step further, it's not what *he* projects but rather what the voter receives. It's not the man we have to change, but rather the *received impression.* And this impression often depends more on the medium and its use than it does on the candidate himself. Politics is much more emotional than it is rational. . . . [W]e have to bear constantly in mind that it's not what we say that counts, but what the listener hears; not what we project, but how the viewer receives the impression.[17]

The essential issue, therefore, comes down to this. The more that campaigning infiltrates into governing, the more we may expect the values of a campaign perspective to overrule the values of a steersman perspective. Rather than maintaining a balance, it means shifting the weights on the scales of the public's business from a longer to a shorter time horizon, from collaborative to adversarial mindsets, from deliberation and teaching to persuasion and selling. Those are serious shifts in the rules of the game for any self-governing people. They are especially serious for a people whose whole constitutional system of representation presupposes the distinction between campaigning and governing. How could that happen?

Creating the Permanent Campaign

As noted at the outset, *permanent campaign* is shorthand for an emergent pattern of political management that the body politic did not plan, debate, or formally adopt. It is a work of inadvertence, something developed higgledy-piggledy since the middle of the twentieth century, much as political parties became part of America's unwritten constitution in the nineteenth century. The permanent campaign comprises a complex mixture of politically sophisticated people, communication techniques, and organizations—profit and nonprofit alike. What ties the pieces together is the continuous and voracious quest for public approval. Elections themselves are only one part of the picture, where the focus is typically on personalities and the mass public. Less obvious are the thousands of orchestrated appeals that are constantly underway to build and maintain favor of the certain publics and targeted elites for one or another policy cause. Thus, while some of the endless appeals for public approval are quite direct, many others are so indirect that "the people" and their thinking are mere fodder for framing issues and controversies for elite consumption. People in government, interest groups at the fringes of government, and networks of collaboration and opposition stretching across both spheres are all part of the nonstop battle for public approval that now occurs throughout the political landscape. In that sense, the permanent campaign is everywhere, and it is nowhere in particular.

We should be careful not to confuse that particularly new aspect of our unwritten constitution with the more general need for public support that has always existed in all forms of government. Philosophers have long argued, with good cause, that the opinion of the governed is the real foundation of all government. David Hume put it this way:

> As force is always on the side of the governed, the governors have nothing to support them but opinion. It is, therefore, on opinion only that government is founded; and this maxim extends to the most despotic and most military governments, as well as to the most free and most popular. The Soldan of Egypt, or the Emperor of Rome, might drive his harmless subjects, like brute beasts, against their sentiments and inclination; but he must, at least, have led his mamelukes, or praetorian bands, like men, by their opinion.[18]

In that intellectual tradition, it is not simply the numerical force of the governed that makes government depend on opinion. Over 2000 years before Hume, Confucius taught that of the three things necessary for government, two—food and military defense—could be given up under duress, because "[f]rom of old, death has been the lot of all men. But a people that has no faith in their rulers is lost indeed."

To the basic ingredients of obedience and trust, waves of democratization during the past two centuries have produced almost universal acceptance for the claim that the only legitimate government is that which is based on the will of the people.[19] It was such consent among equals that Tocqueville saw as being modeled first in

America and then destined to sweep over the world. Indeed, one could claim that the permanent campaign began with the first breath of life drawn by the new American republic. In 1775 the Continental Congress during its first hundred days not only organized the colonies for armed resistance. It also self-consciously produced nine major public addresses and organized a press campaign to win support for the American cause. Each address was carefully crafted paragraph by paragraph and "put to press and communicated as universally as possible," using the precursor of the Post Office that Correspondence Committee chairman Benjamin Franklin was creating.[20] Once the Constitution was in place, policies of the new national government created an extended public sphere for mobilizing political opinion. Among those policies were mail subsidies for the cheap distribution of newspapers, fully nationalized mail routes, and an unprecedented commitment to the publication of government documents.

From those and many other examples, it would clearly be a mistake to think that the dependence of government on public opinion is anything new to government. But the permanent campaign is something different from government's perennial need for public support. Every day is election day in the permanent campaign. Such campaigning is a nonstop process seeking to manipulate sources of public approval to engage in the act of governing itself. American governance enters the twenty-first century inundated with a campaign mentality and machinery to sell politicians, godly policies, and everything in between. Has something important happened? We might recall this chapter's earlier reference to Sam Grafton, who in 1960 considered curious and noteworthy an eastern senator who polled constituents to guide his getting "hot" on certain issues. One is right to think that something important has intervened when, forty years later, another eastern senator famous for his insight retires with a valedictory on "How Polling Has Trampled the Constitution."[21]

The permanent campaign can be described as our unwritten Anti-Constitution. The written Constitution would keep the citizenry at arm's length from the governing process. The Anti-Constitution sees all efforts at deliberation outside the public eye as conspiratorial. The Constitution would normally consider the people as a sum of localities linked to government through representatives who take counsel with each other. The Anti-Constitution sees a largely undifferentiated public where one representative is interchangeable with another so long as he or she takes instructions. The Constitution would submit the results of governing to the people at regular intervals in many different election venues. The Anti-Constitution prescribes instant responsiveness to the continuous monitoring of the people's mass opinion and mood.

Those generalizations about our written Constitution and unwritten Anti-Constitution may seem too extreme, and so they are if taken to be descriptive of any one moment in time. But that view of the unwritten Anti-Constitution is not excessively extreme if one is thinking in terms of timelines and trajectories. It is no exaggeration to think that over the course of time, the permanent campaign does point in a quite different direction from the long-standing vision of constitutional government. The central tendency of the permanent campaign, as it continues, is anticonstitutional. That trajectory is as much about the mentality as the machinery of modern politics.

The mentality involved touches on deep-seated cultural changes, a subject that would take us too far afield to fit into the confines of this chapter. Here, simply note that at the deepest level, cultural patterns underlying the endless campaign raise questions about how we understand the nature of reality and our place in the world. Is "truth" anything more in principle than what I, as well as people like me, can accept? Is public thinking anything more than the sending of messages by communities of interpretation? Is knowledge something that we construct or that we discover? Is man the measure of all things, or is he a participant in meanings far beyond himself? Obviously, those are not issues that we can pursue here.[22]

What we can identify and discuss without doing excessive injustice to the subject are the political instrumentalities that give expression to the deeper developments of political culture. Those features proved important in creating the permanent campaign, and one can conveniently group them into six categories. The point here is not to describe each in detail but to show the logic that has connected those emergent properties into a coherent pattern during the past fifty or so years—the pattern of campaigning so as to govern and even governing so as to campaign.

The Decline of Political Parties. The first feature is a venerable concern of political scientists—the decline of political parties. That is a more complex subject than it first appears, since in some respects America's two national parties are stronger than they were fifty years ago. Where parties have become much weaker is at the level of political fundamentals—generating candidates for office and being able predictably to mobilize blocs of people to vote for them. The cumulative effect of many changes from the late nineteenth century onward—ending the "spoils" system in public employment, electoral reforms and party primaries, suburbanization, and television, to name a few examples—was largely to destroy the parties' control over recruitment and nomination of candidates for office. Concurrently, the general trend since the middle of the twentieth century has been a gradual decline in the strength of voters' identification with the two major parties. Much of that has to do with the replacement of the more party-oriented New Deal and World War II generation by the post–New Deal generations.[23] The twentieth-century change in American parties represents a general shift from party-centered to candidate-centered elections, in an "every man for himself" atmosphere.[24] Since politicians cannot count on loyalties from party organizations, voting blocs of the New Deal coalition, and individual voters, after the 1950s politicians have had every reason to try to become the hub of their own personal permanent campaign organizations. Typically, American politicians now rise or fall not as "party men" but as largely freewheeling political entrepreneurs.

Although much weaker on the recruitment side, political parties have also become stronger in other dimensions that intensify the permanent campaign. In the last quarter of the twentieth century, party coalitions grew more ideologically and socially distinctive. Simultaneously, the national party organizations' ability to raise and distribute money vastly increased. The central headquarters of each party also became more adept at constructing national election strategies and campaign messages to attack the other party. At the same time, two-party conflict in Congress became more ideologically charged and personally hostile. With that development came congressional leaders' growing use of legislative campaign committees to raise money, set agendas, and define the party image. All that has provided the financial wherewithal and career interests for more sustained and polarized political warfare. In short, both where parties have become weaker and where they have become stronger, the effect has been to facilitate a climate of endless campaigning.

Open Interest-Group Politics. A second feature creating the permanent campaign is the rise of a much more open and extensive system of interest-group politics. "Opening up the system" became a dominant theme of American politics after the Eisenhower years. On the one hand, to open up the system meant that previously excluded Americans—minorities, women, youth, consumers, and environmentalists, for example—demanded a voice and place at the table. The civil rights movement was in the vanguard, followed by many others. With the politics of inclusion came more advocacy groups and a nurturing environment for that minority of Americans who were inclined to be political activists. On the other hand, opening up the system also meant exposing all aspects of the governing process to public view. In the name of good government and participatory democracy, barriers between policymakers and the people were dismantled. Open committee meetings, freedom-of-information laws, publicly recorded votes, televised debates, and disclosure and reporting requirements symbolized the new openness. The repeal of public privacy had a sharp edge. After Vietnam, Watergate, and other abuses of government power, deference to public officials became a thing of the past. Replacing that deference were investigative journalism and intense media competition for the latest exposé. People in public life became themselves the object of a new regime of strict ethics scrutiny and exposure—and thus tempting targets in a permanent campaign.

Often the two versions of openness—inclusion and access—were mutually reinforcing. Groups demanded new laws and procedures that would give them greater access to the policymaking system. Greater access to the policymaking system—administrative rule-making, standing to sue in courts, congressional committee hearings, freedom-of-information claims, and so on—encouraged more groups to countermobilize and make their presence felt. With a host of political agendas in play and a declining ability of political parties to create and protect political careers, politicians as a whole became more subject to interest-group pressures and more obliged to engage in continuous campaigning. Then, too, the single-issue groups and social movements that became prominent after midcentury also provided a large pool of potential candidates who were likely to be more policy-oriented than the older breed of party politicians. Thus, the expanding sphere of interest-group politics provided more fuel for the permanent campaign in the form of people who saw campaigning with and against special-interest groups to be the heart of governing.

Here might be a good place to pause and observe some of the permanent campaign's emerging dynamics. While political parties were weakening as linking mechanisms between leaders and the grassroots, mobilized interest groups converged on an increasingly open policymaking system. Politicians' careers became more individually constructed, and governing coalitions became more diffuse and difficult to sustain. Party stalwarts and establishment notables faded into history, while advocacy groups and activists with an agenda crowded onto the public stage. On all sides of the scramble, incentives were growing to turn to the onlooking public and its presumptive opinion for support and bargaining strength in governing. Contrariwise, "moves" and "messages" deployed in governing could be used to shape public reactions in the process of campaigning against opponents. Increasingly, the use and manipulation of public opinion were the politicians' means to get their way. But how could that be done in a mass democracy?

New Communications Technology. A third feature is the new communications technology of modern politics. The rise of television after the 1940s was obviously an important breakthrough in personalizing direct communication from politicians and interest groups to a mass public. Candidates for office could move from retailing their appeals through party organizations to direct wholesaling with the voting public. Likewise, groups could use protests and other attention-grabbing media events to communicate their causes directly to a mass audience. For both politicians and advocacy groups, communication with the public bypassed intermediaries in the traditional three-tiered "federal" structure of party and interest-group organizations, where local, state, and national commitments complemented each other. In place of the traditional structure could grow something like a millipede model—direct communication between a central body and mass membership legs. Of course, the story did not stop with broadcast television but went on to include cable TV, talk radio, the twenty-four-hour news cycle, "narrowcasting" to target audiences, and the Internet. Explosive growth in the electronic media's role in Americans' lives provided unfathomed opportunities to crossbreed would-be campaigners and governors.

Quite apart from its use by politicians and interest groups, the new communications technology had its own powerful reasons to present its expanding audiences with the picture of governing as little more than a continuous process of campaigning. Openness offered ever more information to report, and the expanding market of media consumers intensified competition for public exposure. Given the media's need to attract and hold the attention of a largely passive audience, communication of just any kind would not do. As Walter Lippmann saw in analyzing the popular print media in the early twentieth century, communication must be of a kind that translates into audience shares and advertising dollars. That has meant playing up story lines that possess qualities of dramatic conflict, human interest, immediacy, and strong emotional value. The easiest way for the media to meet such needs has been to frame the realities of governing in terms of political contests. The political-contest story about government makes complex policy issues more understandable, even if the "understanding" is false. It grabs attention with short and punchy dramas of human conflict. It has the immediacy of a horse race and a satisfying resolution of uncertainty by naming winners and losers. In addition, of course, it does much to blur any sense of distinction between campaigning and governing.

Even if the participants themselves do not frame their activities as a political contest, media figures—the new intermediaries in politics—can show that they are too savvy to be taken in. Unmasking the "real" meaning of events, reporters reveal the attempts of one side or another to gain political advantage over its rivals in the governing process. Translating the campaign "spin" and finding the "hidden agenda" can be Everyman's badge of political sophistication in the modern media culture.

Again, if we pause to take stock, what we are watching is not simply the development of a technological marvel of mass communication over the past half-century. We are watching a media system that shapes a public mind that is primed to be ministered to by the permanent campaign. Of course, most of us have a significantly limited attention span and an inclination to prefer dramatic entertainment over complex matters of substance. Modern communication technology allows those individual proclivities to be recast into patterns of public thinking at a mass social level.

New Political Technologies. The fourth feature underlying creation of the permanent campaign is what we might call new political technologies. At the same time as changes in parties, interest groups, and electronic media were occurring, the twin techniques of public relations and polling were invented and applied with ever growing professional skill in the public arena. Together, they spawned an immense industry for studying, manufacturing, organizing, and manipulating public voices in support of candidates and causes. The cumulative result was to impart a much more calculated and contrived quality to the whole political process than anything that prevailed even as recently as the 1950s.

When professional public relations began its break from turn-of-the-century press hacks and publicity stuntmen, it did so in the public sector. The profession's origins lay in the federal government's propaganda offices during World War I. A number of veterans from those public information campaigns went on to found businesses that began turning "counsel on public relations" into a distinct and well-paid profession. The young industry catered mainly to businesses, and it was not until the mid-1930s that corporate America in general embraced the new public relations services as a way to restore its Great Depression– and New Deal–battered image with the public.[25] The effort of business to sell itself, and not just its products, had begun in earnest. Effective public relations reached beyond marketing and advertising; soon it was seen to require strategies that could fundamentally change a business client's practices and policies. By the middle of the twentieth century, the PR man had gained the keys to the executive washroom, and it was roughly at that time that politicians and the new profession began discovering each other. The permanent campaign was about to move from the private to the public sector.

At this point, the story of public opinion polls intervenes. Political polling had its own roots in nineteenth-century straw votes and newspaper ballots, and the later addition of mail questionnaires and then magazine-sponsored telephone surveys did little to improve polls' reliability. It was only in the late 1930s that former newspapermen George Gallup and Elmo Roper pioneered the use of statistical sampling to produce representative surveys of public opinion. The polling industry grew rapidly after the Second World War and found its services in demand by two types of clients. First and most obvious were the media, beginning with print journalism and then vastly expanded by the growing electronic media after the 1950s. By the 1970s Americans were routinely hearing the results of polls sponsored by major media outlets that typically described the popularity of particular viewpoints and personalities as well as dramatic horse-race accounts of elections or, rather, election predictions. Reporting to Americans what they themselves thought turned out to be a popular and readily available source of created news. While seeking to generate news stories by announcing their results, such polls have added little to understanding the complexities of public opinion. Yet they are important to our subject. The media's pervasive polling and financial stake in publicizing the results helped teach Americans of the late twentieth century to read their society as a continuously contested battleground for public opinion.

The second type of client for the new, statistically designed polls was less noticeable to the man on the street. It was the growing industry of public relations consultants. Even more than the media would need polls, pollsters and public relations people needed each other. Elmo Roper described the development to his firm's interviewers in 1949:

> Corporations have become increasingly concerned about their standing in the eyes of the public. . . . The "public relations counsel," who is the expert in advising companies how to act so as to deserve the public's confidence, needs some facts to go on. He needs to know *how* his client does stand with the people and *why* that standing is good or bad. He needs to know what people want and expect from business enterprises beyond good products and values. Public relations research tries to get the answers to those questions.[26]

Those were exactly the kinds of concerns that politicians and interest groups were ready to hear when they started making significant use of the services of opinion-research and public-relations firms after the middle of the twentieth century. The first collaborations were a simple technology transfer from advertising campaigns for consumer products to the marketing of candidates and political causes. As earlier with business clients, however, it soon came about that public relations professionals claimed a strategic view that could affect the practices and policies the client might want to put forward.[27] Over time, consultants and pollsters moved into the political front office. After the 1960s, increasingly specialized political consultant services developed and were fortified by professional polling to cover every imaginable point of contact among politicians, interest groups, and the people being governed. The basic features of the political marketing landscape include the following services: poll and focus-group research, strategic planning, image management, direct-mail marketing, event management, production of media materials, "media buys," opposition research against competitors, and orchestration of "grassroots" citizen campaigns.

Pausing again, one can appreciate the conjuncture of those powerful forces. With the third and fourth features came the technical capability to engage in a kind of politics that would have been unthinkable in the first half of the twentieth century. From small and disparate beginnings, the three great technologies—electronic media, polling, and public relations—converged into immense and mutually supportive industries. For politicians and group activists, they opened the door of opportunity to orchestrate, amplify, and inject the presumptive voices of the American people—that is, "our people"—into the daily management of public affairs. All those trends have made it increasingly possible for politicians and other would-be leaders to know about the public without having any real human relationship with the people in particular. Haltingly at first, and then with much gusto after the 1960s, America stepped through that door into the permanent campaign.

Need for Political Money. The fifth factor in the creation of the permanent campaign amounts to a logical consequence of everything else that was happening. It is the ever growing need for political money. It turns out that most of what political marketing does resolves into spending money on itself—the consultants—and the media. Hence, after the 1960s, an immense new demand grew for politicians and groups to engage in nonstop fund-raising. Even if the people managing the new technologies—media, polling, and public relations—were not in profit-oriented businesses, the new forms of crafted politics would have cost huge amounts of money to create and distribute. As it was, the splendid profits to be made helped add to even larger political billings. For example, in 1994 the fifteen most expensive Senate campaigns in the United States devoted almost three-quarters of their funds to consultants' services.[28]

Legislative reforms in the 1970s aimed to control election contributions but actually had the effect of enhancing the role and costs of political consultants. Now added to the scene were specialists who could master the technical requirements of the law and the fund-raising techniques for extracting large sums in small amounts from many like-minded donors. In 1976 the Supreme Court ruling in *Buckley v. Valeo* determined that political spending was deserving of all the constitutional protections of individual free speech. That ruling guaranteed that the money wells could be drilled ever deeper to nourish the permanent campaign into the foreseeable future. Those with the right skills and mailing lists could design legal channels through the reefs of rules and regulations for virtually any money anyone wanted to put into the permanent campaign. The government steering metaphor took on a new aspect.

To tap into dependable streams of political money, political consultants and operatives now became adept at tailoring a never ending campaign to subgroups of the population with distinctive demographic profiles. In terms of actually mobilizing people in politics, the new impetus was to hunt out support—concentrating resources to search for narrowly targeted groups of predisposed sympathizers—rather than to gather support within general coalitions. Thus, modern technology allowed "list vendors" to assemble computer-generated files of potential supporters who had been profiled by their consumption and other characteristics. From such lists, "personalized" mailings and other direct contacts to raise funds were organized. The responses to those contacts could, in turn, serve as the databases to mobilize periodic grassroots letter-writing and call-in campaigns on special issues. Of course, all those activities called for spending more money to facilitate yet more fundraising.

Stakes Involved in Activist Government. To close the circle of forces behind the permanent campaign, we need to revisit the obvious. Granted a massive and growing need for more political money exists. But why should anyone pony up the money? What we might easily overlook is the obvious point that the permanent campaign exists because there is something big and enduring to fight about. The stakes involved in activist government are what make it worthwhile to pay out the money that keeps the permanent campaign going and growing. At the simplest level, one might call that the Microsoft effect. Only after Bill Gates found that the federal government had an Antitrust Division did Microsoft lobbyists and contributions to both parties begin appearing to demonstrate the company's commitment to civic education and participation.

If the federal government were as small a part of people's lives and of the economy as it was during the first half of the twentieth century, we can be sure that there would be far less interest in the continual struggle to influence the creation, administration, and revision of government policies. Campaigning has become big and permanent because government has become big and permanent. One is speaking here of more than the obvious benefits to be derived from influencing spending and taxation, although with the federal budget approaching $2 trillion, that is not a small consideration. It is not even a matter of the federal government's growing regulatory power over society and the economy. The deeper reality is a pervasive presence of public policy expectations. That is another factor that changed greatly after the Eisenhower years and helped give birth to the permanent campaign.

To say it another way, conceptions of who we are as a people became increasingly translated into arguments about what Washington should do or should stop doing. Abortion is an obvious example, but to see the point more fully one need only to consider Americans' thinking about race, the role of women, crime, religious issues, economic security, education, or people's relation to the natural environment. Emblematic of that trend, both academics and the public after the 1950s began to make unprecedented use of the term *policy* as a category for understanding their society. Writing as domestic policy adviser in 1970 to the newly elected President Nixon, Daniel Patrick Moynihan pointed out that the very way of thinking about government was changing in *postindustrial* society—then a newly minted term. "We are moving from program to policy-oriented government," he wrote.[29] Programs—government officials' traditional focus—were all about delimited activities authorized by statute; they were "inputs." Policy, on the other hand, aims to guide government in accordance with the properties of a "system," which is to say a vast, interconnected body where "everything relates to everything" with frequently counterintuitive results; policy is about "outputs."

The challenge created by that changing perception of government and the body politic was only beginning to dawn on people at the end of the 1960s. If what government does is policy, and if everything relates to everything else, and if whatever ends up happening is output—then policy is without borders, and everyone always has an open invitation to see government as responsible for whatever goes wrong. In words that explain much about the impetus behind permanent campaigning, Moynihan concluded, "It follows that there is no significant aspect of national life about which there is not likely to be a rather significant national policy. It may be a *hidden* policy. . . . But it is policy withal." Here, indeed, was promising territory in which the permanent campaign could take to the field.

Everything was political and poised to break forth into a policy dispute before the national public, from endangered species in the swamps to sexual innuendo in the workplace. Moynihan was simply expressing a policy mentality that shaped expectations of policymakers and public alike for the permanent campaign. "The movement away from program-oriented government toward policy orientedness . . . may be likened to a change in sensibility in cultural matters," he said. And so it was.

Those six features have seemed to take us far afield. The point has been to try to connect the dots so that we might see that what seem to be many things are actually the one thing we are calling the permanent campaign. By giving scant attention to the changing American culture, we have probably not come close to identifying the ultimate causes of the subject in view. Nevertheless, perhaps enough has been said to indicate that the causes must be deepseated and independent of any passing personality—although the Clinton presidency surely did more than its share to spur on the permanent campaign.

The campaign without end is not a story of evil people's planning and carrying out nasty designs on the rest of us. Rather, it is more like a story of things all of us would do, given the incentives and what it takes to win under changing circumstances. The story's central narrative is the merger of power-as-persuasion inside Washington with power-as-public-opinion manipulation outside Washington. The two, inside and outside, governing and campaigning, become all but indistinguishable—as they now are in any one of the big-box lobbying or consulting firms in Washington. The paradox is that a politics that costs so much should make our political life feel so cheapened.

Concluding Unscientific Postscript

We might recall that the second paragraph of this chapter had to correct itself. The permanent campaign is not the way Americans do politics, but the way politics is done to them. Without calling it by that name, the way most Americans do politics is by not doing what they consider "political" but by engaging in a myriad of local volunteer activities—politics in particular.[30] That is all to the good and worth remembering. But it is also true to say that the handiwork of professional consultant-crafted politics is now probably the only version of nonlocal politics that the average American ever experiences.

The pervasiveness of political marketing means that all national politics take place in a context of permanent, professionally managed, and adversarial campaigning to win the support of those publics upon whom the survival of the political client depends. Into the media are poured massive doses of what historian Daniel Boorstin discerned in the 1960 birth of TV politics and called pseudoevents.[31] They are not spontaneous, real events but orchestrated happenings that occur because someone has planned, incited, or otherwise brought them into being for the purpose of being observed and swaying opinion. Leaks, interviews, trial balloons, reaction stories, and staged appearances and confrontations are obvious examples that most of us hardly recognize as "pseudo" anymore. It is difficult to know anything about national affairs that is not subject to the ulterior motives of professionals in political management or in the media, a distinction that itself is tending to dissolve.

What is the result of transforming politics and public affairs into a twenty-four-hour campaign cycle of pseudoevents for citizen consumption? For one thing, the public is regularly presented with a picture of deeper disagreements and a general contentiousness about policy issues than may in fact be true when the cameras and microphones are turned off. Second, immense encouragement is given to the preexisting human tendency to overestimate short-term dramatic risks and underestimate the long-term consequences of chronic problems. Third, public thinking is focused on attention-grabbing renditions of what has gone wrong for which somebody else can be blamed. Thus, any attempt to debate policy continually reinforces a culture of complaint and victimization where seemingly dramatic conflicts never really settle anything or lead anywhere. With artifice everywhere, perhaps one cannot trust anyone. The shrug replaces the vote.

The ultimate result is perhaps most worrisome of all. As Boorstin shrewdly predicted, in the montage of orchestrated happenings, ordinary people are confused—not so much by the artificial simplifications as by the artificial complication of experience. Political news is news made to happen. Meanings are spun. The performance becomes more significant than what is said. Pseudoevents generate competing pseudoevents. What happens becomes enmeshed in what might have been the motives and whether any statement really means what it says. People who are supposed to be self-governing are taught that nothing is what it is. It is only what it seems, and it is as true to say something seems one thing as another. What is one to say about such a situation? Perhaps only that this way madness lies.

The objection can always be raised by defenders of the status quo that the system—more inclusive, openly accessible, and ear-to-the-ground than ever before—is at least responsive. The concept of responsiveness deserves careful consideration, for it returns us to the central confrontations between governing and campaigning. Clearly, what has been described in this chapter is not the *deliberative responsiveness* of the constitutional tradition. Such responsiveness would reflect a picture of representative government in which institutional structures known to the written Constitution hold expressions of popular opinion at a distant arm's length from government discussions. Deliberative responsiveness would leave us still in the normative mind-set of the Founding Fathers. It is the mind-set that argued that the public voice pronounced by the representatives of the people will be more consonant to the public good than if pronounced by the people themselves.[32] In the sense of popular sovereignty, the people and their opinion were to rule, but public opinion was not to govern.

If deliberative responsiveness has not given us direct popular control over policymaking, neither has the permanent campaign done so. Were public opinion such a prime mover of government action—what might be called *mimetic responsiveness*—then we should find policymakers more or less reproducing whatever it is the public wants. Surely, it is difficult to see the political class as pandering automatons in a time when two-thirds or more of the American people consistently claim that elected officials neither pay attention to nor understand what they think and that most government decisions are not the choices the majority of Americans would make. If the permanent campaign were a matter of simply echoing the will of the people, we should not have the legitimacy paradox. In the same period when political leaders have become ever more attentive to and sophisticated in gauging public opinion, the public has become ever more distrustful and alienated from a political process perceived as being out of touch with its constituents.

The same paradox excludes an opposite interpretation. That view would understand the permanent campaign as total manipulation of public opinion through the new technologies of mass persuasion. A "captive public" so enthralled by opinion meisters would surely be too deluded to register the high levels of disenchantment with the political process that now prevail.[33]

The term that perhaps best describes what happens in the permanent campaign is *instrumental responsiveness*.[34] It is a hands-on approach to leveraging and massaging opinion to make it serve one's own purposes. The campaigners do not engage the public to teach people about real-world happenings and thereby disabuse them of false hopes or encourage forbearance against harsh realities. Rather, the permanent campaign engages people to tell them what they want to hear in ways that will promote one's cause against others. Such instrumental responsiveness appears to be the system's functional philosophy, even while mimetic responsiveness—doing the people's will—is its confessional theology.

No one can say how long such instrumental responsiveness may continue to dominate the permanent campaign. Should disasters occur and the people become sufficiently confused and angry, they may stop telling each other to have a nice day. Like a blinded animal, they may turn on their handlers and demand a reign of mimetic responsiveness, no doubt with new demagogues arising to feel their pain and meet their needs. Some hints of such growing public yearning for majoritarianism and democracy by plebiscite already exist.[35]

For the time being, however, all the advantages appear to lie with the immense infrastructure and financial stakes of the permanent campaign. Its momentum takes us into a future of better-orchestrated but shortsighted political warfare. It promises less deliberation and more selling, more preoccupation with political fund-raising, and more puzzlement that nothing can be taken at face value. The permanent campaign is a school of democracy, and what it teaches is that nothing is what it seems, everything said is a ploy to sucker the listener, and truth is what one can be persuaded to believe. Of course, that is not true for every person on every occasion. It surely is, however, the general bent of instruction.

Why should one care? Because our politics will become more hostile than needed, more foolhardy in disregarding the long-term, and more benighted in mistaking persuasions for realities. The case for resisting further tidal drift into the permanent campaign rests on the idea that a self-governing people should not wish to become more vile, myopic, and stupid. Apart from that, there probably is not much reason to care.

Peace and prosperity can deceive, but wartime pressures distill into their clearest essence the dangers of conflating political campaigning and governing. Government-sponsored propaganda campaigns abound under modern conditions of total war. It is disastrous, however, to confuse the propaganda campaign with the realities of the war-making campaign. Failure to govern on the basis of the truths of the situation, as best they can be known, is a sure route to eventual disaster for the governed and rulers alike. History suggests that one major reason the Western democracies were better governed in World War II than their opponents was that their leaders brought their people into the truth of governing the war effort and did not merely campaign to raise morale. While fascist dictators fell into the trap of believing propaganda campaigns they conducted with their own people, leaders such as Roosevelt and Churchill—even if in very general ways—told citizens about the hard truths of their situation. In his first war report to the nation on December 9, 1941, for example, President Roosevelt not only told the people, "So far, all the news has been bad." He also told them, "It will not only be a long war, it will be a hard war." There would be shortages: "We shall have to give up many things entirely." FDR said that he would not tell the people that there would be sacrifices ahead. He said instead that there would be the "privilege" of suffering.[36]

Fast-forward almost sixty years, and we find America in repose and its national politics having ended the century with a major debate on the budget and Social Security. Throughout 1999, Republicans and Democrats contended over how to use the federal budget surplus responsibly, and each side solemnly promised not to let the other side raid the Social Security trust fund. But the great debate was little more than elaborate and well-crafted posturing grounded in polls and focus-group thinking. On any reasonable projection, the budget surplus in the immediate future is merely the calm before the storm of fiscal problems that will be produced by an aging population sustained by accelerating medical break-throughs.

Meanwhile, the long-term financial imbalance of the Social Security system is a monumental problem that has gone unaddressed. Certainly, no national program touches so many Americans in so many ways over such a long period. When the favorable state of the economy and the budget made Social Security remedies relatively easy, when the long lead time to the system's insolvency in 2034 made action relatively painless, why in the governing process did politicians bypass such a golden opportunity? The answer lies in the advantages offered by posturing rather than by deliberating, as politicians looked toward the 2000 elections. It was one more illustration that in America's current political situation, "framing the issue," "setting the agenda," "sending messages," and the like can be at least as important as striking a particular deal to achieve a policy settlement. Long-term settlements appropriate to governing may actually be the last thing wanted by those most committed to the permanent campaign.

It is reasonable to conclude that by the beginning of the twenty-first century, American national politics had gone past a mentality of campaigning to govern. It had reached the more truly corrupted condition of governing to campaign. In other words, among political leaders and their tolerant citizen onlookers, it seemed better to have a campaign issue for the 2000 election than to deal with a vital public issue by actually governing. It is no exaggeration to use the imagery of true "corruption" in its classic sense—something much darker than money or sex scandals. We can know quite well from history when democratic politics is passing from degradation to debauchery. That happens when leaders teach a willing people to love illusions—to like nonsense because it sounds good. That happens when a free people eventually come to believe that whatever pleases them is what is true.

Notes

1. Sidney Blumenthal, *The Permanent Campaign* (New York: Simon and Schuster, 1982), 7.
2. Samuel Grafton, "The Polls Grow—Should They?" *New York Times Magazine,* February 26, 1960, 15.
3. Richard E. Neustadt, *Presidential Power* (New York: John Wiley, 1960).
4. David Mayhew, *Congress: The Electoral Connection* (New Haven: Yale University Press, 1974); Arthur Maass, *Congress and the Common Good* (New York: Basic Books, 1984).
5. Hugh Heclo, "The Presidential Illusion," in *The Illusion of Presidential Government,* edited by Hugh Heclo and Lester M. Salamon (Boulder, Colo.: Westview Press, 1981); Theodore J. Lowi, *The Personal President: Power Invested, Promise Unfulfilled* (Ithaca: Cornell University Press, 1985); Samuel Kernell, *Going Public: New Strategies of Presidential Leadership* (Washington, D.C.: Congressional Quarterly, 1993).
6. Anthony King, *Running Scared: Why America's Politicians Campaign Too Much and Govern Too Little* (New York: Routledge, 1997).
7. Elizabeth Drew, *The Corruption of American Politics: What Went Wrong and Why* (Secaucus, N.J.: Carol Publishing Group, 1998), 25, 29.
8. Lawrence Jacobs and Robert Shapiro, "The Rise of Presidential Polling," *Public Opinion Quarterly* 50 (1995); Paul Brace and Barbara Hinckley, *Follow the Leader: Opinion Polls and the Modern Presidency* (New York: Basic Books, 1992).
9. Charles O. Jones, "Passages to the Presidency: 2000," speech, American Enterprise Institute, Washington, D.C., January 5, 1999.
10. The Platonic dialogue *Gorgias* was studied with special care on this subject.
11. Often in early America this meant literally to stand at the courthouse while the local white male property owners appeared to publicly announce their votes. The account in this section is indebted to Michael Schudsson's *The Good Citizen: A History of American Civic Life* (New York: Free Press, 1998).
12. In 1896 the young Democratic nominee William Jennings Bryan shocked respectable opinion by initiating the first traveling speaking campaign for the presidency. It was only in 1932 that Franklin Roosevelt broke with the tradition of staying at home to be notified and appeared personally before the convention to accept his party's presidential nomination.
13. Before that, Congress passed the Sedition Act in 1798. Among other things, the act made it a federal crime (with a fine up to $2,000 and imprisonment

for up to two years) to "write, print, utter or publish" anything "false, scandalous, and malicious" against the president or Congress "with intent to defame . . . or to bring them . . . into contempt or disrepute; or to excite against them . . . the hatred of the good people of the United States." James Morton Smith, *Freedom's Fetters* (Ithaca: Cornell University Press, 1965).

14. That in itself says nothing about who should govern, only that true forms of government exist for the sake of the governed as a whole. Aristotle, *Politics* 3.6–8.

15. By 1949 there were 2,423 full-time federal employees engaged in public relations activities, a classification that excluded persons doing publication work required by law. Edward L. Bernays, *Public Relations* (Norman: University of Oklahoma Press, 1952), 151 ff.

16. "And though all the winds of doctrine were let loose to play upon the earth, so Truth be in the field, we do injuriously, by licensing and prohibiting, to misdoubt her strength. Let her and Falsehood grapple; who ever knew Truth put to the worse, in a free and open encounter? Her confuting is the best and surest suppression." John Milton, *Areopagitica* (1644).

17. Raymond K. Price, quoted in Joe McGinniss, *The Selling of the President, 1968* (New York: Trident Press, 1969), 192–95 (italics in the original).

18. Quoted in A. V. Dicey, *Law and Public Opinion in England,* 2d ed. (London: MacMillan, 1914), 2.

19. John Markoff, *Waves of Democracy* (Thousand Oaks, Calif.: Pine Forge Press, 1996).

20. James Sterling Young, "America's First Hundred Days," from a forthcoming book on the presidency and nation leading.

21. Daniel Patrick Moynihan, "How Polling Has Trampled the Constitution and Other Mild Observations," *Civilization,* August/September 1999, 68 ff.

22. The intellectual history of this typically "modern" problem is discussed in Charles Taylor's *Sources of the Self: The Making of the Modern Identity* (Cambridge: Harvard University Press, 1989). A recent attempt to rebalance historical explanation between the uncompromising absolutists and uncompromising relativists is Thomas Haskell's *Objectivity Is Not Neutrality: Exploratory Schemes in History* (Baltimore: Johns Hopkins University Press, 1998).

23. Warren E. Miller and J. Merrill Shanks, *The New American Voter* (Cambridge: Harvard University Press, 1996).

24. Stephen A. Salmore and Barbara G. Salmore, "Candidate-Centered Parties: Politics without Intermediaries," in *Remaking American Politics,* edited by Richard A. Harris and Sidney M. Milkis (Boulder, Colo.: Westview Press, 1989), 215–38.

25. The early forays into political consulting are revealing. In 1919 Lithuanian politicians hired one of the nation's first PR firms to persuade Americans to support Lithuanian independence. In 1924 the first White House breakfast with stage and screen stars was orchestrated to soften Calvin Coolidge's public image in the election campaign. Bernays, *Public Relations,* 80–81.

26. Quoted in ibid., 151 (italics in the original).
27. In a 1989 survey, 44 percent of political consultants interviewed reported that their candidate clients were uninvolved in setting the issue priorities in their own campaigns, and 66 percent reported that their candidates were uninvolved in determining the tactics. Marshall Ganz, "Voters in the Crosshairs," *American Prospect*, no. 16 (Winter 1994): 103.
28. *Washington Post*, November 8, 1994.
29. These and subsequent Moynihan quotations are taken from National Goals Research Staff, "Statement of the Counselor to the President," *Toward Balanced Growth: Quantity with Quality* (Washington, D.C.: Government Printing Office, June 4, 1970), 5–7.
30. The Kettering Foundation and Harwood Group, *Citizens and Politics: A View from Main Street America* (Dayton, Ohio: Kettering Foundation, 1991), chap. 5.
31. Daniel J. Boorstin, *The Image* (New York: Macmillan, 1961).
32. "The republican principle demands that the deliberate sense of the community should govern the conduct of those to whom they intrust the management of their affairs; but it does not require an unqualified complaisance to every sudden breeze of passion, or to every transient impulse, which the people may receive from the arts of men, who flatter their prejudices to betray their interests." *The Federalist Papers* No. 71. See also Gordon S. Wood, *The Creation of the American Republic* (New York: Norton, 1972), 596 ff.
33. Benjamin Ginsberg, *The Captive Public* (New York: Basic Books, 1986).
34. I owe this term to Lawrence Jacobs, who contrasts it with *substantive responsiveness*. For the latter I have preferred the more descriptive title *mimetic responsiveness* and would regard substantive features to be more accurately associated with the deliberative process. Lawrence R. Jacobs and Robert Y. Shapiro, *Politicians Don't Pander: Political Manipulation and the Loss of Democratic Responsiveness* (Chicago: University of Chicago Press, 2000).
35. Steven Kull, "Expecting More Say: The American Public on Its Role in Government Decisionmaking," Center on Policy Attitudes, Washington, D.C., May 10, 1999.
36. Harold L. Hitchens, ed., *America Goes to War* (Chicago: Columbia Educational Books, 1941), 51–56.

2

The Press and the Permanent Campaign

Stephen Hess

The modern presidental campaign was invented in 1896 by William Jennings Bryan, a thirty-six-year-old former Nebraska congressman and advocate of the inflationary coinage of silver, whose electrifying "cross of gold" speech at the Democratic National Convention unexpectedly won him the party's nomination, and by Mark Alonzo Hanna, a Cleveland industrialist, who had successfully managed the campaign that captured the Republican nomination for Ohio governor William McKinley and was then named the party's national chairman.

Mark Hanna's contribution was to bring technical management to presidential campaigns. He divided the electorate into voting blocs and assigned a staff and a budget to each, so that within the Republican National Committee there were divisions for women (who had been given the vote only in Colorado, Wyoming, and Utah), African Americans, German Americans, traveling salesmen, and even bicyclists ("wheelmen"). He polled key states again and again to determine changes in public opinion, and what his pollsters missed may have been picked up by his spies at Democratic headquarters. He instituted central purchasing, competitive bidding, and strict audits. He organized campaign financing and levied assessments on the business community—Standard Oil, $250,000; New York Life, $50,000; Illinois Central, $35,000. His speakers' bureau was responsible for recruiting, training, directing, and scheduling 1,400 speakers, a third of them professionals. His Bureau of Publication and Printing distributed 200 million items (fourteen for each voter) in twelve languages besides English. Candidate McKinley, meanwhile, greeted supporters from his front porch in Canton, Ohio.

Nineteenth-century presidential candidates, as historian Gil Troy noted, were expected to stand for office, not run for office.[1] Bryan, however, packed his bag and set out to spread the free-silver gospel. At first, he traveled alone on regular trains and often carried his own luggage. Finally, the Democratic National Committee provided him with a private railroad car, misnamed "The Idler." His audiences were huge: 70,000 listened on the Boston Common. As the first "whistle stop" campaigner, Bryan traveled 18,000 miles and delivered 600 speeches to perhaps 5 million people in twenty-seven states.[2]

Whistle-stop politicking, in turn, gave rise to "pack" journalism. Journalism educator Thomas B. Littlewood described the new press corps:

> Shaped by the psychology of the group, the traveling press corps took on an institutional character. The needs of the press had to be tended to by the campaign organization. Because reporters had to file their news stories at a prescribed time every day, the candidate was compelled to say something new and different each day. Together on the train for day after day, journalists and campaigners learned to exchange confidences and to adapt to one another's needs.[3]

Littlewood also noted that since it was considered inappropriate for a woman to travel unaccompanied on a train, women were discouraged from entering the political press corps. That was also a time when all of the elements were coming together that would form the White House press corps in about the configuration that we know it today.[4]

Reporters who covered our peripatetic national office seekers during the first half of the twentieth century were almost all males of middle years. Of the 127 respondents to Leo Rosten's classic 1936 survey of Washington correspondents, only five were women. They defined their job as accurately transcribing what a candidate said and rank-ordering its importance: "What's the lead?" They prided themselves on their ability to work fast under deadline pressures and protected each other as comrades: cooperation was more useful than competition when information was of routine value. One sub rosa ritual, called "blacksheeting," was the exchange of carbon copies of their stories.[5] They were not paid to be stylists, and most of them were not. But neither were they the egg-on-the-vest scribes covering Chicago police precincts in Ben Hecht and Charles MacArthur's *The Front Page*. Half of the Washington reporters were college graduates when Rosten portrayed them in the midst of the Great Depression. They were comfortably in the middle class, although salaried on the low end of the professions. Still, no one would mistake them for celebrities. The White House, not the press room, established rules of engagement. At the press conferences of Harding, Coolidge, and Hoover, for instance, reporters' questions had to be submitted in advance in writing; FDR allowed oral questioning but could be quoted directly only by permission.[6]

There were, however, other journalists in Washington—newspaper and magazine columnists—who were celebrities. In the period that spanned the presidency from Franklin Roosevelt through Lyndon Johnson, Walter Lippmann, Arthur Krock, David Lawrence, Joseph and Stewart Alsop, Marquis Childs, Roscoe Drummond, and James Reston traveled at the highest reaches of an administration, sometimes supportive, sometimes challenging. Suggestive of their standing, Joseph Kraft wrote of Reston, "His influence, easy to exaggerate and hard to pin down, is impossible to overlook. On some big matters the State Department informs him almost automatically, as it would the representative of a major power."[7] They set a lofty tone and did not view government as an adversary.

The composition of the press corps would change. Daniel Patrick Moynihan, as usual, would be among the first to notice. He wrote in 1971, "One's impression is that twenty years and more ago the preponderance of the 'working press' (as it liked to call itself) was surprisingly close in origins and attitudes to working people generally. They were not Ivy Leaguers. They now are or soon will be."[8] Sociologists could move them up a notch to the upper-middle class in that nearly two-thirds of the Washington press corps now have undergraduate degrees from the nation's most highly selective colleges and universities. Some 40 percent of them are women, up from 20 percent in 1978.[9] These are folks with a keen interest in stylish writing and analysis. They did not become journalists to be stenographers.

After John F. Kennedy defeated Richard M. Nixon, the press had a new template for covering a presidential campaign. Its creator, Theodore H. White, had had a distinguished career as a foreign correspondent for *Time* and was a successful novelist as well. "*The Making of the President 1960* was a revelation to us," recalls David S. Broder, "especially to a kid reporter like myself who was covering that presidential race for the first time on the press bus."[10] White brought a novelist's eye to his work. In his first campaign book, recounts White's biographer:

> The story begins at midnight. Conflict and suspense start building in the opening sentences, which speak of mystery, power, and secrets. Plot and characters start to take shape in hazy outlines. The focus sweeps from a New Hampshire village across the American landscape, then travels back through history to Rome and Athens—all on the first page.[11]

White's romantic view of political leaders was combined with a firm grasp of politics, the back-room deals, the strategies and tactics, and the role of the handlers. "It took from eight to twelve years for the newspapers to accept White as an institution," wrote Timothy Crouse, "but by 1972 most editors were sending off their men with rabid pep talks about the importance of sniffing out inside dope, getting background into the story, finding out what makes the campaign tick, and generally going beyond the old style of campaign reporting."[12] Journalists competed to out-White White in the opinion of Albert Hunt, columnist for the *Wall Street Journal*, who wrote after the 1984 election, "The press gets so caught up in trying to report the story behind the scenes that major speeches or position papers on the substance of a campaign receive relatively little attention."[13]

Nowhere was the new style of strategy reporting more evident than in presidential debate coverage with its emphasis on why candidates said what they said rather than on what they said. After one Bush-Clinton debate in 1992, a *New York Times* front-page story began, "One way to score a presidential debate is to ask: What did each candidate need to achieve and did he do it?" Quotes from the candidates' "spin doctors," a hallmark of strategy reporting, turned the likes of George Stephanopoulos, Bob Squier, Ed Rollins, Paul Begala, James Carville, and Mary Matalin into household names.[14]

The view into the inner workings of campaigns opened wider when Nixon's media advisers in 1968 allowed a young writer named Joe McGinniss to be a fly on the wall as they plotted advertising strategy. Choosing a title reminiscent of White's series, *The Selling of the President 1968* was an instant bestseller in which 100 pages consisted of purloined campaign documents. Readers were fascinated; they expressed shock at a candidate's manipulative efforts to troll for votes.

The new emphasis on the machinery of politics, combined with the usefulness of quantification to reporters, made polling an ever more important element of campaign stories. Straw polls had been around at least since the 1820s, when taverns and coffee houses kept blank books in which customers wrote their preferences, which were then reported in the press.[15] But with scientific polling, the frequency of the horse-race story ("Who's ahead? Who's behind?") increased exponentially. It doubled in the *New York Times* from 1948 to 1992, and the three television networks paid more attention to the horse race in 1996 than in 1992, even though Clinton was unopposed for one of the major party nominations.[16] By the 1996 election, there were more than 800 media-sponsored polls.

The Boys on the Bus, Timothy Crouse's account of the press corps at work during the 1972 Nixon-McGovern presidential campaign, proved that Americans' fascination with the nuts and bolts of politics extended to fascination with the journalists who covered the politicians. While once the mainstream press limited news of itself to stories about winning awards, now David Shaw of the *Los Angeles Times* won a Pulitzer Prize for commentary on how the press conducted its business, Howard Kurtz was given a weekly column in the *Washington Post* to expound on press peccadillos, the *New York Times* featured media news in its Monday business section, CNN delved into journalists' habits on a program called *Reliable Sources,* and Terence Smith was named media correspondent for *The NewsHour with Jim Lehrer.*[17]

TV correspondents, depending on their ability to affect ratings, became valuable commodities: Barbara Walters at ABC was the first to get a million dollars a year in 1976.[18] Journalists no longer settled for being anonymous scribblers; *Time,* the proud inventor of group journalism, was forced to give bylines to its correspondents. Steven Brill founded a glossy-paged monthly magazine on the premise that journalists are celebrities, just as John F. Kennedy, Jr., founded a glossy-paged monthly magazine on the premise that politicians are celebrities. But the journalists who turned journalists into movie stars were Carl Bernstein and Bob Woodward (played by Dustin Hoffman and Robert Redford in *All the President's Men*), whose Watergate stories would inspire and instruct other reporters on how campaign dirty tricks could be uncovered.

Increasingly, the race for the presidency seemed like a permanent condition. It was now so expensive that candidates needed to start earlier to raise funds, especially since "front-loading" had pushed together more and more state primaries into the winter months of the election year. David Brinkley told his listeners in early 1983, "The Constitution calls for electing a president every four years, but it does not say we have to spend the whole four years doing it."[19] In Washington, however, politics had become a permanent campaign, even when the campaign was not about an election. Presidents framed their legislative initiatives and journalists framed their coverage in campaign terms and used the same tools and techniques that they had been perfecting since the late 1960s. That was especially evident in Clinton's effort to get a health care bill through Congress in 1994. The White House created a War Room, just as it had in the 1992 presidential campaign, and staffed it with the same pollsters and media consultants. The insurance industry countered with its own focus groups and TV commercials, including the now-classic "Harry and Louise" advertisement:

Louise: "Having choices we don't like is no choice at all."
Harry: "They choose."
Louise: "We lose."[20]

An immensely complicated issue was often reduced in the press to an exposition of competing strategies. And after the Republicans captured the House of Representatives in the 1994 election, the next four years were reported as a saga of Clinton versus Gingrich in much the same manner as foreign correspondents once framed the world as USA versus USSR. "Prospects for a major tobacco law grow dimmer daily," began a Knight-Ridder report, "even though everyone from President Clinton to House Speaker Gingrich says he wants one."[21] Clinton and Gingrich turned up in leads, even when the stories were not about them.

Along with changes in the way journalists covered campaigns, changes in the journalists who covered campaigns, and changes in what constituted campaign coverage, there were changes in the technology of the media, the components of the media, and the economics of the media that would also affect why and how politics and government came to be reported as part of a permanent campaign.

Network television happened upon a special moment in political history to begin altering the basic mix of where Americans go for news. The first time presidential conventions were nationally tele-vised, in 1952, was also the last time the nation would not know who the nominees would be when the conventioneers convened. Television was so unimportant that CBS Radio refused to surrender Edward R. Murrow to be the TV anchor, and instead the network recruited a young reporter, Walter Cronkite. The dramatic selection of Adlai Stevenson by the Democrats and Dwight Eisenhower by the Republicans, covered gavel-to-gavel by CBS (139 hours) and NBC (151 hours), mesmerized those who had access to a TV set.[22] NBC's turn to use the conventions to transform obscure broadcasters into superstars came in 1956, when its coverage was coanchored by Chet Huntley and David Brinkley. While the Huntley-Brinkley team (John Chancellor, Sander Vanocur, and Robert MacNeil) and the Cronkite team (Roger Mudd, Mike Wallace, and Charles Kuralt) had a personal flair that was not required in anonymous print journal-ism, otherwise their journalistic practices and standards were car-ried over from newspaper and radio. Add the relative immobility of the equipment, which limited the visual scope, and TV news of that period might be thought of as illustrated newspapers.

Network news divisions were not expected to make money. The nightly programs, documentaries, and such special events as key congressional hearings and election nights were loss leaders meant to put a serious face on an entertainment medium that could afford to trade some profits for prestige. Marvin Kalb recounts a 1962 meeting in which

> William Paley, who created CBS, outlined his ambitious plans for the future of CBS News to a small group of CBS correspondents. One of them, Charles Collingwood, cautioned that this could be very expensive. Paley responded: "You guys cover the news; I've got Jack Benny to make money for me."[23]

Then, in what Ken Auletta describes as "the blink of an eye in 1986," ABC was acquired by Capital Cities (later to be sold to Disney), CBS was taken over by Laurence Tisch and Loews (later to be sold to Westinghouse), and General Electric acquired NBC.[24] The loss-leader concept was repugnant to the new owners, two of whom had never been in the news business. Indeed, the philosophy of redundancy, which is basic to news gathering—that is, amassing more information than can be used in a story—was considered an unhealthy business practice, and news operations were seriously downsized.[25]

The new owners eventually figured out a way to turn their news divisions into "profit centers." It was called the newsmagazine. Even though CBS's *60 Minutes* on Sunday night was by 1979 the most widely viewed program in the nation, the inspiration for turning over prime-time weekday programming to newsmagazines was *A Current Affair,* a sensationalist show introduced in 1987 by Rupert Murdoch for his Fox stations and quickly imitated by other syndicators with such tabloids as *Inside Edition* and *Hard Copy.* The networks followed suit with *Prime Time Live, 20/20, West 57th, Dateline, 48 Hours,* and *60 Minutes II.* Because the programs were cheaper to produce than sitcoms and dramas, they could generate greater profits with lower ratings. Moreover, unlike the sitcoms, the newsmagazines were owned by the networks. They consisted of gotcha segments, often using hidden cameras, and celebrity interviews. "All right, was it really the best sex you ever had?" asked Diane Sawyer of Marla Maples on *Prime Time Live.*[26] Newsmagazines avoided the topics that were once the staple of network documentaries; a 1998 study showed that only 8 percent of their stories concerned "the combined areas of education, economics, foreign affairs, the military, national security, politics or social welfare issues."[27] By the fall 1999 season, ABC, CBS, and NBC ran a dozen newsmagazines a week in prime time. The success of those shows became the driving force of the news divisions; it affected personnel and resources and increased the number of evening news features with names like *Eye on America* that replaced hard-news stories.

Changes on the evening news also reflected changes that technology made possible. Replacing film with tape created the opportunity for instant editing. Stories could be faster paced. Presidential candidates' sound bites shrank from 43.1 seconds in 1968 to 25.2 seconds in 1972 to 18.2 seconds in 1976 to 9.8 seconds in 1988 to 8.2 seconds in 1996.[28] For politicians the accent would have to be on the short and snappy if they were to make the evening news. "Read my lips, no new taxes!" was the quintessential sound bite. Also, as stories became shorter, the percentage of the stories in which the correspondents were speaking—rather than the candidates—became larger, and the percentage of correspondents expressing opinions—rather than giving information—also increased.[29] Celebrity correspondents and anchors were the networks' signature. They required airtime. Moreover, as stories became more and more correspondent-centered, they became less and less deferential to politicians and officials and increasingly negative.[30] Political consultant Mike Murphy imagined the Gettysburg Address on today's television as a sound bite "immediately subsumed by some blowhard reporter saying, 'Lincoln campaign insiders said the speech was an attempt to win support from veterans' groups and a test of a new, shorter speaking format.'"[31]

In 1979 Ted Turner created a twenty-four-hour cable news channel; at first derided as the Chicken Noodle Network, CNN gained worldwide credibility with its coverage of the 1991 Gulf War. CNBC was launched in 1989; MSNBC and Fox News Channel were launched in 1996. A great deal of airtime had to be filled. One public affairs format, invented by John McLaughlin in 1981, consisted of his presiding over four journalists, supposedly divided between liberals and conservatives, who shouted opinions and predictions at each other.[32] Clones of *The McLaughlin Group* had names like

The Capital Gang and *Inside Washington*. Their weekly predictions, scholars proved, were as reliable as flipping a coin.[33] Writing in the *New York Times,* Walter Goodman considered the format the political equivalent of TV wrestling: "One imagines the combatants being poked and provoked by their keepers before being unleashed."[34] Yet the combatants included such luminaries of Washington journalism as Albert Hunt (*Wall Street Journal*), Jack Germond (*Baltimore Sun*), Eleanor Clift and Howard Fineman (*Newsweek*), Margaret Carlson (*Time*), Gloria Borger (*U.S. News & World Report*), Morton Kondracke (*Roll Call*), Mara Liasson and Nina Totenberg (National Public Radio), Juan Williams (*Washington Post*), Steven V. Roberts (*New York Daily News*), and Fred Barnes (*Weekly Standard*). The number of journalists engaged in those extracurricular activities was small, perhaps forty or fifty, yet their acquired celebrity made them hot commodities on the lecture circuit and raised a troubling question: Could journalists maintain their intellectual rigor when hired as performance artists?[35] The answer was no. Political commentary on commercial channels apparently demanded simplified explanations of complex events, most often cast in terms of contests or strategies or both.

McLaughlin's intoxicating formula spread to the Sunday network programs, even the venerable *Meet the Press*. Originally designed for reporters to ask questions of politicians, the program added a concluding segment of opinionating journalists. The weekday morning programs—*Today* and *Good Morning America*—likewise added panels of Washington insiders. TV's political "opinionating" increasingly combined journalists with public officials—or former politicians who were now journalists with former journalists who were now public officials—and thus blurred the lines between the two. Could consumers tell the difference? It did not matter for the politicians. But the journalists were challenged to be "objective" during the week and "partisan" on the weekend—reporters from 9:00 A.M. to 5:00 P.M. and partisan analysts after dark.

The broadcast networks had new worries as cable penetration passed 50 percent in 1987 and rose to 67 percent by mid-1997. For ABC, CBS, and NBC, the loss of market share would be reflected in how they chose to cover political events: Reagan in his second term became the first president of the United States to have a request to televise a speech turned down; low-rated presidential news conferences were rotated so that only one of the three networks needed to be burdened at any time; and the great party conventions, which had consumed more than 100 hours of network time in 1980, dropped to less than 16 hours in 1996—one hour Monday through Wednesday and two hours on Thursday night when the presidential nominees gave their acceptance speeches.

Newspapers also sought ways to adjust to an electronic age. When Eisenhower was elected in 1952, the combined morning and evening circulation of daily newspapers was 54 million. By the Clinton presidency, there were 100 million more Americans, the average home was being offered fifty-seven or more TV channels, and newspaper circulation was virtually unchanged.

One way to challenge TV was to create a newspaper that was a print version of TV. *USA Today,* the paper that Gannett's Al Neuharth invented in 1982, was built around many short articles, lots of photographs and charts, lots of sport scores and statistics, imaginative graphic design, vivid color—including a weather map that would be widely imitated—and national circulation like a network. Even the paper's blue and white newsracks looked like giant TV sets on pedestals.[36] By 1997 its paid circulation of 1.7 million was 700,000 ahead of the *New York Times* and a million more than the *Washington Post.*

Other newspapers took a very different approach to competition from TV. Americans now first learned about events from television, so the "facts" would be known by the time the morning paper arrived; subscribers instead should be offered greater analysis. Yet the more interpretive the reporting became, the more biased it was perceived to be. The more biased it was perceived to be, the more press credibility declined. Consumers' assessment of bias is based on whether what they read is "wrong," as measured by what they believe.[37] By standards of neutrality the press often got high marks from scholars.[38] But what about that biased article on the PLO, IRA, or AIDS? Magazines of opinion, on the other hand, largely went to people who shared a magazine's opinions; nineteenth-century newspapers had likewise gone to partisans as when Joseph Pulitzer wrote of the *New York World,* "Every column of our paper tells the story of our devotion to the principles of the Democratic party."[39]

Raising the level of interpretation also expanded the possibilities for "attitude" or "edge" to creep into daily journalism. In a brilliant essay on "what made the press so snide and aggressive," the *New Yorker's* Adam Gopnik wrote: "Yesterday's edge becomes today's tedium, and the only way to get more attention is to continually up the ante."[40] Reporting with attitude or edge nicely fitted the needs of those who aspired to be celebrity journalists as well as cable TV's need to fill time, network TV's need to compete with cable, and print's need to recapture consumers whose tastes were increasingly shaped by TV. The firewall of so-called objective reporting had been breached.

"The problem is not that the press has become more aggressive or even more abusive," explained Georgetown University professor Deborah Tannen. She asserted:

> Historians can unearth examples of astounding venom and vituperation hurled against politicians and other public figures from the time journalism began. But in earlier times, those who attacked public figures did so with a purpose: They were ideologically opposed to what their opponents stood for, and they loudly proclaimed that conviction. Aggression was a weapon in a war against specific wrongs. The spirit of the attack today . . . is disinterested, aimed at whoever is in the public eye. And a show of aggression is valued for its own sake.[41]

It was not journalists who invented the permanent campaign. Those in "governance" have increasingly borrowed techniques developed in elective politics as the means to accomplish their ends. The permanent campaign is there to be reported, which is the reporter's job. Yet it is not the only way a story can be framed. "Framing," as defined by Joseph N. Cappella and Kathleen Hall Jamieson, "is a kind of sense-making that creates one interpretation of political events while ignoring others."[42] When Washington journalists frame a story in terms of politics and its techniques, they are moving an issue into a realm they understand. Here they know the players, the pollsters, consultants, advertising people, and party apparatchiks. Rather than acquire specialized knowledge, they can turn to what is convenient and safe. And Washington is a city that rewards the political journalists. Their faces are most seen on interview shows. They get the best speaking engagements. Their invitations are from the A-list. Moreover, governance interpreted as political campaign fits the reconfigured media, the shortened sound bite, confrontational angle, point-counterpoint of cable TV, and talk radio.

Blurring the lines between political operative and political reporter as they move from campaigning to governing suggests political scientist James Q. Wilson's observation that organizations come to resemble the organizations with which they are in conflict—later reformulated as the Iron Law of Emulation by Daniel Patrick Moynihan from his Washington experience. Moynihan was originally noting how the burgeoning bureaucracy of the legislature had begun to look like the burgeoning bureaucracy of the executive branch.[43] The interface between politician and journalist is most starkly seen when individuals cross and recross the once impassable line between news organizations and government entities. More subtle is the shared mind-set of the Washington insider. "And around and around, within virtually a closed loop of the same people talking to each other, we would go again and again," recalled Lanny Davis, the White House aide whom President Clinton assigned to talk to reporters during his Whitewater investigation.[44] Blurring the line that once separated campaigning and governance may well serve the interests of journalists and officials, as we have noted. But a consequence, as reflected in a recent Pew Research Center poll, is that a large majority of Americans—68 percent—rightly see "bickering and opposing" getting worse in Washington.[45]

Notes

1. Gil Troy, *How They Ran: The Changing Role of the Presidential Candidate* (New York: Free Press, 1991), 7.
2. Stephen Hess, "The Making of the President, 1896," *The Nineties* (New York: American Heritage, 1967), 30–35, 130–38. See also Ralph M. Goldman, "Stumping the Country: 'Rules of the Road, 1896,'" *Journalism Quarterly* (Summer 1952): 303–6. Goldman unearthed in the Bryan papers a document written by the traveling reporters for their collective amusement that is remarkably similar to what future generations of "boys on the bus" would concoct. Designed as the mock bylaws of "the Amalgamated Society of the United-Associated Newspaper Correspondents," its section

on "literary style," for example, stated, "No correspondent shall be permitted to describe the 'soulful sadness of the October season,' unless he can show that his is really a soulful sadness and not the cravings of an empty stomach."

3. Thomas B. Littlewood, *Calling Elections* (Notre Dame, Ind.: University of Notre Dame Press, 1998), 63.

4. "By the end of the [nineteenth] century," wrote Martha Joynt Kumar, "the president and his staff and the reporters had developed a set of common understandings serving as the base of their relationship." See her "White House Beat at the Century Mark," *Harvard International Journal of Press/Politics* 2 (Summer 1997): 22.

5. According to Leo Rosten, "The stories on Herbert Hoover's acceptance of the Republican Presidential nomination, which appeared in the Baltimore *Evening Sun* and the New York *Herald Tribune* in August of 1932, were practically identical and betrayed the undiscriminating use of the Blacksheet." See his *Washington Correspondents* (1937; reprint ed., Arno Press, 1974), 89.

6. Stephen Hess, *Presidents and the Presidency* (Washington, D.C.: Brookings Institution Press, 1996), 115.

7. Joseph Kraft, *Profiles in Power* (New York: New American Library, 1966), 78. In a political satire of that time, Meg Greenfield wrote of "a top-secret National Security Council paper prepared three months ago for James Reston and recently leaked to President Johnson." See her "Problem Problem," *Reporter,* February 25, 1965, 31. Two other columnists during that period reached celebrity status through routes other than commentary: Walter Winchell (gossip) and Drew Pearson (exposés).

8. Daniel Patrick Moynihan, *Coping: Essays on the Practice of Government* (New York: Random House, 1973), 319; first published in *Commentary,* March 1971, 41–52.

9. My thanks to Andrew Kohut and Molly W. Sonner of the Pew Research Center for the People and the Press for extracting those figures for me from a survey they released on March 30, 1999. For comparative purposes, see Stephen Hess, *The Washington Reporters* (Washington, D.C.: Brookings Institution, 1981). College selectivity is based on a rating devised by James Cass and Max Birnbaum, *Comparative Guide to American Colleges,* 15th ed. (New York: HarperCollins, 1991).

10. David S. Broder, interview with author, January 24, 2000.

11. Joyce Hoffmann, *Theodore H. White and Journalism as Illusion* (Columbia: University of Missouri Press, 1995), 107.

12. Timothy Crouse, *The Boys on the Bus* (New York: Ballantine Books, 1974), 36.

13. Quoted in E. J. Dionne, Jr., "Did Teddy White Ruin Coverage of Presidential Campaigns?" *Media Studies Journal* 11 (Winter 1997): 79.

14. Stephen Hess, *The Little Book of Campaign Etiquette* (Washington, D.C.: Brookings Institution Press, 1998), 46–48.

15. Littlewood, *Calling Elections,* 20.

16. The *New York Times* figures come from John Zaller, "Negativity and Bias in Media Coverage of Presidential Elections, 1948–1992," a paper delivered at the annual meeting of the American Political Science Association, August 30, 1996.

17. That should not imply that the news industry is now a beehive of self-criticism. As Sidney H. Schanberg wrote, "There are roughly 1,500 daily newspapers in this country. Only a handful—at most a dozen, including *The [Washington] Post*—actually have a reporter who covers the press full-time as a beat." See his "News No One Dares to Cover," *Washington Post,* August 29, 1999.

18. According to "1999 Salary Report," compiled by *Brill's Content,* May 1999, 86–87, Walters now makes $10 million, followed by Peter Jennings, $8.5 million to $9 million, Ted Koppel, $8 million, and Diane Sawyer, Dan Rather, and Tom Brokaw, $7 million each.

19. David Brinkley, *Everyone Is Entitled to My Opinion* (New York: Knopf, 1996), 25.

20. Haynes Johnson and David S. Broder, *The System: The American Way of Politics at the Breaking Point* (Boston: Little, Brown, 1996), 205, 614–15.

21. "Prospects Dim for Tobacco Bill as Political Differences Multiply," *Boston Globe,* April 26, 1998.

22. Martin Plissner, *The Control Room: How Television Calls the Shots in Presidential Elections* (New York: Free Press, 1999), 35–40. Only 39 percent of the nation's households had a television in 1952.

23. Marvin Kalb, "The Rise of the 'New News,'" Discussion Paper D-34, October 1998, Shorenstein Center, Kennedy School of Government, Harvard University, 10.

24. Ken Auletta, *Three Blind Mice: How the TV Networks Lost Their Way* (New York: Vintage Books, 1992), 15.

25. Dean Alger, *Megamedia* (Lanham, Md.: Rowman & Littlefield, 1998), 173–77; see also Stephen Hess, *News and Newsmaking* (Washington, D.C.: Brookings Institution Press, 1996), 103–5.

26. Quoted in Carl Bernstein, "The Idiot Culture," *New Republic,* June 8, 1992, 24.

27. Tom Rosenstiel, *Changing Definitions of News: A Look at the Mainstream Press over Twenty Years* (Washington, D.C.: Project for Excellence in Journalism, March 6, 1998), 5–6.

28. Daniel C. Hallin, "Sound-Bite News: Television Coverage of Elections, 1968–1988," *Journal of Communications* 42 (Spring 1992): 5–24, and "Campaign '96 Final," *Media Monitor* 10 (November/December 1996): 2. See also Kiku Adatto, "Sound-Bite Democracy: Network Evening News Presidential Campaign Coverage, 1968 and 1988," Research Paper R-2, June 1990, Shorenstein Center, Kennedy School of Government, Harvard University.

29. Catherine A. Steele and Kevin G. Barnhurst, "The Journalism of Opinion: Network News Coverage of U.S. Presidential Campaigns, 1968–1988," *Critical Studies in Mass Communication* 13 (September 1996): 187–209.

30. Thomas E. Patterson, *Out of Order* (New York: Knopf, 1993), 20–21.
31. Quoted in Joe Klein, "Where's the Music?" *New Yorker*, September 27, 1999, 42.
32. Jack W. Germond, "Confessions of a McLaughlin Group Escapee," *Brill's Content*, September 1999, 84–87.
33. Lee Sigelman, Jarol B. Manheim, and Susannah Pierce, "Inside Dopes? Pundits as Political Forecasters," *Harvard International Journal of Press/Politics* 1 (Winter 1996): 33–50.
34. Walter Goodman, "Dependable Partisans Celebrate Fifteen Years of Sparring," *New York Times*, June 23, 1997.
35. Alicia C. Shepard, "The Pundit Explosion," *American Journalism Review* (September 1995): 24–29.
36. For an interesting account of the paper's history, see Peter Prichard, *The Making of McPaper: The Inside Story of* USA Today (Kansas City, Mo.: Andrews, McMeel & Parker, 1987).
37. Russell J. Dalton, Paul A. Beck, and Robert Huckfeldt, "Partisan Cues and the Media: Information Flows in the 1992 Presidential Election," *American Political Science Review* 92 (March 1998): 111–26.
38. See, for example, Michael J. Robinson and Margaret A. Sheehan, *Over the Wire and on TV: CBS and UPI in Campaign '80* (New York: Russell Sage Foundation, 1983).
39. Stephen Hess, "Credibility and the Bottom Line," *Presstime* 20 (July/August 1998): 25.
40. Adam Gopnik, "Read All about It," *New Yorker*, December 12, 1994, 93.
41. Deborah Tannen, *The Argument Culture* (New York: Ballantine Books, 1998), 58.
42. Joseph N. Cappella and Kathleen Hall Jamieson, *Spiral of Cynicism* (New York: Oxford University Press, 1997), 229.
43. Daniel Patrick Moynihan, *Counting Our Blessings: Reflections on the Future of America* (Boston: Atlantic Monthly Press, 1980), 115–37.
44. Lanny J. Davis, *Truth to Tell* (New York: Free Press, 1999), 35.
45. See Morton M. Kondracke, "Pennsylvania Avenue," *Roll Call*, May 4, 2000, 6.

3

Polling to Campaign and to Govern
Karlyn Bowman

By the time Iowans went to their caucuses on January 24, 2000, the major national pollsters had asked more than 1,000 questions about the election. But that number does not begin to tell the story of their activity. For some of the media pollsters, the 2000 campaign started before the last presidential election ended. In 1995 Gallup, CNN, and *USA Today* asked people what they would like to see Colin Powell do in the 2000 presidential contest if he declined to enter the 1996 one. In September 1996 the ABC News/*Washington Post* poll asked people whether they would be satisfied with the choice between Democrat Al Gore and Republican Jack Kemp in the 2000 election. In October the Yankelovich Partners/*Time*/CNN poll asked respondents whether they would vote for Kemp or Gore if "the year 2000 election for President were being held today." Also in October, the *Los Angeles Times* asked whether Kemp should be the nominee of the Republican Party in 2000, and, separately, whether Gore should be the nominee of the Democratic Party. Roughly seven in ten voters sensibly chose the response "too early to say." The pollsters' practice of advancing the campaign calendar is not limited to national contests. By the summer of 2000, state pollsters had asked questions about thirty-eight different senatorial and gubernatorial races—in 2002!

Private polling for political candidates is flourishing as well. Vice President Gore has used the services of seven experienced pollsters in his campaign, and George W. Bush has employed two veterans to direct his campaign's survey work. Writing about the 2000 contest in August 1999, the reporting team of Jules Witcover and Jack Germond asserted that never before has there been "a presidential campaign shaped by polls as thoroughly as this one. Survey data [have] defined the campaign to the point that it seems stripped of any purpose."[1]

A half century after the polling debacle in the 1948 election nearly destroyed the credibility of the adolescent survey research business, the industry is thriving, but the pollsters face credibility problems of different kinds. Polls are now a commonplace of political life. Virtually every aspect of the modern campaign is poll-tested, and private polling has become a prominent feature of governing for those inside the White House and those outside who seek to influence them. Meanwhile, the media pollsters use the "Who's winning? Who's losing?" formula that they employ in campaigns to judge the performance of elected officials and the success of their policies.

This chapter describes the growth of polls in presidential campaigns, during transitions to elected office, and finally, during the process of governing. The review is necessarily a superficial one, and it relies heavily on the work of scholars who have examined those areas in more detail. I am indebted particularly to David Moore, whose book *The Superpollsters* provides a thorough introduction to the practitioners and their practices. Robert Eisinger, Lawrence Jacobs, and Robert Shapiro are leaders among a small band of scholars whose research in presidential archives is providing a more complete picture of polling activity for presidential candidates and for presidents than has existed before.

The Candidates

Given the importance of public opinion in a democracy, it is hardly surprising that the device that purports to measure public opinion accurately is widely used. One indication of the growth of polling comes from the collection of surveys housed at the Roper Center at the University of Connecticut. Most of the major survey firms that release data publicly send their polls to the center for archiving.

There are 9,157 individual questions from polls in the archive from the 1960s. During the 1990s, the archivists added more than 132,000 questions to the center's database. In the 1960s questions from the Gallup and Harris polls made up slightly more than three-quarters of the collection; their combined contributions in the 1990s represented just 22 percent of the entries. In the 1960s nine firms archived their data with the Roper Center; today, eighty-six are represented.[2] Not all the questions in the archive are political ones, of course, but they represent a substantial portion of the collection.

Starting in the 1930s, surveys as we know them today added a "scientific" cachet to politicians' efforts to win elections and govern successfully. It was not until the 1960 campaign, however, that candidate John F. Kennedy used a pollster to conduct private surveys for his campaign. According to campaign chronicler Theodore H. White, Louis Harris "polled more people across the country than had ever been done by any other political analyst in American history."[3]

Although the level of sophistication of Harris's effort pales in comparison with what candidates and political parties use today, his polls were used, as they are today, in virtually every aspect of the 1960 campaign, from helping to chart a campaign strategy, to scheduling the candidate's appearances, and to dealing with the touchy issue of resistance to a Catholic president in the White House.[4] Harris, like his successors, polled about potential vice presidential candidates. He has described his role as being on the candidate's strategy committee, briefing him about public attitudes before each debate, helping the campaign team devise a campaign theme, and writing newspaper ads.[5] Harris polled in thirty-nine states at least once. He did not poll in states where opposition to a Catholic president would make it difficult for Kennedy to win. Jacobs and Shapiro reported that Harris conducted "66 polls during the primary and general election campaign, 26 of them between September and November 1960."[6] Two decades later, in the 1980 campaign, during the period from late August to election day, Patrick Caddell, working for Jimmy Carter, conducted 133 separate state surveys, fourteen national polls, three waves of qualitative work, and two market tests of commercials. In the same time period, Richard Wirthlin, polling for Ronald Reagan, conducted sixty-four separate state polls, more than a half dozen national surveys, and several small-sample surveys in response to critical campaign events. In addition, Wirthlin used a sophisticated computer program to track the voting intentions of more than 10,000 likely voters.[7]

David Moore observed that Harris's advice to Kennedy to confront the issue of his religion as he campaigned for the West Virginia primary may have been "the first notable influence of a pollster on a campaign," although he and others suggested that a stronger case could be made for the advice Patrick Caddell gave to Democratic candidate George McGovern to enter the Ohio primary in 1972, because Caddell's poll-based guidance much more closely reflected the actual outcome than Harris's.[8]

Anyone who studies the evolution of polls must be impressed by how changes in technology have changed the business and its role in politics. Jacobs and Shapiro reported that Harris's data on policy issues "took on average two weeks to reach Kennedy for much of the campaign."[9] Today, data collection is almost instantaneous. Harris and his young assistant, the now-prominent Democratic pollster Peter Hart, used slide rules to make election night calculations at the Kennedy compound in Hyannis Port, Massachusetts. In that campaign it took Gallup two weeks to tell the country who had won the late September Kennedy-Nixon debate. In 1976 the Associated Press reported results of a panel study on reactions to the presidential debate the night of the debate. In 1992 CBS News reported results of the second presidential debate within fifteen minutes of its conclusion.[10]

While technology has changed political polling in fundamental ways, some continuities exist from the work of forty years ago to the work being done for candidates today. During the 1960 campaign, Harris asked people about the most important problem facing the nation. He followed up by asking them what could be done about it. Today, pollsters frequently ask those questions. Many of the concerns Americans have today are not very different from their concerns forty years ago. Moore, for example, noted that Kennedy "hammered at education themes," after he had learned from his polling that 80 percent of American families hoped to send their children to college, though fewer than 30 percent did so then.[11]

Beginning in 1964, the pollsters' story could be told from the Democratic or the Republican perspective, as each campaign used private polling in its decisionmaking. The strategic blueprints and poll findings a Democratic and a Republican pollster provide are often mirror images of one another. In 1984 Peter Hart, polling for Vice President Mondale, and Richard Wirthlin, polling for President Reagan, said that they compared notes after the election and that from September on, their "figures never varied from one another by more than 2 percent."[12]

In 1972, according to Moore, both presidential campaigns did "daily interviewing, rotating the samples from state to state." Those surveys were a "precursor of the tracking polls"[13] that the candidates and media pollsters use today. Although the advertising agency that worked for the Eisenhower campaign in 1956 used telephone polls, the first campaign pollster to use them was Robert Teeter in 1972. Teeter, who was director of research for the Nixon reelection effort, also continued to conduct in-person interviews. The 1972 campaign was also the first campaign to use audience-reaction meters to calibrate people's reactions to candidates' speeches.[14] Although it is hard to pinpoint what year focus groups were used for the first time in private polling efforts for a presidential candidate, they have been used in the commercial world for decades.

Modern surveys are so sophisticated that they can be used in a myriad of ways, not all of them salutary for democracy. Patrick Caddell, armed with data about an electorate alienated from national political life, contributed to a campaign strategy designed to depress voter turnout in the 1986 California senate contest. It worked, and his candidate won, but the exercise caused Caddell to withdraw temporarily from the business when he realized the effect his poll-based advice had had on the election.

The influence of pollsters in presidential campaigns is unique because the special expertise they bring to campaigns is indispensable in most aspects of modern campaigns. This is often combined with long-standing personal relationships with the candidates they serve. Harris's first poll about the Kennedy-Nixon race was conducted in 1957 for Richard Lee, the New Haven, Connecticut, Democratic mayor who introduced Kennedy and Harris that year. Patrick Caddell met Governor Jimmy Carter in 1972 when he was polling for presidential candidate George McGovern, and over time he developed a friendship with Carter and his wife. Richard Wirthlin met Ronald Reagan in 1968, when Reagan was governor. That pattern of long association continues to cement those relationships.

The work that the pollsters do for presidential candidates gets a great deal of media attention. Still, the business is a relatively small one. Mervin Field, founder of one of the longest running state polls, the Field poll in California, argued that when Teddy Kennedy geared up his campaign in 1980, he had "50 to 100 ad agencies to choose from, firms that could measure up to a national race . . . but [only] two or three" names of possible pollsters.[15] Today, there are only about two dozen men or women who could direct the polling operation in a presidential campaign.

This account of changes in polling during presidential races is only a partial picture of the polling activity in campaigns. In the early 1960s Louis Harris estimated that more than two-thirds of the men running for the U.S. Senate in the 1962 elections used private polling in their campaigns.[16] In 1984, when the *National Journal* published the first comprehensive survey of political consultants and their clients in Senate and gubernatorial contests, it reported that "every serious candidate in a contested race had hired both a pollster and a media consultant."[17] In addition, the national party committees and the congressional and senatorial campaign committees poll continually.

Media Polls

The polling-media-politics connection is as old as the polling business itself. In part to boost their commercial research businesses, George Gallup, Archibald Crossley, and Elmo Roper published their new "scientific" poll results in newspapers and magazines. The editors of *Fortune,* in introducing their survey in July 1935, argued that "the survey technique is not only as well adapted to journalistic use as to other uses, but considerably better adapted."[18]

In its first survey in October 1935, Gallup asked whether people had voted for Roosevelt in 1932 and, separately, whether they would vote for him today. In January 1936 the organization asked people whether they would vote for Roosevelt or the Republican. In January 1936 the editors of *Fortune* noted, in prose that is familiar to us today, that "[t]he season for the preelection counting of political noses opened early last fall with more [straw] polls than can be conveniently kept track of, and more conflicting results than can be reconciled by any theory other than the old cliche 'you can prove anything with figures.'" In the poll, Roper asked a four-part question that probed the intensity of people's feelings about Roosevelt's reelection. *Fortune* editorialized that "the spirit of prophecy was not upon *Fortune*'s editors when they set out to explore the public attitudes toward the Roosevelt administration."[19]

That disdain for prophecy notwithstanding, *Fortune* touted the accuracy of its predictions after the election was over—a practice that continues today: "No national forecaster (barring *Fortune*) predicted a greater proportion of the popular vote for Mr. Roosevelt than he received in 1932." Although the results were a source of institutional satisfaction, the editors thundered:

> Rightness or wrongness in the quadrennial game of forecasting elections should not be regarded as something tremendous in itself partly because it would not be healthy that the game should become endowed with exaggerated importance, partly because it is not really a primary function of journalism.[20]

By 1948 Gallup was mailing "four releases a week to 126 newspapers with 20 million readers."[21] The first state poll was conducted in Texas, and by the 1940s, a dozen pollsters were working on other state polls. The *Washington Post*, the first newspaper to subscribe to Gallup's "America Speaks" column, polled locally in 1945.[22]

The media-polling partnerships that are most familiar to us today began about a quarter of a century ago when CBS News and the *New York Times* joined forces. They used their surveys for independent assessments of the claims made by the candidate pollsters, political consultants, and government officials. Today, the country's leading newspapers all poll, as do the five major networks, many local affiliates, and the major news magazines. In addition to the CBS News/*New York Times* poll, there are ten other major national media polls in the field on a regular basis.[23] The *Hotline,* a daily news briefing for political junkies that began in 1987, publishes the results of new national, state, and local political polls every day. The *Hotline* also conducts polls of its own.

Not only has the number of media polls grown over the past twenty-five years, but so too has the amount of activity by the individual organizations. CBS News and the *New York Times* sent 1,586 questions to the Roper Center archive in the 1970s; in the 1990s they sent more than 12,000. One indication of the growth in the political work done by the media pollsters comes again from the Roper Center's archive. It includes 118 questions that mention *both* Richard Nixon and George McGovern in the same question, 222 that include the names Gerald Ford and Jimmy Carter, 480 about Jimmy Carter and Ronald Reagan, 701 about Ronald Reagan and Walter Mondale, 939 about George Bush and Michael Dukakis, 1,475 about George Bush and Bill Clinton, and 2,125 about Bob Dole and Bill Clinton.[24]

The media pollsters and scores of others are active during all the phases of the presidential campaign—the jockeying before the primaries, the primaries, the conventions, and finally the stretch until election day. CBS News began surveying the delegates to the national conventions in 1968, and other media pollsters have followed suit. Both Gallup and Roper asked questions about Wendell Willkie's challenge to debate Franklin Roosevelt in 1940. In 1960, according to Sidney Kraus and Melanie Ross, the pollsters asked fourteen questions about the presidential debates.[25] In 1996 they asked more than 130 questions about the debates. In 1980 poll standings were used as a criterion for participation in the debates.

Not only are the media polls influential throughout the campaign, but they are also used to explain the results. In 1967 CBS conducted what is generally thought to be the first systematic exit poll of voters as they left the polls, in the Kentucky gubernatorial contest.[26] In 1984 and 1988 CBS, NBC, ABC, and the *Los Angeles Times* were conducting separate exit polls at enormous expense to the individual networks. To keep costs down, CBS, NBC, ABC, and CNN formed an exit polling consortium known as Voter Research and Surveys. In 1990 that new entity conducted its first exit poll. In 1996 Fox News and the National Election Service, the operation that counts actual votes, joined the consortium, now called the Voter News Service. For just a seat at the table today, each of the five participating networks pays on average more than $1 million a year to VNS. Despite that price tag, the pool arrangement has saved the networks millions of dollars over the election cycle. Exit polls are conducted in presidential and off-year contests, in primary and general election campaigns.

Predictable patterns of growth and stagnation exist in campaign polling activity. In years when an incumbent runs, fewer questions are usually asked about the preferences of his party's followers. In years with significant third-party candidates, the total number of questions increases. The total number of questions asked about the presidential candidates between 1976 and 1996 for the oldest major media pollster, CBS News and the *New York Times,* tripled. Much of the growth in the number of questions asked during each election cycle has occurred in the past eight years, in part because several pollsters started taking daily soundings at different stages in the past two campaigns.

Transitions

The polling conducted privately by campaigns and publicly by media pollsters does not come to a halt after election day. Although the advice that private pollsters provide presidents-elect rarely becomes public, the *Washington Post* obtained a copy of a memo Patrick Caddell provided Jimmy Carter soon after the 1976 election. Caddell was one of a handful of campaign insiders to write memos to Carter about the transition. His 10,000-word, fifty-one-page "Initial Working Paper on Political Strategy" described in essence the permanent campaign. Caddell himself recalls coining the term, but it is generally credited to Sidney Blumenthal, who wrote a book with that title.[27] "In devising a strategy for the Administration," Caddell wrote, "it is important to recognize we cannot successfully separate politics and government. . . . Essentially it is my thesis that governing with public approval requires a continuing political campaign." The memo included a poll-derived analysis of voter alienation from national political life. In addition, it suggested "cutting back on imperial frills and perks," using symbolic actions such as "fireside chats" during the preinaugural period, "ostentatious use of guests such as Bob Dylan, Martin Luther King, Sr., and perhaps an older conservative to make some points" at the time of the inauguration, and "town meetings" during the early months of the presidency. Caddell argued that the administration needed to "buy time quickly," because "given their mood today, the American people may turn on us before we ever get off the mark."[28]

The memo also included a discussion about implementing a working group to begin planning the 1980 campaign. Caddell suggested using the Democratic National Committee to identify and "coopt the people who might help staff opposing political campaigns."[29] In a presidential news conference a few days after portions of Caddell's memo appeared in the Washington Post in May 1977, President Carter was asked several questions about Caddell's poll-based advice.[30] So central had the role of the "pollster-as-adviser" become that he was the subject of a presidential press conference.

Like Caddell, Richard Wirthlin submitted an initial action plan to Ronald Reagan in 1980. Wirthlin argued that the campaign principals knew "with a great deal of certainty what [Reagan] wanted to do. . . . The purpose of the plan was to put in sharp relief how that might best be accomplished." At the request of the president, Wirthlin briefed the cabinet members on public attitudes and "the reasons and rationale for the presidential win."[31]

Whether Caddell was right or not about buying time, he knew that the pollsters would soon begin charting the new president's fortunes. Although the pollsters have long probed people's expectations about new presidents, a question asked by Yankelovich, Skelly, and White for Time in 1981 appears to be the first question that asked people specifically to assess a president-elect's standing during a transition: "Regardless of how you voted, have your impressions of Ronald Reagan improved, stayed the same, or gotten worse as a result of his performance during the transition period between administrations?" In 1992, sixteen days after the election, Gallup asked whether people approved of the way Bill Clinton was handling the transition. By inauguration day, five other pollsters had asked similar questions, some more than once. Questions were also asked about how George Bush was handling the transition to private life and whether Hillary Clinton was playing too great a role in her husband's transition operation. In November 1994 Gallup asked people how the Republican leaders were handling the transition from Democratic to Republican control of Congress.

The presidential job-approval question that Gallup inaugurated measures whether the president is up or down, winning or losing. With more pollsters in the field, that question is being asked more frequently and thus cements the notion of a permanent campaign. Table 3-1 documents the increase in the pace of polling activity during a president's first 100 days. In 1969 three pollsters asked eight job-approval questions during the first 100 days of the Nixon presidency. By 1993 ten pollsters asked thirty-seven job-approval questions in the first 100 days of the Clinton administration. We have gone from one job-approval sounding every 12.5 days to one every 2.7 days. As for presidents themselves, John F. Kennedy received from Louis Harris, a document, "Public Reaction to President Kennedy during the First 60 Days," with the results of two polls Harris had conducted. The memo included a job-approval question and views about Kennedy's positive and negative characteristics and his actions.[32]

Governing

President Roosevelt, who became "an instant devotee of the new, more scientific polls"[33] after they predicted his landslide in 1936, was the first president to use private polling, although the objectives that the polling was designed to serve are different from what they are today. Roosevelt's polling operation was secretly run by Hadley Cantril, director of the Office of Public Opinion Research at Princeton University, who did original surveys for the White House (often with White House input on question wording) and provided data from Gallup and Roper polls, some of which were never released publicly. In his memoir Cantril said:

Table 3-1 Number and Frequency of Job-Approval Questions during the First 100 Days in Office

	1945	1953	1961	1964	1969	1974	1977	1981	1989	1993
President	Truman	Eisenhower	Kennedy	Johnson	Nixon	Ford	Carter	Reagan	Bush	Clinton
Number	1	4	4	6	8	11	14	15	27	37
Frequency	100+	(every 25 days)	25	16.67	12.5	9.09	7.14	6.67	3.7	2.7
	Gallup	Gallup	Gallup	Gallup	Gallup	Gallup	Gallup	Gallup	Gallup	Gallup
					Harris	Harris	Harris	Harris	Gallup/Pew	Gallup/CNN/ *USA Today*
					ORC	ORC	CBS/NYT	CBS/NYT	Harris	Gallup/Newsweek
						Yankelovich	NBC	NBC/AP	CBS/NYT	Harris
								ABC/WP	NBC/WSJ	CBS/NYT
								LAT	ABC/WP	NBC/WSJ
									LAT	ABC/WP
									Yankelovich	*LAT*
									Gordon Black	Yankelovich
										PSRA/Pew
										PSRA/Newsweek
										Wirthlin
										Tarrance/Mellman/ Lazarus/Lake

Note: Questions are not worded identically.

[The president] regarded the reports . . . the way a general would regard information turned in by his intelligence services as he planned the strategy of a campaign. As far as I am aware, Roosevelt never altered his goals because public opinion appeared against him or was uninformed. Rather he utilized such information to try to bring the public around more quickly or more effectively to the course of action he felt was best for the country.[34]

Robert Eisinger, who has studied the Roosevelt polling effort, had a less benign assessment: "Roosevelt's advisers used polls as vehicles to advance the president's agenda and as instruments to measure the popularity of policies not yet codified and candidates not yet announced."[35] Roosevelt had, for example, information about public attitudes toward Lend-Lease before the program was announced. Eisinger and Jeremy Brown argued that Roosevelt's polls gave him independence from other powerful political actors of the day, particularly the Democratic Party, Congress, and the media.[36]

Given his own experience with the polls that predicted Tom Dewey's victory in 1948, Truman did not pay as much attention to them as his predecessor, although he did receive poll reports from government departments. New scholarship has suggested that the Eisenhower campaign and White House "routinely received poll data" and used it for public relations purposes.[37] Louis Harris talked to Kennedy "two or three times a week," although he said that he believed that it was a conflict of interest to poll for an elected official for whom he had worked during the campaign.

Jacobs and Shapiro have provided the most comprehensive account of the use of polling in the Kennedy, Johnson, and Nixon administrations, a period in which they argued that "public opinion analysis became an integral part of the institution of the presidency." Not only did White Houses become "veritable warehouses for public opinion data" during those presidencies, but analysis of the data became routine and regular, and additional staff were assigned to conduct that analysis. Presidents Kennedy and Johnson tacked questions onto polls being conducted for other clients, but President Nixon was "the sole sponsor of polls, enabling him to control the timing, frequency, content and dissemination of the findings."[38]

Jacobs and Shapiro believed that the differences among the three presidents in their use of polls were less important than the trend in all three administrations toward "developing a public opinion apparatus as an institutional component of the modern presidency." Jacobs and Shapiro maintained that each of those presidents used "their public opinion analyses to make and sell the president and his policies."[39]

All presidents since Nixon have continued to poll privately, although the more recent ones await their Eisinger, Shapiro, or Jacobs to chronicle their use of polls. Richard Wirthlin met with Ronald Reagan more than twenty-five times in the first twenty-nine months of the administration and delivered memoranda on the results of over forty public opinion studies to the president's top three aides.[40] Stanley Greenberg, polling for President Clinton in his first term, said that early in the admininstration he did monthly tracking surveys and met with the president about once a week for fifteen minutes during Clinton's first year in office.

The pollsters in recent presidencies have differed more in style than in the technical work they do for presidents. The young polling *wunderkind* Patrick Caddell generated considerable media interest. Robert Teeter, Richard Wirthlin, Fred Steeper, and Stanley Greenberg had lower media profiles, perhaps because of their dispositions and perhaps because the role they play is now more familiar to the public. Dick Morris, President Clinton's campaign strategist and pollster, claimed that his polling extended to areas such as presidential vacation spots. President Clinton admitted that Morris told him of a poll he conducted that showed that Americans would be more willing to forgive the president for adultery than for perjury or obstruction of justice, although it is not clear that the White House commissioned that survey.

Shadowing the work of the presidents' pollsters have been the public pollsters, whose coverage of presidents has risen substantially in the past fifty years. Gallup asked the presidential job-approval question 119 times during Eisenhower's two terms and 135 times during Reagan's terms. Between January 1993 and December 1999, with one year still to go in the Clinton presidency, Gallup asked the question 201 times.

Although they are fairly crude exercises, searches of the Roper Center's database provide a snapshot of the explosion of polling on issues with which presidents must deal. The words *Vietnam* or *Vietnam War* appear 1,397 times in questions in the Roper Center's database in the fourteen years from 1961 through 1974. With more pollsters in the field, the Roper Center's database includes nearly 800 questions about the Gulf War in the eight months from August 1990 through March 1991. Seventeen Gallup and Harris questions about Medicare appear in 1965, the year the legislation passed. In 1994, the year Clinton's health care plan failed, 1,417 questions appear in the database about health care (in 1993, there are 1,824 questions). In all of 1973 and 1974, 103 questions in the archive used a variant of the word *impeach.* In 1998 and 1999 the database has 1,290 such questions. Several polling organizations tracked President Clinton's standing daily at different points during the impeachment drama. During the final weeks of the Clarence Thomas confirmation battle, during the Gulf War, and during the height of U.S. involvement in Kosovo, so many pollsters were in the field asking questions that several soundings each week were available. The pollsters described those issues in terms very similar to the ones they use in campaigns to measure the ups and downs of candidates. Was Thomas up, or was he losing ground? Would the president win or lose public support on the Gulf War and Kosovo? Policy issues can be made into a thousand little elections. Slightly more than 400 questions appear in the archive about all the first ladies from Eleanor Roosevelt through Barbara Bush. From 1992 through 1998, 1,202 questions about Hillary Clinton appear. Approximately 100 questions appear about Democratic Speakers Tip O'Neill and Jim Wright together. More than 800 were asked about Newt Gingrich between 1994 and 1998.

Conclusion

For several years the survey research community has been engaged in a debate about online polling. Two of its proponents, Humphrey Taylor, chairman of Louis Harris and Associates, and George Terhanian, director of Internet research at Harris Black International, have argued that the online research business is "an unstoppable train [that is] accelerating."[41] Although Taylor and Terhanian asserted that not all methodologies are appropriate for all kinds of research, they have started, and plan to continue, online polling in political contests. In 1998 they conducted online polls in fourteen Senate and gubernatorial contests, in part to increase their understanding of the challenges the new technology would pose. They planned to poll in all the major Senate and gubernatorial races in 2000. CBS News, with the assistance of InterSURVEY, conducted an online poll of views on President Clinton's January 27, 2000, State of the Union address and reported results the same night as the speech.

New technologies often meet resistance, and those used in survey research are no exception. Online polling may be the new frontier, but methodological hurdles remain in using the technique in elections. Although serious questions are being raised about the problem of rising refusal rates in telephone surveys,[42] for the most part the modern survey techniques used by candidates, presidents, parties, interest groups, and the media are widely accepted, and those individuals and groups will continue to use the techniques. As for the effects of public polls on voters, Michael W. Traugott, who has both contributed to and reviewed the literature, argued that although a wide range of effects of media polls can be documented, "large-scale shifts in voter preference or actual voting behavior based on information about what other citizens are thinking or doing . . . cannot be demonstrated conclusively."[43]

Candidates will continue to poll privately in their campaigns, and the work of their pollsters will continue after they are elected. President Roosevelt received polling information secretly, and it helped give him autonomy from the parties, his media critics, and Congress. Although political parties today pay for surveys for presidents, the surveys still provide the White House with private independent assessments. Roosevelt used polls to understand the mood of the country and to help him advance his policies. His successors have done the same. Whether polls are used to make policy depends on the convictions of the officeholder sponsoring the polls.

In part because the polls and the pollsters have become more prominent, they have become prominent targets even among politicians who use them. Michael Dukakis mentioned polls in just under one-fifth of his speeches in 1988, Bob Dole mentioned them in a third of his.[44] Journalist Walter Shapiro noted a subtle change of emphasis in the antipolling chorus in 1999. He cited George W. Bush's speech at the Iowa straw poll in August 1999 as an indication: "I know how to lead," said Bush. "I don't run polls to tell me what to think. The most important, most influential job in America should be the president, not the president's pollster."[45] The attack on "government by polls" may simply be a fresh assault on a familiar target, and it may be a reflection on the Clinton administration's voracious appetite for polls. It may also be a commentary on the proliferation of polls.

The media polls are the public face of the industry, and they are now a permanent feature of the permanent campaign. Polls are news, and they shape and color media coverage of campaigns. Poll standings contributed to decisions by two candidates to drop out of the 2000 race months before a caucus or primary had taken place. In the competitive media-polling environment, pollsters blur the lines between campaigning and governing, in part because they chart the performance of elected officeholders the same way they cover the fortunes of candidates.

The abundance of polls also magnifies problems inherent in polling. While substantial continuity in attitudes exists in many areas, other areas exist where attitudes are tentative and unformed. With so much competition in the media-polling business, pollsters are delving into many areas and reporting opinion as if that opinion is firm when it is not. We know that early in 2000 many Americans had not given much thought to the 2000 presidential contest. Yet opinions about the race, as about many other political issues, were reported as if they had been settled.

The race to be first degrades the polling enterprise. I began this chapter by citing polls taken in 1995 and 1996 about the 2000 presidential race. The media pollsters need to ask themselves what news value those polls have. Polls that help to advance the campaign calendar may make life interesting for political insiders, but such polls trivialize the contests for ordinary citizens. Just because pollsters *can* ask questions years before an election takes place, just because they *can* provide virtually instantaneous readings of public reactions to presidential debates, just because they *can* track the preferences of citizens on a daily basis during campaigns, and just because they *can* conduct polls online does not mean that they *should* do so.

The media polls have also indulged in sensationalism. In 1997 one of the major media pollsters asked a graphic question about a court-ordered examination of President Clinton's genitals in connection with the Paula Jones lawsuit. During the impeachment drama, a number of the pollsters asked questions about Monica Lewinsky's motivations. One asked whether she was a tramp. What constitutes oral sex was another subject of poll inquiries, as was the question whether the president was a sex addict. It is tempting to think that those kinds of questions were a one-time occurrence, but the practice by pollsters of focusing on the sensational is not limited to President Clinton's behavior.

When something becomes common, it loses value. Although little evidence exists of public hostility to polling, rising refusal rates may be a rough verdict on the way polls are being conducted today. Public attitudes are, as the editors of *Fortune* said in introducing their poll over sixty years ago, "the raw material of politics." If pollsters permit the competitive pressures of the media business to drive the survey business, both the public credibility of the polls and the deeper understanding polls can provide of the nation's rich and complex political life may suffer.

Notes

1. Jack W. Germond and Jules Witcover, "Polls Haven't Replaced Voters—Yet," *National Journal* (August 14, 1999): 2392.
2. Lois Timms-Ferrara of the Roper Center at the University of Connecticut provided this information. The data are through April 1999.
3. Quoted in David W. Moore, *The Superpollsters* (New York: Four Walls Eight Windows, 1995), 79.
4. In 1937 the Gallup Organization asked, "If your party nominated a generally well-qualified person for president who happened to be Catholic, would you vote for that person?" In 1937 60 percent said they would, but 30 percent said they would not. In May 1960 71 percent said they would, but 21 percent said they would not.
5. Louis Harris, Patrick Caddell, Richard Wirthlin, and Stanley Greenberg, panel discussion, American Enterprise Institute Annual Policy Conference, Washington, D.C., December 8, 1993.

6. Lawrence R. Jacobs and Robert Y. Shapiro, "Issues, Candidate Image, and Priming: The Use of Private Polls in Kennedy's 1960 Presidential Campaign," *American Political Science Review* 88, no. 3 (September 1994): 530.

7. Mark R. Levy, "Polling and the Presidential Election," *Annals of the American Academy of Political and Social Science* 472 (March 1984): 89, n. 5.

8. Moore, *The Superpollsters,* 86, 134–35.

9. Jacobs and Shapiro, "Issues, Candidate Image, and Priming," 531.

10. For 1960 and 1992, Kathleen A. Frankovic, "News Media Polling in a Changing Technological Environment," lecture, Northwestern University School of Speech, May 25, 1994, 11. For 1976, conversation with Evans Witt, fall 1999.

11. Moore, *The Superpollsters,* 79.

12. "Moving Right Along? Campaign '84's Lessons for 1988," interview with Peter Hart and Richard Wirthlin, *Public Opinion* 7, no. 6 (December/January 1985): 59.

13. Moore, *The Superpollsters,* 223.

14. Ibid.

15. William J. Lanouette, "When a Presidential Candidate Moves, a Pollster May Be Pulling the Strings," *National Journal* (December 15, 1979): 2093.

16. Robert King and Martin Schnitzer, "Contemporary Use of Private Political Polling," *Public Opinion Quarterly* 32, no. 3 (1968): 433.

17. Jerry Hagstrom, "Soul of a New Machine," *National Journal* (June 18, 1984): 1458.

18. "The Fortune Survey," *Fortune,* July 1935, 66.

19. "The Fortune Survey," *Fortune,* January 1936, 47, 141.

20. "The Fortune Survey," *Fortune,* January 1937, 86.

21. Richard Jensen, "Democracy by the Numbers," *Public Opinion* 3, no. 1A (February–March 1980), 59.

22. Kathleen A. Frankovic, "Public Opinion Polling: The U.S. Experience," speech at Fifth Latin American Marketing Research Conference, Santiago, Chile, April 1999.

23. ABC News and the *Washington Post*; NBC News and the *Wall Street Journal*; Gallup, CNN, and *USA Today*; Fox News and Opinion Dynamics; Zogby International and Reuters. The *Los Angeles Times* polls alone. Yankelovich Partners polls for CNN and *Time*; Princeton Survey Research Associates polls for *Newsweek*. A bipartisan polling team called Battleground releases quarterly surveys, some of which have been done for *U.S. News & World Report*. National Public Radio has begun a collaboration with the Kaiser Family Foundation and Harvard University. Princeton Survey Research Associates also polls for the Pew Research Center for the People and the Press.

24. This search of the Roper Center archive was done in 1999. In part because of the many different ways questions are asked and responses coded, the

kind of searches we have done for this chapter produce a solid count of the questions described in the text, although it may not be a precise count.

25. Sidney Kraus and Melanie Ross, "Polling on the Debates," *Public Perspective* 7, no. 5 (August/September 1996): 59.

26. Moore, *The Superpollsters,* 255.

27. Harris, Caddell, Wirthlin, and Greenberg, panel discussion.

28. Quoted in Sidney Blumenthal, *The Permanent Campaign: Inside the World of Elite Political Operatives* (Boston: Beacon Press, 1980), 38–39, 42.

29. Nancy Collins and Robert G. Kaiser, "The Scenario: Most of Carter's Early Moves Charted in 1976 Caddell Memo," *Washington Post,* May 4, 1977.

30. *Public Papers of the Presidents: Jimmy Carter, 1977,* vol. 1 (Washington, D.C.: Government Printing Office: 1977), 864–65.

31. Harris, Caddell, Wirthlin, and Greenberg, panel discussion.

32. Robert M. Eisinger, "The Illusion of Certainty: Explaining the Evolution of Presidential Polling," Ph.D. dissertation, University of Chicago, 1996, 130.

33. Jensen, "Democracy by the Numbers," 59.

34. Quoted in Seymour Sudman, "The Presidents and the Polls," *Public Opinion Quarterly* 46 (1982): 303.

35. Robert M. Eisinger, "Pollster and Public Relations Adviser: Hadley Cantril and the Birth of Presidential Polling," manuscript, University of Chicago, n.d., 3.

36. Robert Eisinger and Jeremy Brown, "Polling as Means toward Presidential Autonomy: Emil Hurja, Hadley Cantril, and the Roosevelt Administration," *International Journal of Public Opinion Research* 10, no. 3 (1998): 237.

37. Eisinger, "The Illusion of Certainty," 90.

38. Lawrence R. Jacobs and Robert Y. Shapiro, "The Rise of Presidential Polling: The Nixon White House in Historical Perspective," *Public Opinion Quarterly* 59 (1995): 166, 173.

39. Ibid., 192.

40. Richard S. Beal and Ronald H. Hinckley, "Presidential Decisionmaking and Opinion Polls," *Annals of the American Academy of Political and Social Science* 472 (March 1984): 72.

41. Humphrey Taylor and George Terhanian, "Heady Days Are Here Again: Online Polling Is Rapidly Coming of Age," *Public Perspective* 10, no. 4 (June/July 1999): 23.

42. The Council for Marketing and Opinion Research, the industry association, conducted studies in 1995 and 1997 to examine the dimensions of the problem. Both studies put the refusal rate at 58 percent for telephone surveys done using random digit dialing and lasting ten to twenty minutes. Industry-sponsored studies in the 1980s found refusal rates in the range of 38 to 46 percent.

43. Michael W. Traugott, "The Impact of Media Polls on the Public," in *Media Polls in American Politics,* edited by Thomas E. Mann and Gary R. Orren (Washington, D.C.: Brookings Institution, 1992): 145–46.

44. Information compiled from the election databases of the Annenberg School at the University of Pennsylvania by Kathleen A. Frankovic and reported in a speech, "Defending the Polls: Three Challenges for 2000 and Beyond," New York Association of Public Opinion Researchers, N.Y., 1999.

45. Cited in Walter Shapiro, "Pollster Bashing Now a Campaign Trend," *USA Today*, August 18, 1999.

4

Running Backward: The Congressional Money Chase

Anthony Corrado

No aspect of the modern political process is as emblematic of the permanent campaign as the constant fund-raising that now takes place inside the Capital Beltway and beyond. Members of the House, facing reelection contests every two years, are essentially campaigning and raising money all the time, one election bid merging into the next, with little or no respite between. Members of the Senate, who have traditionally enjoyed some break from campaigning owing to their longer terms of office, have also felt compelled to begin fund-raising earlier and earlier in an election cycle, and most incumbents now raise money throughout the course of their six-year terms. Indeed, the quest for campaign dollars has become so persistent and pervasive that members of Congress are commonly described as being entrenched in a "money chase" or a "fund-raising arms race" to which there is no end in sight.

To gauge the emphasis placed on fund-raising in Washington, one need only take note of the schedule of events at the private clubs and restaurants around Capitol Hill on any given weekday that Congress is in session. On most mornings, a number of campaign fund-raising breakfasts are being held, usually sponsored by individual corporations, trade associations, or other lobbying organizations. The evenings are filled with candidate receptions, sometimes as many as a half-dozen or more per evening, honoring various members at a cost for each attendee of anywhere from $250 to $1,000 or more. In addition are party fund-raising events, political action committee receptions, and even fund-raising efforts conducted by PACs or political committees either established by or affiliated with specific members of Congress. Over the past decade, that search for cash has increasingly spilled over into the weekends, with members raising money not only back home in their states or districts, but also in major cities and at upscale resorts where they participate in weekend ski or golf getaways for lobbyists and other large contributors that are hosted by each party's congressional campaign committees.

It was not always that way. While Congress has always been an electorally sensitive institution with members undoubtedly mindful of the need to finance their campaigns, fund-raising was never so constant or frenetic as it is now. Rising campaign costs, changing political tactics, and shifting congressional mores have combined to enhance the significance of fund-raising and the role of money in the political process. As a result, political currency on Capitol Hill is increasingly measured in terms of cash and fund-raising prowess, as opposed to tenure in office, legislative expertise, or public popularity. Legislators place greater and greater emphasis on building political war chests to finance their elections, to discourage challengers, and to assist colleagues and fellow candidates. Lobbyists and other political donors find it easier to convert their financial resources into access to policymakers. The public and the media, meanwhile, raise more and more questions about the effect of all that money on legislative decisionmaking and the quality of representation provided by elected officials.

The permanent campaign for political money has thus generated important and alarming concerns about the effects of fund-raising and the influence of money on both the process of campaigning and the process of governing. This chapter seeks to address those questions by identifying the major factors that have contributed to the new "money politics" and by highlighting the recent changes that are obscuring the lines between campaigning and governing. In doing so, the chapter will make the case that members of Congress are raising more money earlier than ever before and using their positions as incumbents to raise money for purposes that are increasingly related more to the legislative process than to the electoral process.

Filling the Gap: The Growth of Off-Year Fund-Raising

In the 1960s and early 1970s and for the first years after the adoption of the Federal Election Campaign Act Amendments in 1974, a perceptible distinction existed between the campaign season and the legislative season and between the end of one campaign and the beginning of the next. Once the campaign season was over, the vast majority of the members of the incoming congressional class did not feel that they had to start raising money again *immediately*. Although legislators understood the need to maintain and build their electoral coalitions,[1] the beginning months of the congressional session were a time for a break from the rigors of campaigning and a respite from the task of soliciting donations. Instead, the focus of attention was on the agenda of the new Congress, legislative politics, and constituency work. While some members would begin raising money early in the off-election year, most would wait until later in the year to resume their solicitations.

By the mid-1980s, however, many members had begun raising money early in the off-election year or soon after arriving in Washington. In 1987 Senator David Boren (D-Oklahoma), in advocating a campaign finance reform bill, observed that "we have people . . . who come to [Congress] and have their first fund-raisers in this town before they ever cast their first votes as members of the House or Senate."[2] Similarly, Senator Robert Byrd (D-West Virginia), a long-time observer of Senate behavior, complained that one of his biggest problems as Senate majority leader was trying to accommodate his colleagues' need for more time away from the Senate chamber. In testimony before the Senate Rules Committee in 1987, Byrd noted that members wanted Mondays off and an early close on Fridays so that they could spend more time at home or elsewhere campaigning and raising money. "They have to go raise the money and they don't want any roll-call votes," Byrd complained. "Now how can a majority leader run the Senate under such circumstances?"[3] Byrd's criticism was sincere, and for him the culprit was clear: rapidly escalating campaign costs. But his question proved to

Table 4-1 Congressional Campaign Expenditures, 1974–1998

Election Year	Total Expenditures ($ millions)	House Candidates ($ millions)	Senate Candidates ($ millions)	Mean Expenditures House Incumbents ($)	Mean Expenditures Senate Incumbents ($)
1974	88.2	53.5	34.7	56,539	555,714
1976	115.5	71.5	44.0	79,398	623,809
1978	194.8	109.7	85.2	111,159	1,341,942
1980	239.6	136.7	102.9	165,081	1,301,692
1982	342.4	204.0	138.4	265,001	1,858,140
1984	374.1	203.6	170.5	279,044	2,539,929
1986	450.9	239.3	211.6	362,103	3,374,602
1988	457.7	256.5	201.2	378,544	3,748,126
1990	446.3	265.8	180.4	422,124	3,582,136
1992	678.3	406.7	271.6	594,699	3,852,428
1994	724.0	405.6	318.4	561,441	4,691,617
1996	759.1	472.5	286.6	678,556	4,236,694
1998	735.8	448.3	287.5	632,716	4,733,793

Sources: Figures on aggregate expenditures were based on data reported in Herbert E. Alexander and Anthony Corrado, *Financing the 1992 Election* (Armonk, N.Y.: M. E. Sharpe, 1995), and Federal Election Commission, "Reports on Congressional Fundraising for 1997–98," April 28, 1999. Figures on mean expenditures were based on the data reported in Norman J. Ornstein, Thomas E. Mann, and Michael J. Malbin, *Vital Statistics on Congress, 1984–1985* (Washington, D.C.: American Enterprise Institute, 1984), and *Vital Statistics on Congress, 1997–1998* (Washington, D.C.: Congressional Quarterly, 1998). The figures for 1998 were calculated by the author on the basis of the data reported in the Federal Election Commission's 1997–1998 report. All data for mean expenditures were based on the amounts spent by incumbents who ran in the general election of the year noted.

be largely rhetorical. In 1988 the Senate's work schedule was altered to give members time off to campaign and attend fund-raisers.[4]

Fund-raising became a more frequent and persistent feature of congressional life primarily in response to rising campaign costs. As noted in table 4-1, the amounts spent on congressional elections have grown dramatically over the past twenty-five years. Between 1974 and 1998, the total amount spent in House races rose from $53.5 million to $448.3 million, while total spending in Senate contests increased from $34.7 million to $287.5 million. Aggregate spending in House elections therefore increased at a slightly faster rate than in Senate elections (to approximately 8.5 times the 1974 total in the case of the House versus about 7.5 times for the Senate), but in both instances spending rose at a rate that is more than twice the size of the increase in the consumer price index occurring over that period.

The data in table 4-1 also indicate that the growth in campaign expenditures has been spurred by the sums spent by incumbents, whose spending rose at an even greater pace than the rate of total expenditures. For example, table 4-1 presents the mean expenditures of House and Senate incumbents who ran for reelection and made it to the general election for every election cycle since 1974. The figures show that while aggregate spending in House contests increased more than eightfold, the average amount spent by a member of the House seeking reelection rose elevenfold, from a little more than $56,000 to more than $630,000. In Senate races, the average amount spent by an incumbent grew from about $555,000 to more than $4.7 million, an increase greater than the total rise in Senate campaign spending. Incumbent spending thus led the way in the escalation of congressional campaign spending.

Moreover, those mean spending figures, which are used because they provide a better sense of the "typical" campaigns of members of Congress, obscure the fact that many incumbents spend far more than those figures suggest. For example, senators seeking reelection in the most populous states, such as California, New York, Texas, Florida, and Illinois, now spend $8 million or more in a campaign. In 1998 Barbara Boxer (D-California) spent over $15 million defending her seat, while Carol Moseley Braun (D-Illinois) spent over $9 million in losing hers. Republican Al D'Amato of New York raised the bar even higher; he disbursed over $27 million in a losing bid against his opponent, then-Representative Charles Schumer, who spent over $16 million.[5]

Those House members who run in competitive districts, where the winner receives 60 percent of the vote or less, also spend significantly more than the averages suggest. In 1996, for example, the average amount disbursed by the hundred incumbents who won in marginal races was over $995,000, while the twenty-one who were defeated in the general election spent an average of $1.1 million. In comparison, the average expenditure for all 382 House incumbents in the general election that year was less than $680,000. In 1992 the ninety-one House members who won reelection with less than 60 percent of the vote spent on average more than $780,000, while the twenty-four who lost marginal races averaged $890,000. In contrast, the average for the whole pool of 349 incumbents was about $595,000.[6]

As the financial demands of congressional campaigns have increased, so has the length of the campaign season. Candidates must devote more time and effort to fund-raising with each new election cycle, a factor that has lengthened the campaign period in recent decades and extended it to the point where it now basically encompasses the length of a congressional term. To raise the sums normally spent in congressional races, representatives have to raise an average of more than $7,000 a week, while senators have to raise more than $15,000 a week. Legislators involved in more competitive contests or those running in large states may have to raise two or three times as much. That is a sizable task, even for the most well-entrenched and well-heeled incumbents.

Although most legislators do not approach fund-raising on some sort of "weekly quota" basis, the rising demands of campaign fund-raising have encouraged legislators to make fund-raising a part of their congressional routine, a regular task that is basically considered "part of the job." Consequently, legislators are raising larger shares of their campaign budgets in the year or years preceding an election and taking advantage of the fund-raising opportunities that Washington offers.

Early Fund-Raising in the House. The "front-loading" of the campaign fund-raising process can be discerned by examining the changes in off-year financial activity that have characterized congressional elections in recent decades. The extent of those changes is suggested by the data in table 4-2, which offer a representative sample of the off-election-year financial activity conducted by House members who ran in the 1980, 1988, and 1998 elections.

Before the 1980 election, House members were raising about 12

Table 4-2 Financial Activity of House Members: Selected Off-Election Years

Year		1st 6 Months ($ millions)	2d 6 Months ($ millions)	Off-Year Total ($ millions)	% of Election Cycle Total[a]	% of Incumbent Total[b]
1979	Receipts	6.4	10.5	16.9	11.7	23.1
	Expenditures	5.9	6.7	12.6	9.2	19.0
	Cash on Hand	N/A	N/A	N/A	—	—
1987	Receipts	24.3	33.6	57.9	20.8	33.0
	Expenditures	17.7	21.9	39.6	6.5	25.3
	Cash on Hand	54.3	66.3	120.6	—	—
1997	Receipts	54.9	60.8	115.7	23.4	39.4
	Expenditures	35.4	35.2	70.6	15.6	27.5
	Cash on Hand	85.4	110.8	196.2	—	—

a. These are off-year finances as a share of the total amounts raised and spent by all congressional candidates in the election cycle.

b. These are off-year finances as a share of the total amounts raised and spent by all House members seeking reelection in the election cycle.

Source: The numbers are based on data reported by the Federal Election Commission.

81

percent of all the monies received by congressional candidates and about 25 percent of their own campaign funds in the year before the election. By the 1998 election cycle, those percentages had almost doubled, with incumbents' raising close to a quarter of all the monies generated in the congressional election cycle and almost 40 percent of their own campaign funds in the off-election year. The total amount of money received rose from $16.9 million to $115.7 million, which is about a sevenfold increase in a period of about two decades. The amount of campaign money spent during the off-year also grew significantly, from $12.6 million in 1979 to $70.6 million in 1997.

Not only were those House members increasing the scope of their off-year campaigning, but they were also engaging in that activity earlier and earlier and increasing the amount of fund-raising conducted in the earliest months of the election cycle. For example, as indicated in table 4-2, House members seeking reelection in 1980 raised about $6.4 million in the first six months of 1979 and another $10.5 million in the second part of that year. For those seeking reelection in 1988, the amount raised in the first six months rose to $24.3 million and ten years later, in the 1998 cycle, grew to $54.9 million. The sums realized in the second part of those pre-election years were $33.6 million in 1987 and $60.8 million in 1997. So, by the late 1990s, the amount of money raised in the first six months of the cycle was nearly nine times greater than it was two decades earlier, while the sum for the next six months was almost six times greater. The campaign season had become increasingly "front-loaded," at least as far as fund-raising was concerned, and more and more members were raising money throughout the entire period of their two-year term in office.

The advent of that permanent campaign activity provided members of the House with a major resource advantage over their future opponents. In fact, in recent election cycles, incumbent fund-raising in the off-election year has surpassed the amounts achieved by their challengers in the entire election cycle. At the end of the 1970s, the early financial efforts of incumbents seeking reelection were the equivalent of less than half the financial activity of their eventual general election challengers. In the 1980 election cycle, for example, those House members who sought reelection raised $16.9 million and spent $12.6 million in the off-year of 1979. In comparison, their general election challengers raised a total of about $37.8 million and spent about $36.3 million over the course of the two-year cycle.[7] Legislators' off-year activity was the equivalent of about 45 percent of their general election opponents' final receipts and about a third of their final expenditures.

By the late 1980s, the early fund-raising of House incumbents had begun to outmatch the sums raised by their eventual opponents. In the 1988 election cycle, members of the House raised $57.9 million in the preelection year of 1987 and spent $39.6 million. Their eventual general election challengers raised $15 million less, about $42.3 million, over the course of the entire campaign, while they spent a total of $41.6 million, or only $2 million more than the incumbents spent before the election year even got underway.[8]

The trend evidenced by those patterns continued into the 1990s, so that by the end of the decade, the funds generated by early incumbents' fund-raising were much greater than the sums raised by their opponents. In the 1998 cycle, incumbents raised $115.7 million in the year before the election, or about $36 million more than the $79.6 million raised by their general election challengers during the entire campaign. They spent $70.6 million in that first year, a sum that fell less than $8 million short of the total $78.2 million spent by their challengers in both years.[9] More important, incumbents were entering the election year with ever larger war chests to spend against their opponents. Although they were spending more money early, the success of their early fund-raising, combined with the surpluses retained from previous campaigns, allowed members to enter the election year with substantial amounts of money. At the start of 1988, for example, House members had about $120 million in cash on hand to put toward their campaigns. At the beginning of 1998, their counterparts had amassed more than $196 million in cash to spend on their elections (see table 4-2). By engaging in nonstop campaigning, they had helped to ensure that, in most instances, they would not have to campaign hard against even well-financed opponents to keep their seats.

Early Fund-Raising in the Senate. As might be expected, the trend toward early fund-raising among members of the Senate is not as dramatic or pronounced as the trend exhibited by members of the House, since senators have longer terms of office that provide them with significantly more time to raise the monies needed for the next election. Senators have the luxury of being able to scale down their campaigning significantly in the year or two after an election, because even if they do, they still have at least four years to gear up for the next contest. Nonetheless, many of those politicians have also begun to raise more money earlier in the election cycle and thus follow the pattern of the permanent campaign.

The shift toward early campaigning can be seen from the results in table 4-3, which analyzes the financial activity in selected off-election years for two different Senate classes. Because a relatively small number of senators are up for reelection every two years and because the costs of Senate campaigns vary greatly, depending on the state and the level of competition, Senate campaign finance is not as open to simple comparisons as is the case with the House. In an effort to provide a comparable basis for assessing off-year Senate financial activity, I examined the amounts raised and spent by specific Senate classes in successive elections and disaggregated the data into three separate two-year election cycles. For the purposes of the analysis, I considered the first two cycles, or the first four years of the six-year Senate term, to be off-election-year efforts. In that way, the findings present data for campaigns involving the same seats, comparable time periods, and, for the most part, the same candidates. While the data are not comprehensive, they do provide evidence of a move toward a permanent campaign mentality in the upper chamber.

In the early 1990s, senators raised and spent more money in the off-election years than they did in the comparable period in the prior decade. For example, in the 1986 election cycle, the members of the Senate who sought to defend their seats and who ran in the general election raised about $4.5 million in the first two years of the cycle and around $9.7 million in the second two years, for a

Table 4-3 Financial Activity of Senate Members: Selected Off-Election Years

Election Cycle		Receipts ($ millions)	% of Total	Disbursements ($ millions)	% of Total
1986 (n = 26)	1981–82	4.54	4.6	4.81	5.2
	1983–84	9.71	9.8	4.14	4.5
	1985–86	84.90	85.6	83.25	90.3
	Total	99.15	100.0	92.20	100.0
1992 (n = 25)	1987–88	10.15	9.2	10.55	9.7
	1989–90	16.74	15.3	8.15	7.6
	1991–92	82.87	75.5	89.55	82.7
	Total	109.76	100.0	108.25	100.0
1988 (n = 26)	1983–84	6.60	5.8	6.31	5.8
	1985–86	12.29	10.8	4.99	4.6
	1987–88	94.83	83.4	97.79	89.6
	Total	113.72	100.0	109.09	100.0
1994[a] (n = 21)	1989–90	6.06	6.1	6.33	6.5
	1991–92	9.91	10.0	5.54	5.7
	1993–94	83.43	83.9	85.77	87.8
	Total	99.40	100.0	97.64	100.0

a. This includes Kay Bailey Hutchison of Texas, who won a special election in 1993 and ran as an incumbent in 1994.

Source: The numbers are based on data reported by the Federal Election Commission.

total of about $14.2 million, which represented a little more than 14 percent of their total receipts for the entire election. In the 1992 cycle, when the seats in that class were again up for reelection, the incumbents took in about $26.9 million over the first four years (around $10.2 million in the first two years and $16.7 million in the second two years), which represented almost 25 percent of their total receipts for the campaign. Similarly, the amounts spent early in the cycle rose from $9 million in the first four years of the 1986 term, or almost 10 percent of total spending, to $18.7 million in the comparable period of the 1992 term, which represented more than 17 percent of total spending.

Thus, with respect to both receipts and expenditures, early financial activity doubled between 1986 and 1992, with the share of total incumbent financial activity represented by early efforts growing significantly. Moreover, in the first two years of a new term of office, which is the period when senators are thought to be most likely to enjoy a reprieve from campaigning, the amounts raised and spent more than doubled.

The change in financial activity between the 1988 and 1994 elections is not so stark as in the case of 1986 and 1992. Even so, the change supports the notion of the permanent campaign. At first glance, relatively little change seems to occur between the 1988 and 1994 election cycles. In advance of the 1988 election, senators seeking reelection raised $18.9 million in off-election-year monies—$6.6 million in the first two years of the term and another $12.3 million in the second two years—which represented almost 17 percent of their total receipts. They spent slightly more than $11 million, or around 10 percent of the total amount they disbursed over the course of the entire election. In contrast, the senators seeking reelection in 1994 raised about $16 million in the first four years of their terms, or almost $3 million less than their counterparts six years earlier. Yet, as in 1988, those early receipts still represented slightly more than 16 percent of the incumbents' total funding. Early expenditures were slightly higher in the 1994 term than in 1988.

It is important to note, however, that the number of sitting members of the Senate who ran in the general election in 1994 was significantly lower than the number in 1988. In 1988, twenty-six incumbents contested the general election, as compared with only twenty-one in 1994. The early financial activity of those twenty-one incumbents, therefore, was on average greater than that of the candidates who ran six years earlier. While the aggregate fund-raising totals for the off-years is comparable in the two cycles, the average amount solicited by each of the candidates in 1994 in the first four years of the cycle was around $761,000, as compared with an average of about $727,000 for the class of 1988. The increase, however, is less than 5 percent, which is significantly lower than the rate of increase exhibited by the 1986 and 1992 classes.

The pattern in Senate races is thus somewhat more mixed than that for House races, but it does tend to reinforce the argument that members of Congress are raising and spending more money earlier and creating a permanent campaign that has blurred the transition between campaigning and governing. Moreover, the relatively modest growth in Senate elections, as compared with House races, might be due in part to the time periods used in the analysis. The evidence might be even more compelling if the final two-year cycle were further disaggregated to examine the financial activity in the fifth year of a senator's term as compared with the sixth year.

What is most significant about those patterns, however, is that they document the resource advantage that sitting senators enjoy as a result of their early financial activity. In the 1980s and 1990s, the only Senate candidates who were raising money in the off-years were incumbents. In almost every circumstance, challengers generally did not focus on a race and begin raising money until the year before the election. That allowed incumbents to start filling their campaign coffers long before any opposition surfaced. In fact, the only challengers to begin raising money in the off-years in the four elections reviewed above were Democrat Russell Feingold of Wisconsin, who solicited about $98,000 in 1989–1990 in anticipation of his 1992 bid against Senator Robert Kasten (R-Wisconsin), and Democrat Joel Hyatt of Ohio, who raised over $709,000 in 1991–1992 in preparing for an open-seat race in 1994. The only other Senate contenders who began raising money early were "permanent campaigners" from the lower house, Representatives Rick Santorum (R-Pennsylvania) and Dave McCurdy (D-Oklahoma), who each generated surpluses in their House campaign committees and transferred more than $100,000 to their Senate campaign accounts when they sought Senate seats in 1994.[10] Otherwise, early money was incumbent money in Senate contests that served to create yet another obstacle to those who were considering a future challenge.

The Sources of Permanent Fund-Raising

The expansion of the campaign fund-raising season and the consequent elimination of any practical temporal distinction between campaigning and legislating are the product of a number of factors that have come together to convince members of Congress that they need to spend more time on fund-raising than ever before. While it is difficult to establish the relative contribution of any one of those causes, the major incentives encouraging more fund-raising have become so prominent that they are easy to identify. Most of the factors have served to reinforce each other and have created a vortex that has drawn legislators deeper and deeper into an unending round of campaign fund-raising.

The simplest reason for the growing emphasis on fund-raising is the imbalance between the amounts of money now spent in congressional elections and the limits on political giving established by the provisions of the Federal Election Campaign Act Amendments. The amendments, adopted in 1974, set contribution limits for all congressional campaigns at $1,000 per election for individuals and $5,000 for PACs. Those limits are not adjusted for inflation, nor do they correspond to the real costs of campaigns. So, while the inflation rate has increased by more than 200 percent and campaign spending by over 700 percent, the contribution limits have remained static.

The contribution limits compel candidates to solicit larger numbers of gifts in each successive election to generate the sums they feel are necessary to finance their campaigns. That usually means that they need to begin raising money earlier and need to capitalize on their ability to raise money from the Washington lobbying community. For some members, it also means that they have to spend significantly more time and effort raising money, since the donor bases in their home districts or states do not provide all the monies the members believe necessary for their upcoming campaigns. The members have to spend time traveling outside their districts and states to gather campaign cash wherever they can. Most focus on locales that have proved to be fruitful sources of candidate funding. Those include New York City, Chicago, Miami, Houston, Beverly Hills, and, most recently, Silicon Valley. All those locations are becoming traditional stops on the congressional money trail.

Another dimension of rising costs that influences the proclivity toward early campaigning is the indebtedness of House and Senate winners. While most incumbents seeking reelection end a campaign with significant cash surpluses, a growing number of challengers and open-seat candidates who win election for the first time, as well as some incumbents in marginal races, end their bids with substantial debts. In some cases, candidates make up the difference simply by loaning money to their campaigns from their own pockets, thereby owing themselves the money, but usually the indebtedness is in the form of unpaid bills, a bank loan, or even a second mortgage on a home. Those debts represent a decision by each candidate to spend the money and incur debt in an effort to win, rather than to maintain a set of balanced books and face the possibility of losing. The level of risk in such an approach is balanced by the prospect of victory and is also mitigated by the knowledge that a victorious candidate can quickly pay back any obligations by raising additional funds as a new member of the House or Senate. In most cases, a few Washington "welcome events" are all that are needed for a campaign committee to get back into the black.

The data in table 4-4 indicate the extent to which candidate debt played a role in the fund-raising discussed earlier in this chapter. The table summarizes the net debt position of candidates who won House seats in the elections before the off-election years of 1987 and 1997 or who won Senate seats in the election before the start of the 1992 or 1994 election cycles. For example, the data for the 1986 House election show the number of candidates who won in 1986 who had a net debt position at the start of the 1988 election cycle. The only candidates included there are those who were elected to office and had outstanding loans or debts that were greater than the amount of cash available in the campaign bank account.

According to table 4-4, candidate debt may have been a contributing factor to the growth of early fund-raising between the elections of the mid-1980s and mid-1990s, but the debt in no way accounts for the increase in fund-raising, especially in the first part of the election cycle, that occurred during the period. The net debt of winning House candidates was significantly higher after the 1996 election than it was after the 1986 election. At the start of 1997, ninety-nine members of the House had a total net debt of about $12

Table 4-4 Net Debt Posture of Winning Candidates: Selected Election Cycles

Election	Chamber	No. of Candidates	Debts Owed	Cash on Hand	Net Debt
1986	House	86	$6,607,684	$1,282,057	$5,325,627
1996	House	99	$13,543,616	$1,508,034	$12,035,582
	House (adjusted)	97[a]	$10,221,498	$1,504,993	$8,716,515
1986	Senate	10	$1,552,399	$538,275	$2,014,124
1988	Senate	11	$5,952,006	$512,425	$5,439,581
	Senate (adjusted)	10[b]	$2,193,006	$472,279	$1,720,727

a. This excludes Ellen Tauscher of California, who loaned $1,673,346 to her campaign from personal resources, and Christopher Cannon of Utah, who loaned $1,446,133 to his campaign.
b. This excludes $3.62 million in debt carried over from the 1982 election cycle by Senator Frank New Jersey); the sum represents personal funds loaned to his 1982 campaign.

Source: The numbers are based on Federal Election Commission data.

million, as compared with eighty-six members who had a total net debt of about $5.3 million at the beginning of 1987. But the difference of roughly $7 million constitutes a relatively minor portion of the $58 million difference between the monies received in 1987 and the monies received in the comparable period in 1997. (See table 4-2.) Moreover, the total debt of $12 million overstates the growth of candidate indebtedness or at least the average growth of candidate indebtedness. Over a quarter of that amount, about $3.3 million, represents the net debt of only two candidates, Ellen Tauscher (D-California) and Christopher Cannon (R-Utah), who basically self-financed their campaigns for open seats in 1996 by loaning about $1.5 million to their respective campaigns. If the net debt figures are adjusted for those two atypical contenders, the total net debt for 1996 is around $8.7 million, or only $3.5 million more than ten years earlier. Thus, candidate debt is not what is driving the level of early fund-raising taking place in recent House elections.

Candidate debt was also not a significant factor in explaining early campaigning in Senate contests. Of the candidates who won

Senate seats in 1986, only ten had a net debt posture at the start of 1987, and the net amount owed was roughly $2 million. That sum does not account for the $10 million raised in 1987–1988, or the $6 million increase in the amounts raised when the first two years of the 1986 cycle are compared with the first two years of the 1992 cycle. Debt retirement might have been a greater consideration at the start of the 1994 election cycle, since eleven of the candidates who won Senate seats in 1988 had an aggregate net debt of $5.4 million, or more than twice the amount of the 1986 class. And that figure was inflated by the $3.6 million in debt being carried over from the 1982 election by Senator Frank Lautenberg (D-New Jersey), who loaned those funds to his campaign in his earlier bid for office and did not repay himself during the course of the 1988 election cycle. If Lautenberg's personal debt is omitted from the total, the adjusted net debt figure for the winners in 1988 is about $1.7 million, which is less than the debt figure for the class of 1986. Yet, the senators raising money in 1989 and 1990 amassed over $6 million.

If candidates are not raising most of their money to pay off debts, for what are they raising it? What has stimulated the financial demands that have made permanent campaigning necessary? While no single factor explains the rising costs of campaigns, one of the most important influences on spending is the professionalization of congressional campaigns. Most congressional candidates have moved away from the traditional, grass-roots, volunteer-oriented style of electioneering that is based on door-to-door campaigning, volunteer mailings, and appearances at local meetings and community events. Instead of volunteer organizations based on local party support, those candidates rely on professional consultants, paid staff, polling, phone banks, computerized direct mail, and broadcast communications. That kind of personnel and political operation costs significant amounts of money.

Incumbents have been in the vanguard of the professionalization of campaigning. They rely on more sophisticated and expensive campaign techniques than their less well financed opponents. For example, a study of the 1992 congressional campaigns conducted by Paul Herrnson examined the use of paid consultants or professional staff to carry out nine separate campaign activities, including campaign management, fund-raising, press relations, polling, and media advertising, as well as the legal and accounting tasks required by federal campaign finance laws. The survey found that the average House campaign used paid staff or consultants for five or six of the nine functions, while the "typical incumbent campaign" used skilled professionals to carry out seven of the functions. Nonincumbents were less reliant on professional assistance, with candidates in uncompetitive races significantly less professional in their operations.[11]

The professionalism of contemporary congressional campaigns is reflected in their allocation of resources. As Herrnson has noted, the "typical" major-party House candidate in a contested general election race spends almost one of every five dollars, about 18 percent of the total campaign budget, on overhead, including staff salaries, fund-raising, and other administrative costs. Another 18 percent is spent on direct mail and yet another 18 percent on television, with 11 percent allocated to radio. The major difference between those House contenders and their Senate counterparts in terms of budget allocations is that the Senate campaigns allocate about 30 percent of their money to television.[12]

The overhead costs are even higher for the typical incumbent campaign, since those contenders usually have more professional staffs and raise more money, which means that they spend larger amounts to raise funds. While those costs vary depending on the financial requirements of the campaign and the fund-raising methods being used, incumbents generally may devote an average of 15 to 20 percent of their budgets to fund-raising activities. According to an analysis of campaign spending in the 1990 House races, incumbents spent over 27 percent of their campaign monies on overhead and another 18 percent on fund-raising, about a third of which was spent on direct mail. In the 1990 Senate contests, incumbents allocated about 23 percent of their budgets to overhead and another 30 percent to fund-raising, two-thirds of which went to direct mail.[13] A similar analysis of the 1992 campaigns found that House incumbents devoted 25 percent of their funds to overhead and about 15 percent to fund-raising (about 20 percent of that portion going to direct mail), while members of the Senate allocated 25 percent to overhead and 21 percent to fund-raising, with about half going to direct mail.[14]

So, as campaigns have become more professionalized, they have become more expensive. That, in turn, has forced candidates to spend more money raising funds, which has further increased the total costs of a campaign. To meet that increased expense, legislators have begun soliciting contributions earlier in the election cycle, which has placed additional financial demands on their campaigns, since it has required them to maintain a campaign organization, albeit a scaled-down one, throughout the entire election cycle. At a minimum, members of Congress need to maintain the fund-raising apparatus for their campaigns: their fund-raising staff and consultants, the professional services needed to fulfill federal legal and accounting requirements, and, in some instances, a professional direct-mail firm. Accordingly, members of Congress must now finance much higher "organizational maintenance" costs through their campaign budgets than they did twenty years ago. For example, according to one estimate, the average House incumbent spent roughly $207,600 on organizational maintenance during the two years leading up to the 1996 election. The average Senate incumbent spent even more. In the six-year period leading up to the 1994 election, the typical senator spent almost $1.1 million in overhead to maintain a campaign organization.[15] Permanent campaigns require expensive permanent campaign organizations.

Another factor that is usually associated with rising campaign costs is enhanced electoral competition. More competitive campaigns tend to be more expensive campaigns, since those contests are viewed as swing seats that attract greater interest from voters and donors alike. Yet one of the more remarkable aspects of the growth of early campaigning is that it has taken place during a period in which most incumbents were safe bets for reelection most of the time. Increasing electoral competition, especially with respect to the campaigns of incumbents, is therefore less a factor than one might expect.

The level of competition in congressional elections certainly increased in the 1990s. But for the most part, that more competitive electoral environment was focused in fifty to sixty congressional districts in each election cycle and was largely due to a greater number of highly competitive open seats. Some incumbents did prove to be vulnerable—in 1992 nineteen House incumbents lost primaries, a post–World War II record, and in 1994 thirty-four lost in the general election, the most since 1974.[16] Further, over half the House members in the 105th Congress (1997–1998) and three-fourths of the Senate had won at least one election with less than 55 percent of the vote.[17] But even with that renewed level of competition and the electoral uncertainty that those outcomes might instill in legislators, the majority of incumbents faced relatively easy reelection campaigns. Over 90 percent of those House members who sought reelection were returned to office, and from 1974 to 1998 at least two-thirds of incumbent contenders held onto their seats with at least 60 percent of the vote.[18] Senate elections generally were more competitive, with the majority of winning incumbents' receiving less than 60 percent of the vote in each of the elections since 1992. Even so, since the election of 1982, an average of 80 to 90 percent of those seeking reelection have remained in office.[19]

More than improved competition, the growth in early fundraising is due to a desire to stifle competition. That motive, which has influenced congressional behavior throughout the past few decades, continues to be a driving force in congressional campaign activity. In short, sitting members of Congress have come to recognize that one of the best strategies for reelection is to run against a weak opponent or, even better, no opponent at all. Members therefore seek to build large accumulations of cash early in the election cycle in an effort to discourage potentially strong challengers from running against them. They hope that large amounts of ready cash will prove to be a formidable obstacle that, combined with the other advantages an incumbent usually enjoys (such as higher name recognition and an established constituency base), will serve to convince potential challengers to wait for a better opportunity to seek a seat.

The reasoning behind that "preemptive fund-raising" strategy is fairly compelling and helps explain why so many incumbents have come to embrace the strategy. Richard Fenno explained it best in his observations two decades ago on behavior in the Senate. He noted:

> The appearance of electoral vulnerability can be disastrous for an incumbent, since potential challengers and the elites who fund them base their decisions partly on the perceived vulnerability of an incumbent. Moreover, they will be making their calculations in the fifth year. One way to appear invulnerable is to raise a lot of money early.[20]

Academic studies have confirmed that candidate war chests do play a role in discouraging serious challengers. They have also demonstrated that those candidates facing the strongest potential opposition are among the most active early fund-raisers.[21] That behavior has also been reinforced by the congressional party leadership. The shift in partisan control in 1994 and the declining margins determining majority control since then—which by 1999 had reached a point where a handful of contests in 2000 might decide which party forms the majority in the 107th Congress—have induced party leaders to emphasize early fund-raising. In recent Congresses, the party leaders on both sides of the aisle have urged their members to concentrate on fund-raising in the early months of the legislative session, in hopes of reducing the number of vulnerable incumbents and discouraging competition for seats held by first-term representatives, who are generally considered more vulnerable than their more senior colleagues. That strategic advice has fueled the chase for early dollars and has created an environment in which members are often as concerned about where the next big donor is to be found as they are about when the next major vote is to be held.

As if that were not pressure enough, changes in the broader electoral environment have further exacerbated the desire for campaign dollars. The changing electoral tactics of organized groups and of party organizations have made even well-established members of Congress question whether they will have enough funding to defend their seats in the next campaign. Incumbents, especially those in marginal districts and those otherwise considered vulnerable, now must be concerned about not only the resources available to their primary or general election opponents, but also the resources that might be used against them by organized groups or an opposing party committee. Such considerations add a multidimensionality to strategic planning that makes it more difficult to envision the dynamics of a race and thereby enhances the uncertainty of electoral outcomes. In that way, the new electoral environment tends to convince candidates and the party leaders who advise them to take what appears to be the only rational solution to the problem: raise as much money as possible to be prepared for any eventuality.

The advent of issue-advocacy advertising by interest groups and party committees, in particular, has significantly raised the financial stakes in House and Senate campaigns: that kind of outside intervention in a race can force a candidate who is the target of such advertising to spend tens of thousands, if not hundreds of thousands, of dollars responding to those attacks. That has been the lesson of recent elections, which have featured a dramatic increase in the use of issue advertising. The tactic first became prominent in the 1996 election cycle, when the AFL-CIO began an advertising campaign early in the election year in at least seventy-five congressional districts that was targeted at seats held by freshmen Republicans or open-seat races. In all, the AFL-CIO spent roughly $20 million on advertising alone, including about $10 million in the final weeks of the campaign in a narrower group of twenty-one marginal districts, and millions more on organizational and get-out-the-vote activities.[22] The effort became a model for other groups and for party organizations. By the time of the general election, more than a dozen interest groups and both party organizations had undertaken issue-advertising campaigns of their own and had spent an estimated total of $135 million to $150 million over the entire campaign period.[23]

By 1998 issue-advocacy advertising had become a standard weapon in the campaign arsenals of interest groups and party organizations alike. The party committees used those ads to supplement the monies they were directly contributing to candidates and the funds they were spending on their behalf in the form of coordinated expenditures. According to an analysis by the Annenberg Public Policy Center, over 70 percent of the issue ads broadcast during the general election period were produced by Democratic and Republican party committees.[24] The National

Republican Congressional Committee spent $21 million in its "Operation Breakout" on combined media campaigns (television, radio, cable television, newspaper advertisements, and direct mail) in an effort to influence the outcomes in fifty-eight competitive House elections in thirty-six states. The National Republican Senatorial Committee spent $7.3 million on ads in connection with five Senate contests. The Democrats engaged in less extensive efforts, but still spent substantial amounts of money on the races they targeted. The Democratic Congressional Campaign Committee spent $6 million on issue advocacy in twenty-five House races, while the Democratic Senatorial Campaign Committee spent about $8 million in eleven closely contested Senate elections.

As this discussion suggests, the changes taking place in the electoral environment have increased the prominence of the Capitol Hill campaign committees and their role in the financing of congressional campaigns. The Capitol Hill committees have become important intermediaries in the fund-raising process by assisting candidates—especially challengers and open-seat contenders—with such essential tasks as developing a donor base, soliciting PAC contributions, and planning fund-raising strategies. They often serve as brokers between donors and promising candidates and in recent years have increasingly relied on their congressional leaders and committee chairs to assist them in their fund-raising efforts. For example, the committees have developed "buddy systems" that match committee chairs and other powerful incumbents with financially needy members holding marginal seats or with promising nonincumbents, so that the more powerful leaders can use their influence with PACs and other donors to leverage funds into their buddies' campaigns. In 1996 Speaker Newt Gingrich supposedly used such a system to convince 150 House members from safe seats to raise $50,000 each for colleagues in jeopardy of losing their seats or for competitive nonincumbents.[25] Congressional leaders are also expected to attend committee fund-raising events, to participate in private briefings and receptions that are held for big givers and contributors to special donor clubs, and to solicit their own campaign donors for contributions to the party committee funds.

More important, the role of congressional leaders and other

incumbents in Capitol Hill committee fund-raising has involved them in soft-money fund-raising to an extent never seen in the 1980s or even the early 1990s. The primary reason that the party committees have incorporated issue advocacy advertising, as well as other generic campaign activities such as voter turnout drives, into their campaign strategies is that such advertising can, for the most part, be financed with soft-money funds not subject to the contribution limits of federal law.[26] Soft money, which was largely a national committee phenomenon from 1980 to 1992, has thus become a staple of Capitol Hill committee fund-raising. The Capitol Hill campaign committees use the access they can provide to the Senate and House leadership, committee chairs, and other powerful legislators to secure large contributions from corporations, lobbying groups, and wealthy individuals with business before Congress. That fund-raising approach has proved to be very effective, and, as a result, the amounts of soft money raised and spent by those committees have grown dramatically. For example, in 1992 the National Republican Senatorial Committee and the National Republican Congressional Committee raised a combined $15.2 million in soft money. By 1996 that sum had more than tripled to about $47.5 million and in 1998 grew again to about $64.8 million, or more than four times the amount of soft dollars received only six years earlier. The Democratic Senatorial Campaign Committee and the Democratic Congressional Campaign Committee have experienced even greater growth in their soft-money deposits. In 1992 those committees received a combined total of less than $5 million in soft-money funds, but by 1996 that total had increased to $26.5 million. In 1998 it rose further and reached a total of $42.7 million, or more than eight times the amount realized only six years earlier.[27] Such lofty totals could never have been achieved without the fund-raising assistance of the sitting members of Congress.

Besides soliciting funds for the party and devoting time to party committee events, an increasing number of legislators are also engaged in soliciting funds for their own personal PACs. Those member-sponsored PACs are known as "leadership PACs" because they were originally PACs sponsored by or affiliated with congressional leaders or individuals who aspired to leadership positions.

They are another financial vehicle that has become an increasingly common component of congressional life. The first such committee was established by Congressman Henry Waxman (D-California) in 1978, but throughout the early 1980s relatively few of such committees were established and actively raising meaningful sums of money.[28] By 1986 at least thirty-five of those committees were associated with members of Congress, and they donated a total of more than $3.1 million to federal candidates.[29]

Since then, the number and size of leadership PACs have exploded. In 1998, for example, at least ninety-five leadership PACs were operating under the aegis of sitting members of Congress and contributed a total of about $9 million to federal candidates in that year.[30] Notably, the PACs included only the committees formed at the national level and registered with the Federal Election Commission. Still others have been established at the state or local level, where disclosure is often less effective and contribution rules more lax, so that members can solicit soft-money funds as well as federally regulated funds, an option not available to PACs established under federal law.

Basically, congressional leaders and members aspiring to a leadership position are almost expected to have a PAC or some other type of subsidiary political organization to supplement their campaign committees. Such organizations can raise additional monies from campaign donors and other political givers who have already contributed the allowable maximum contribution to a campaign. The monies raised can be used to defray the costs of a member's political travel, fund-raising activities, and organizational maintenance expenses. They can also be used to curry favor with junior colleagues, colleagues in jeopardy of losing a seat, or prospective legislative newcomers, by providing those candidates with contributions from the PAC's funds. In the contemporary political environment in Washington, cash is what is in demand, so legislators capable of amassing cash and directing it to others are those who are likely to build up political currency that can be translated into votes for leadership positions or other legislative benefits. In that way, the more powerful members have learned to apply the lessons they mastered in campaigning at home to their internal political campaigning in Congress. They have learned to convert their own capacity to raise funds into a broader political asset.

The Permanent Campaign and the Election of 2000

The early stages of the 2000 election, especially with respect to the House races, provide a clear example of the money politics that now characterizes the national legislature. Given the slim margins determining majority control (a shift of six seats could return the Democrats to the majority) and the expectation of a highly competitive federal election season, legislators engaged in an aggressive early fund-raising campaign, with vulnerable incumbents' raising money at an unprecedented pace. The leadership in both parties pushed members to build war chests in anticipation of a complement of challengers who would be stronger than usual. House Republican leaders urged incumbents who already had a significant challenger or who won in 1998 with less than 55 percent of the vote to try to have $200,000 in the bank by the end of June 1999. The Democratic leadership urged their vulnerable members, including all the freshmen, to set a goal of $150,000 in the bank by the end of June.[31]

The congressional leadership aided those efforts by joining in the sweepstakes and appearing at fund-raising events on behalf of colleagues or in support of the Capitol Hill campaign committees. Speaker of the House Dennis Hastert (R-Illinois), for example, spent most Mondays, Fridays, and weekends during the early months of the legislative session hopscotching around the country. His aides estimated that, by the middle of June 1999, he had already raised $6 million for candidates and the party committees. House minority leader Richard Gephardt (D-Missouri) was also on the campaign trail early and raised an estimated $4 million for candidates in the first six months of 1999. Republican Tom DeLay of Texas, the House majority whip, also chipped in, not only by appearing at fund-raisers but also by organizing the Republican whip structure into a program called ROMP, or Retain Our Majority Program. The purpose of the program was to commit each member of the whip organization to raise $30,000 each for each of the Republicans' ten most vulnerable incumbents.[32] Thus, the internal party organizational structure in Congress, which is usually used to solicit and count votes, was turned outward to solicit and count dollars. Such tactics make it difficult to distinguish campaign work from legislative work.

As a result of those intense fund-raising efforts, members of Congress generated record sums of early cash. In many cases, the differences from even the previous election cycle were remarkable. In the 1998 cycle, for example, Democratic freshmen had an average of $74,000 in the bank after the first six months of their first year in office; for 2000, the freshmen average climbed to $206,000 in cash on hand after the first six months. Similarly, on the Republican side, freshmen had banked an average of $109,000 in the first half of 1997. In the first part of 1999, they almost doubled that amount with an average of $203,000.[33]

Incumbents, however, are not the only 2000 contenders who are raising money earlier and more often. Challengers are also finally catching on. They, too, are getting a head start on fund-raising, especially in those districts likely to be competitive. Many of those contenders recognize that an early start is needed to amass the sum needed to wage a viable campaign. They are also being encouraged to start early by party leaders or staff professionals at the Capitol Hill campaign committees, who have an interest in seeing those hopefuls achieve victory on election day. Consequently, those with the best prospects of becoming members of Congress are learning the lessons of the permanent campaign before they are even elected to serve in government.

As a result, many challengers are raising substantial amounts of money relatively early in the process. By midyear 1999, sixteen Democratic hopefuls challenging incumbents or seeking open seats had already received over $100,000, as compared with only three who reached that level at the same point in 1997. Of those, six had already raised over $200,000. Among Republicans, at least eighteen nonincumbents had reached $100,000, and five had surpassed the $200,000 mark.

Meanwhile, the campaign committees on Capitol Hill have been raising money, especially soft money, at a record rate. With congressional leaders actively participating in the solicitation of funds, both parties enjoyed great early success. For the first time, the Democratic Congressional Campaign Committee established a $100,000 donor club in an attempt to follow in the footsteps of the national committees by bringing in the big dollars. By the end of the first six months of 1999, the committee, in part because of the aggressive fund-raising efforts of Gephardt and Democratic Congressional Campaign Committee chair Patrick Kennedy (D-Rhode Island), had raised about $9 million in soft money, an increase of 373 percent over the same period in 1997. The Republicans kept pace, with the National Republican Congressional Commmittee raising about $9.4 million in soft money during the first six months of the cycle—an increase of 77 percent over the first part of 1997.[34] No one, however, could match the Herculean efforts of House Majority Whip Tom DeLay (R-Texas), who before year's end had already personally collected more than $15 million for Republican candidates, including $1 million for his own reelection campaign and leadership PAC, more than $12 million for the National Republican Congressional Committee, and more than $1.3 million for ten vulnerable Republican incumbents.[35]

The 2000 election thus constitutes the latest step on the path of rising off-election-year financial activity. By the end of 1999, the 417 House challengers who had filed reports with the Federal Election Commission had raised a total of about $24.8 million, as compared with around $14 million for the 284 challengers who had registered by the end of 1997. But their prospective opponents, all of whom currently serve in the House, did even better. In all, the 416 incumbents soliciting campaign funds in 1999 generated over $144 million in receipts, an increase of more than 25 percent over the amount raised in 1997. As in the case of each of the elections at the end of the previous two decades, a larger number of candidates raised substantially more money in the preelection year than was the case in the decade before.

Conclusion

The permanent campaign appears to be a phenomenon that will be part of the national political landscape for the foreseeable future. Members of Congress are constantly raising money for their own campaigns in an effort to retain their positions. When they are not, they may be found raising money for the party. That is especially true for the leadership and safe incumbents. When they are not raising money for the party, they may be raising it for a "buddy" or some other candidate. When they are not raising money for some other candidate, they may be raising money for their personal PAC or some other political committee with which they are affiliated.

Over a decade ago, then–Senate majority leader Robert Byrd advocated reform of the campaign finance system because, in his view, members of the Senate had become "full-time fund-raisers, instead of full-time legislators."[36] And that was before the situation worsened and soft money became an essential component of congressional campaign finance.

The system has now reached a point where it essentially feeds upon itself. Members raise ever increasing sums of money in an effort to deter quality challengers or to ensure that they will be able to mount a defense against any electoral challenge that might come along, regardless of the source. Those who face little threat of losing their seats devote their time and efforts to raising funds for others in an attempt to determine their own position and status on Capitol Hill by preserving or securing majority control for their party. No one is exempt from the demands of the process, including challengers, who are becoming "permanent campaigners"—even before they are elected to the positions they seek.

One positive aspect of the current state of affairs is that it has served to generate substantial funding for incumbents in jeopardy and nonincumbents with good prospects, a development that has helped to enhance the quality of the candidates and the level of competition in those districts considered marginal and capable of being won by one party or the other. The problem is that those districts usually represent less than a quarter of the House races and less than half of the Senate contests in any given election year. So, instead of encouraging greater numbers of qualified candidates to seek office and enhancing competition across a broad array of districts, the current incentive structures tend to concentrate a large share of the vast financial resources into a relatively small number of contests. Those contests tend to feature candidates who are already well financed. The aggregate effect, therefore, is that the rich get richer and the poor get poorer; the financial gap between most incumbents and their challengers grows wider, while the amounts spent in competitive districts rise ever higher. How those rising costs will affect the pool of potential candidates in the future is a question that remains to be answered.

Given the changes that have taken place over the past three decades, it is little wonder that most of the public has come to believe that members of Congress are always busy raising money and are more concerned about the "special interests" in Washington than the folks back home. It is certainly the case that the financial demands of the process and the constant attention to fund-raising have provided lobbyists, organized interests, corporate groups, and labor unions with greater access to elected officials, better opportunities to meet legislators in more informal settings, and an improved ability to have their views heard and to participate in the political process. How that affects legislation and what influence it has on policy outcomes are matters of scholarly debate. The public, however, has come to conclude that "money talks" on Capitol Hill and that policy is too often shaped by campaign contributions.

What is clear is that such permanent campaigning is diminishing the quality of representation in Washington. Legislators are spending excessive amounts of time on fund-raising and electioneering. Their focus on campaigning comes at the expense of the legislative craft; if they are spending more time raising money, they are spending less time learning legislative practice, understanding the details of major policy debates, or becoming acquainted with their professional colleagues. But in the current culture on Capitol Hill, such a development should not come as a surprise, since the old norms of legislative excellence and policy expertise as means to congressional status are giving way to the new norms of fund-raising prowess and expertise in electoral tactics. That, perhaps more than any other factor, explains why candidates are enduring the demeaning demands of fund-raising and participating in the permanent campaign.

Notes

The author thanks Robert Biersack of the Federal Election Commission and Sarah Ward and Janet Bordelon of Colby College for their assistance in preparing this chapter. Some of the research for this chapter was supported by a Colby College Social Sciences Research Grant.

1. See, generally, David Mayhew, *Congress: The Electoral Connection* (New Haven: Yale University Press, 1974), and Richard F. Fenno, Jr., *Home Style: House Members in Their Districts* (Boston: Little, Brown, 1978).

2. Quoted in *Congressional Campaign Finances: History, Facts, and Controversy* (Washington, D.C.: Congressional Quarterly, 1992), 22.

3. Cited in ibid., 23.

4. Ibid.

5. Federal Election Commission, "FEC Reports on Congressional Fundraising for 1997–98," press release, April 18, 1999.

6. The data in this paragraph are from Norman J. Ornstein, Thomas E. Mann, and Michael J. Malbin, *Vital Statistics on Congress, 1997–1998* (Washington, D.C.: Congressional Quarterly, 1998), 81, 88–89.

7. The data on challenger financing, which include only those challengers facing incumbents in the general election, are based on the amounts reported in Federal Election Commission, *FEC Reports on Financial Activity, 1977–1978: Interim Report No. 5, U.S. Senate and House Campaigns* (Washington, D.C.: June 1979), 56, 58.

8. The data on challenger financing, which include only those challengers facing incumbents in the general election, are based on the amounts reported in Federal Election Commission, "FEC Reports on Congressional Fundraising for 1997–98."

9. Ibid.

10. See the summaries of individual Senate campaign activities in Federal Election Commission, "1994 Congressional Fundraising Climbs to New High," press release, April 28, 1995.

11. Paul S. Herrnson, *Congressional Elections: Campaigning at Home and in Washington,* 2d ed. (Washington, D.C.: Congressional Quarterly, 1998), 65.

12. Ibid., 68, 71.

13. Sara Fritz and Dwight Morris, *Gold-Plated Politics: Running for Congress in the 1990s* (Washington, D.C.: Congressional Quarterly, 1992), 18, table 1-3, and 20, table 1-4.

14. Dwight Morris and Murielle E. Gamache, *Gold-Plated Politics: The 1992 Congressional Races* (Washington, D.C.: Congressional Quarterly, 1994), 22, 28.

15. Herrnson, *Congressional Elections,* 2d ed., 60, 70.

16. Ibid., 24–25.

17. Ornstein, Mann, and Malbin, *Vital Statistics on Congress, 1997–1998,* 68.

18. Ibid. In two elections during this period, the percentage of incumbents reelected with at least 60 percent of the vote was not quite two-thirds. In 1992 the percentage was 65.6 percent, and in 1994 it was 64.5 percent.

19. Ibid., 62, 69.

20. Richard F. Fenno, Jr., *The United States Senate* (Washington, D.C.: American Enterprise Institute, 1982), 31.

21. See, among others, Janet M. Box-Steffensmeier, "A Dynamic Analysis of the Role of War Chests in Campaign Strategy," *American Journal of Political Science* 40 (May 1996): 352–71; Peverill Squire, "Preemptive Fund-Raising and Challenger Profile in Senate Elections," *Journal of Politics* 53 (November 1991): 1150–64; and Philip L. Hersch and Gerald S. McDougall, "Campaign War Chests as a Barrier to Entry in Congressional Races," *Economic Inquiry* 32 (October 1994): 630–42. But see also Jonathan S. Krasno and Donald Philip Green, "Preempting Quality Challengers in House Elections," *Journal of Politics* 50 (November 1988): 920–36; and David Epstein and Peter Zemsky, "Money Talks: Deterring Quality Challengers in Congressional Elections," *American Political Science Review* 89 (June 1995): 295–308.

22. Anthony Corrado, "Financing the 1996 Election," in *The Election of 1996,* edited by Gerald Pomper (Chatham, N.J.: Chatham House, 1997), 162–63.

23. Diana Dwyre, "Interest Groups and Issue Advocacy in 1996," in *Financing the 1996 Election,* edited by John C. Green (Armonk, N.Y.: M. E. Sharpe, 1999), 203.

24. The 1998 Annenberg Public Policy Center analysis is available on the Web at www:appcpenn.org/issueads/report.htm (viewed January 20, 2000).

25. Herrnson, *Congressional Elections,* 2d ed., 93.

26. For background on the law governing issue advocacy and soft-money financing, see Anthony Corrado et al., *Campaign Finance Reform: A Sourcebook* (Washington, D.C.: Brookings Institution, 1997), especially chaps. 6 and 7.

27. The data are based on figures reported by the Federal Election Commission. See Robert Biersack and Melanie Haskell, "Spitting on the Umpire: Political Parties, the Federal Election Campaign Act, and the 1996 Campaigns," in *Financing the 1996 Election,* 172; and Federal Election Commission, "FEC Reports on Political Party Activity for 1997–98," press release, April 9, 1999.

28. Paul S. Herrnson, *Congressional Elections: At Home and in Washington,* 3d ed. (Washington, D.C.: Congressional Quarterly, 2000), 98.

29. Center for Responsive Politics, *Money and Politics: Spending in Congressional Elections* (Washington, D.C., 1998), 31–33. The figures do not include the PACs associated with presidential candidates.

30. The figures are based on the listing of leadership PACs constructed by the Center for Responsive Politics, excluding the PACs affiliated with politicians or retired politicians who are not current members of Congress. The listing can be found at www.opensecrets.org/pacs/indus/1998/Q03.htm (viewed May 2, 2000).

31. Alison Mitchell, "Congress Chasing Campaign Donors Early and Often," *New York Times,* June 14, 1999.

32. Ibid.

33. Ruth Marcus and Juliet Eilperin, "Battle for House Fuels Cash Race," *Washington Post,* August 11, 1999.

34. Susan B. Glasser, "Soft Money Paves the Way," *Washington Post National Weekly,* October 25, 1999, 7.

35. Juliet Eilperin, "The Hammer DeLay Whips the Lobbyists into Shape," *Washington Post National Weekly,* October 25, 1999, 8.

36. Quoted in Andy Plattner, "Nobody Likes the Way Campaigns Are Financed, but Nobody's Likely to Change It, Either," *U.S. News & World Report,* June 22, 1987, 30.

5

The American Presidency: Surviving and Thriving amidst the Permanent Campaign

Kathryn Dunn Tenpas

Written in 1982, Sidney Blumenthal's book, *The Permanent Campaign,* clearly reflected an inexorable trend occurring within the institution of the presidency. This chapter examines the institutional adaptation of the presidency to the permanent campaign—how presidents have responded to it, and what they have done to fuel it.

The presidency has been transformed over the past thirty years by the addition of "outreach" offices designed to buttress the president's popular support,[1] the expansion of the president's advisory network to include professional political consultants and pollsters, and the use of campaign-like tactics to govern. Modern presidents have responded to the permanent campaign by acquiring the resources necessary to compete in a vastly altered political and policymaking arena. The permanent campaign mentality not only has affected individual presidents, but also has had an enduring effect on the institution of the presidency.

Scholars of White House staffing are well aware of the growth and specialization within the office,[2] with both a sudden increase in the number of specialized policy offices (domestic, environmental, urban, science, and trade) and an emphasis on constituent outreach. Beginning in the Nixon administration, three major outreach units were added to the White House—the Office of Communications, the Office of Public Liaison, and the Office of Political

Affairs.[3] Each pays attention to critical groups within the president's electoral coalition while striving to maintain and expand presidential support. During that same time, the president's advisory network took on a significant addition—the professional political consultant. Since President Nixon, those pollsters and campaign experts have provided continuing advice to sitting presidents on matters of both politics and policy. While presidential political consultants are neither formal members of the White House staff nor U.S. government employees, they have access to the president's most senior advisers and often to the president himself. Having acquired the necessary resources to compete in the permanent campaign environment, presidents are increasingly using campaign-like tactics for governing. The final section of this chapter identifies instances of the permanent campaign at work and concludes with a normative assessment of this era. The chapter reveals the influence of the permanent campaign ethos by drawing on archival sources, interviews, and relevant secondary sources. In the process, it demonstrates how the permanent campaign manifests itself in day-to-day White House operations.

Outreach in the White House

Changes in the composition of the White House staff since the Nixon administration have significantly expanded the ability of the president to reach out to key constituencies—the media, interest groups, and local party officials.[4] Take, for example, three entities that continue to play key roles in the administration: the Office of Communications, the Office of Public Liaison, and the Office of Political Affairs.[5] The primary function of those outreach offices is to enhance the president's popularity among key constituents in an effort to gain support for a governmental program, policy, or campaign.[6] In short, the modern White House is now able to perform many of the same tasks that a party organization or political campaign would carry out in the course of daily business. The following discussion does not provide detailed explanations of each office and its functions but instead draws attention to those White House activities with direct parallels to campaigning.

Office of Communications. President Nixon was the first to appoint a director of communications to coordinate news flow within the executive branch. That office, independent of the press office, was designed with an eye toward controlling the administration's message and press access to administration officials. According to one study of the Office of Communications:

> Communications Director Klein was responsible for the larger coordination of news flow from the executive branch, for maintaining links with local editors, publishers, and broadcasters, and for scheduling interviews and television appearances by administration officials and other proadministration spokespeople (such as members of Congress and party officials).[7]

Since that position was separate from the press office, it freed the director to formulate long-term communications strategies while providing liaison to members of the press—particularly at the local level. The latter was of particular concern to President Nixon: "Nixon felt that local broadcasters and editors could be used as yet another means of circumventing the 'establishment' media and taking his message directly to the people."[8] That ability to appeal directly to the people, also referred to as "going public," has proved to be an indispensable component of modern presidential communication.[9] Fostering friendly press relations at all levels is integral to any presidency hoping for positive coverage. Thus, the Office of Communications seeks not only to control the administration's message, but to cultivate relations with members of the press and to provide a contact point for that critical constituency.

Since President Nixon, successive presidents have maintained the Office of Communications with some variation across administrations in terms of size and composition. Presidents and candidates alike seek centralized control over communication and aim to influence the media and public in a positive manner. Despite the obvious differences between White House and campaign, the Office of Communications and a presidential campaign press operation possess identical goals and often use similar techniques to achieve those goals.

Office of Public Liaison. Although a nascent public liaison operation emerged in the Nixon White House, President Ford formally established the Office of Public Liaison.[10] To paraphrase John Hart, the function of that office is to lobby the lobbies. The office reaches out to key constituencies to gather support for the administration's legislative proposals.[11] In addition, during election season, the office might be responsible for rounding up key blocs of supporters—labor, blue-collar workers, Jewish organizations, the elderly, and youth. By establishing ties with various interest groups, the White House seeks to persuade opposing groups as well as to nourish relations with previously supportive groups in hopes that such assistance might one day be reciprocated.

Those efforts are not unlike the ones used in political campaigns to reach voters at the precinct level or to obtain key endorsements. Just as the campaign needs to assemble a winning coalition for election day, the White House needs to assemble a winning coalition on a number of policy measures at the congressional level. Having the support of key interest groups is critical to presidential and electoral success, and obtaining that support requires constant maintenance.

Office of Political Affairs. With the declining role of the party in the president's reelection campaign came the increasing centralization of campaign planning within the White House.[12] One forthright attempt to maintain control of the president's reelection campaign has been the addition of the White House Office of Political Affairs, formally established during the Reagan administration (although semblances existed during the Nixon, the Ford, and especially the Carter administrations). The staff members are responsible for maintaining and expanding the president's electoral coalition by keeping in contact with party officials and key constituents across the country.[13] In effect, they provide a point of access for that critical group of supporters—a "casework" office, much like the staff in a congressional office. After the midterm elections, staff members switch their focus to the reelection campaign, and many ultimately move to the campaign headquarters. The Office of Political Affairs, now a mainstay in the White House office, is exactly what Sidney Blumenthal was referring to when he pointed out that the permanent campaign had "remade the government into an instrument designed to sustain an elected official's popularity."[14] No White House office comes closer to achieving that goal than the Office of Political Affairs.

As presidents became less tied to the party organizations and officeholders, they needed to improve their ability to reach out to the citizenry. The capacity to communicate with the press, party officials, office holders, and other key constituencies has been useful in situations where the president was trying to pass a key legislative initiative, promote the candidacy of a Supreme Court nominee, or simply maintain or improve his popularity ratings.[15] Such efforts are not uncommon in a presidential campaign and serve to illustrate the similarity between governing in the modern White House and campaigning.

Expansion of the President's Advisory Network: Outsiders or Insiders?

A related phenomenon that also began with President Nixon was the expansion of the president's advisory network to include political consultants and pollsters. The practice started when President Nixon hired two political pollsters to conduct surveys related to significant policy issues such as the Vietnam conflict, inflation, busing, and the admission of China to the United Nations.[16] Since President Nixon hired academician David Derge and pollster Robert Teeter, sitting presidents have sought the continuous advice of professional campaign consultants. Unlike the informal "kitchen cabinet" advisers associated with FDR, Truman, and Eisenhower, these consultants market themselves as campaign experts skilled in the arts of polling, spin control, creating the perfect sound bite, and devising a successful campaign strategy.

The presidential political consultants and pollsters for Presidents Nixon, Ford, Carter, Reagan, Bush, and Clinton were not formal members of the White House staff, but rather external political consultants paid for by the national party organization or the campaign committee. President Nixon's consultants included David Derge (1969–1972) and Robert Teeter.[17] President Ford was advised by Robert Teeter and Stuart Spencer. President Carter's consultant was Patrick Caddell. President Reagan's consultants were Stuart Spencer and Richard Wirthlin. President Bush was advised by Robert Teeter and Fred Steeper. The presidency of Bill Clinton represents the zenith of that development, as demonstrated by his numerous and wide-ranging band of political consultants coupled with their influence on politics and policy: James Carville, Paul Begala,[18] Mandy Grunwald, and Stanley Greenberg (1993–1995); Richard Morris (1994–1996); Robert Squier, Hank Sheinkopf, and Marius Penczer (1995–1996); and Mark Penn (1994–present).[19]

Preliminary research on the role of political consultants as presidential advisers indicates that they have played an influential role at the senior staff level by using their campaign expertise to provide advice on issues pertaining to governance.[20] As mentioned above, the formal use of political consultants as presidential advisers on a continuous basis began with President Nixon. Jacobs and Shapiro pointed out:

> Kennedy and Johnson's private polls were generally offered as a low- or no-cost favor in which the pollster "piggybacked" a few general questions onto surveys conducted for other political candidates. . . . In contrast, the Nixon administration was generally the single sponsor of its polls. . . . In short, Derge and especially Teeter introduced innovative and technically sophisticated methods for analyzing public opinion and political behavior; the methods used to advise Nixon and his senior aides were genuinely state-of-the-art—a level of expertise that was never approached under Kennedy or Johnson.[21]

All presidents since Nixon have sought the continuous advice of professional political consultants, whether they were considered polling experts, media consultants, or general strategists. And, in all cases, the campaign pollsters went on to become the presidential pollsters.[22] President Clinton set a new record with the sheer number of external consultants he employed. Moreover, some observers argue that Clinton's consultants were unusually influential. Political journalist Elizabeth Drew asserted:

> The role of the consultants in the Clinton administration was without precedent. Previous Presidents had pollsters and other outside political advisers, but never before had a group of political consultants played such an integral part in a Presidency. Clinton's consultants were omnipresent, involved in everything from personnel to policymaking to the President's schedule.[23]

Presidential scholar Charles O. Jones noted that Clinton's "penchant for travel and campaigning induced his political consultants to participate in devising policy strategy to a greater extent than normal."[24] It is simply too soon to tell whether President Clinton's extensive reliance on political consultants is the logical extension of a phenomenon that began with Nixon, whether it simply reflects President Clinton's personal style, or both. What is clear, however, is that President Clinton's use of political consultants is part of an important trend occurring within the institution of the presidency.

Another indicator of the consultants' increasing influence and stature is the amount of money that the Democratic National Committee and the Republican National Committee spent subsidizing political consulting. Expenditure records beginning with the Ford administration are available from the Federal Election Commission and reveal an unusual and interesting pattern.[25] Preliminary estimates of party expenditures (converted to 1997 constant dollars) indicate that over the course of Ronald Reagan's two terms, the RNC spent roughly $16 million on consultants Richard Wirthlin and Robert Teeter. (See table 5-1.) Not far behind and for just five years of President Clinton's eight-year stint, the DNC spent roughly $12.5 dollars on Clinton consultants. With all the press that the Clinton band of consultants received, one would have expected the Clinton administration to outspend all prior administrations by a huge margin.[26] Other administrations in which presidents served a single term or less pale by comparison: the DNC spent roughly $4 million on President Carter's pollster Pat Caddell, and the RNC spent $2 million on President Bush's pollster Bob Teeter and less than $1 million for President Ford's partial term in office (approximately $960,000).[27]

To gain a greater appreciation for the magnitude of expenditures for the Clinton presidential political consultants, it is worthwhile to compare the DNC consultants' expenditures with the salaries of senior White House staff members. In 1995 the salaries for President Clinton's fifteen most senior White House staff members totaled approximately $1.8 million (with the highest annual salary of $133,600).[28] During that same year, the DNC spent over $2.9 million dollars on seven sets of consultants—Stanley Greenberg, James Carville (and Paul Begala), Mandy Grunwald,[29] Mark Penn,[30] Robert Squier, Hank Sheinkopf, and Marius Penczer.[31] Notably, that figure excludes the principal presidential consultant Dick Morris,

Table 5-1 Party Expenditures for Presidential Polling
(converted to 1997 constant dollars)

President	Total	Mean Annual Expenditures
Ford	$960,000	$480,000
Carter	$4,000,000	$1,000,000
Reagan	$16,000,000	$2,000,000
Bush	$2,000,000	$500,000
Clinton[a]	$12,500,000	$2,500,000

a. The totals include only five of eight years in office.

whose salary was paid by the Clinton-Gore reelection campaign organization. It also excludes Morris's advertising commissions that represented a substantial portion of his total consulting income. That exclusion suggests that the difference between the payments to the sixteen most senior White House staff members and the presidential political consultants is, if anything, understated.

The campaign experts' advice to presidents is costly, but why? What is it exactly that they do for the president? Relationships between presidents and their consultants vary—some have proximity to the president, while others are on the periphery of the inner circle. In addition, the consultants' area of expertise—media, polling, or general strategy—varies. Nevertheless, a general pattern of activity emerges. Set out below is a discussion of the consultants' primary duties.

Reelection Advice. Many of the consultants under study conducted polls or provided strategic advice pertaining to the president's reelection campaign.[32] In fact, during the Ford administration, Stuart Spencer's only role was to provide campaign advice. Keep in mind, however, that during a presidential reelection campaign, the separation between campaign politics and governance is negligible. Presidents and their advisers must constantly consider the electoral impact of policy decisions. So, while Spencer was nominally there to provide campaign advice, his input inevitably affected policy. Demonstrating that point, one news report forthrightly stated, "Stuart Spencer, well-known California political consultant . . . was brought aboard to advise on policy and strategy."[33] Similarly, political consultant Dick Morris was retained to focus on President

Clinton's reelection campaign in the aftermath of the disastrous 1994 midterm elections. And, as with Spencer during the Ford and Reagan reelection campaigns, such advice extended well beyond the campaign and into the policymaking realm. Other campaign advisers like James Carville continued in a less formal advisory role as campaign strategists.[34] In addition, pollsters continued to take the pulse of the electorate—albeit more frequently during the campaign season. The consultants' provision of reelection-related advice is not surprising since their expertise lies in campaigning. Nevertheless, the consultants' "outside the beltway" advice and public opinion data are critical to a president. Fearing that their presidential duties have served to distance them from the electorate or that their White House aides have not been able to provide candid advice, presidents find that their trusted consultants' advice is invaluable.

Domestic Policy Input. Examples of consultants' advice on policy choices and content abound. Over the course of President Carter's term, pollster Patrick Caddell, author of the *Cambridge Report,* published a number of policy-related surveys on issues such as consumer protection, defense, economic stimulation, energy conservation, political reform, race relations, and unemployment. He also conducted surveys solely for the Carter administration that pertained to agriculture, government regulation, bilingual education, health care policy, government reorganization, inflation, the energy crisis, and such economic issues as tax reform and Social Security. In fact, it appears that the bulk of Caddell's surveys were related to issues rather than to image, performance, or reelection.[35] According to senior staff members, data from those surveys were ultimately incorporated into the administration's policy discussions.[36]

President Reagan's pollster, Richard Wirthlin, frequently took the public's pulse on key domestic issues: impoundment of federal funds, interest rates, balanced budgets, the air traffic controllers' strike, and tuition tax credits.[37] As with Carter, the number of issue-related surveys appears to outweigh simple performance-approval surveys, although those were also abundant.[38] Wirthlin's data circulated among the president's most senior aides and likely found its way into policy discussions.[39]

Most recently, Dick Morris was credited with prodding Clinton to pursue a number of domestic issues, in particular, his own version of a balanced-budget plan, which served to annoy congressional Democrats.[40] With the assistance of polling data from Mark Penn, Morris also convinced Clinton to make frequent public announcements about smaller domestic programs such as public school uniforms, the V-chip (to screen out violent programming on television), and college-tuition tax credits.

Foreign Policy Input. Consultants play a much more limited role in foreign policy than in domestic policy, although their advice remains critical. Carter pollster Pat Caddell surveyed American attitudes toward Israel, Rosalynn Carter's trip to Latin America, and later in the term, the Iranian hostage crisis. Republican consultant Stuart Spencer coached Reagan on how best to deal with the Soviet Union and the aftermath of the Marine barracks bombing in Lebanon.[41] Meanwhile, Richard Wirthlin conducted tracking polls about foreign policy in the Middle East, Poland, the grain embargo against the Soviet Union, the Iran-Contra affair, and American policy toward the Soviet Union more generally.[42] That interaction shows that presidents were deeply interested in the public's opinion on such issues. Rather than rely on consultants for substantive policy ideas and options, presidents are more apt to seek consultants' advice on gaining popular support for a foreign policy decision or for tips on how to explain a policy or action to the American people. Demonstrating the consultants' limited role in foreign policy, Morris indicated that President Clinton used the polling data not for formulating foreign policy, but for determining how to sell it.[43]

Speech Content. Consultants are frequently asked to draft, rewrite, and review speeches. The most important speech each year is the State of the Union Address, although political consultants also provide advice on less visible speeches to Congress or on issue-specific speeches to the American public. The most notable address of the Carter administration, the "Crisis of Confidence" speech, was based on the analysis of his pollster Patrick Caddell. That speech, delivered in the summer of 1979, was the result of a ten-day gathering at Camp David in which the president invited leading citizens to the mountaintop for candid conversations about the state of the union. According to scholar Robert Strong, Caddell's analysis "became the model for much of what went on at the Camp David domestic summit."[44] One senior administration official also noted, "You know it was Caddell, among others, who persuaded President Carter to cancel his energy speech and go to Camp David. That was primarily Caddell's idea, and then he kind of orchestrated that week up there to a large extent."[45] Demonstrating Caddell's input and influence, President Carter, in a handwritten note to Caddell after the speech, wrote, "Your analysis was a masterpiece, and your advice was crucial. Stick with me during the coming weeks. We will win together. You're a great ally to have in fighting our crisis of confidence."[46]

Consultants also provide polling advice in relation to forthcoming speeches. Consider the following depiction offered by Clinton consultant Dick Morris:

> I called the president and suggested that we formulate the speech the same way we used to do it in Arkansas: he would tell me what he wanted to say and what he was thinking of proposing, I would test it in a poll, we would agree to analyze the results together, and then I would draft a speech.[47]

The pretesting of speech themes is a frequently used technique. One method is called the "mall intercept," in which members of the consultant's team rent a storefront at a shopping mall and ask shoppers to offer their opinions on various themes and phrases for the president's upcoming speech—the most popular of which are then added to the speech. That technique provides presidents with an edge in that they can be relatively confident about the substance of their message and focus more on the delivery. In the case of the Reagan administration, pollster Richard Wirthlin tested reactions to the president's State of the Union Address during and after the speech. In the course of delivering the speech, Wirthlin gathered an audience and provided members with a handheld computer terminal with which they could express their approval or disapproval of Reagan's entire speech. Wirthlin subsequently produced a graph entitled "Speech Pulse" that indicated the high and low points of the speech in terms of relative importance and performance.[48] Wirthlin also provided the president with a video of the speech that displayed viewers' responses as the speech was delivered.[49] In post-speech surveys, Wirthlin extracted proposals from the speech and asked respondents whether they approved or disapproved. Those innovations have become part and parcel of the modern president's speechwriting process.

Public Spokesperson. Many of the consultants have appeared as representatives and advocates of the president on television or in print. Historian Theodore White characterized Pat Caddell as the Carter administration's main spokesman: "[B]y the time of the Carter administration's gas crisis in 1979, [Caddell] had become the administration's chief unofficial spokesman to the press—far more so than Jody Powell, the nominal and administrative press secretary."[50] Fast forward to the Clinton administration and witness consultant Paul Begala defending the administration's opposition to an independent counsel in the Whitewater matter. In addition, he represented the administration's health care position to press secretaries on Capitol Hill: "He met with a roomful of press secretaries on the second floor of the Senate and gave a tutorial on how to boost the Clinton health care plan."[51] Campaign-veteran-turned-political-consultant James Carville also played the role as administration advocate when he defended President Clinton's 1993 economic package. At one particularly frustrating point with the White House staff, Carville stated:

> I can't go on *Meet the Press* without a message. And the only thing I get is deficit reduction stuff, and no one ever told me this was the message. And for better or for worse, and whether you guys like it or not, I have been dubbed as kind of a spokesperson for the administration.[52]

Since President Nixon, the visibility of the president's political consultants has greatly increased (as has the televised appearance of "talking heads" more generally) and has made consultants like James Carville and Dick Morris household names. Such a development is quite a contrast to earlier years when President Johnson fired a pollster named Oliver Quayle because he had become too publicly visible.[53]

Scheduling and Personnel Issues. Consultants also provide strategic advice about how and where a president should spend his time and what to do with problematic staff members. Since the president's time is his chief commodity, consultants provide insight into the opportunity cost of spending time in one city as against another or of delivering a televised speech before a large audience instead of addressing an informal and intimate gathering of key donors.

The shuffling of White House aides throughout the president's term is a prime opportunity for consultants to offer their advice. Is the aide leaking sensitive information to the press? Is an aide pulling the president too far to the left or the right? Is the aide performing his or her job inadequately? For example, during Reagan's second term in office, Chief of Staff Donald Regan was under severe criticism, and President Reagan sought the advice of his trusted political consultant, Stuart Spencer.[54] According to Spencer, "Ronald Reagan couldn't fire anybody . . . so usually me and somebody else, usually me, would go back and try to figure out what the strategies [were], how to get rid of a person. It's not easy."[55] The outsider consultant is often the best person for the president to assign such dirty tasks since the consultant's eyes are not set on ascending to the top of the White House staff hierarchy; nor will the consultant have to deal with the uncomfortable and possibly hostile fallout from firing a presidential aide.

As the previous discussion shows, political consultants have used their campaign expertise for a broad array of presidential business. Clearly, presidents are not hiring pollsters simply to track their popularity or secure reelection, but rather with an eye toward understanding public attitudes on key policy issues. Confidence in polling has rebounded considerably in the aftermath of two disasters: the failed forecasts of the FDR-Landon election in 1936 and the Truman-Dewey race in 1948. Modern-day pollsters' expertise is based on state-of-the-art statistical and survey techniques. These days, pollsters offer an array of sophisticated sampling and survey options: polling, focus groups, mall intercepts, and pulse meters. In addition to those techniques, external political consultants provide a different and valued perspective:

When you're in there [the White House] all the time, you can be overwhelmed by the daily routine and the demands of the work, whereas when
you're out of it and have a little distance from it, you can sort of pick and
choose the spots that you want to weigh in on. . . . [S]o I think there is some
objectivity which is gained from that distance and perspective.[56]

Recent presidents' tendencies to reach beyond the formal advisory
network suggest that the external political consultants' perspective
is a necessity. Note that the consultants' advice to the president is
rooted in their campaign instincts, and that perspective provides
evidence of the permanent campaign ethos permeating the presidency.

Illustrations of the Permanent Campaign in Action

With the White House's having acquired the resources to adapt to
the permanent campaign, how does the resulting mentality play out
in day-to-day operations? Examples abound, and a comprehensive
overview could be a book unto itself. Recent practices include the
use of the party organization to promote the president's legislative
agenda, the establishment of the various "war rooms" to promote
policies, and finally the development of and adherence to the White
House line of the day.

The National Party Organization as Presidential Lobbyist. The
Democratic National Committee, which was once primarily
engaged in planning the president's reelection campaign and generally held in low esteem by the White House, emerged in the early
days of the Clinton administration as a central lobbyist for the president's legislative agenda, particularly the economic package of
1993 and the health care reform initiative. Although that incarna-
tion as policy lobbyist was short-lived, it demonstrates the permanent campaign at work.

The DNC spent over $3 million promoting the budget package,
mobilizing local party organizations, organizing house parties
around key events, setting up phone banks, and coordinating media
appearances. In an effort to advance the health care initiative, the
DNC set up the National Health Care Campaign, an attempt to create a nationwide network of support with field directors in twenty-
four states.[57] The principal goal, set by the White House, was to

advance a multimedia lobbying campaign on behalf of health care reform. Amid much controversy and mixed signals emanating from the White House, the NHCC ultimately folded, and the DNC launched a $4 million advertising campaign.[58]

As this brief discussion suggests, the difference between a political campaign and a policy campaign is negligible, and the tactics are indistinguishable—field directors, for example, or phone banks. Moreover, the party's promotion of legislative proposals demonstrates the importance of two key campaign skills: public relations and grassroots activities. The heightened importance of such campaign skills in the effort to achieve legislative success is evidence of the transference of campaign skills to governing.

Moving beyond the policy realm, the DNC actively campaigned on behalf of President Clinton's reelection bid well over a year before the election. With oversight from the White House, the DNC discovered a legal loophole that freed it from campaign finance limits so that it could unleash a barrage of "issue advertisements." Those issue advertisements did not explicitly promote President Clinton's campaign or the defeat of Bob Dole but sought to highlight the weaknesses of the Republican-controlled Congress and the achievements of the Clinton administration. Many thought that such "issue advocacy," estimated to have cost $34 million dollars before June 1996,[59] was the key to President Clinton's early lead over Republican rival Bob Dole. Such support was not unusual, given that the winning of elections is a primary function of the party organization and given the rationale that what is good for President Clinton is good for the DNC. But the degree to which the DNC provided early assistance to President Clinton was unique.

The DNC's efforts may also have been deleterious in some instances. In the aftermath of the 1996 election, front-page news reports of campaign finance abuse coupled with congressional hearings and investigations dominated the news, and the DNC was forced to return numerous donations—an act that further drained an already heavily indebted party organization. In the case of health care reform, once the program became associated with the DNC, it lost all chance of becoming a bipartisan issue; rather, it became the program that the Republicans sought to defeat and later to exploit as an issue in the 1994 elections. Furthermore, the use of finite DNC resources for the promotion of President Clinton's policy agenda diminished the DNC's ability to assist other Democratic candidates in the 1994 midterm elections and probably contributed to devastating Democratic losses at all levels. While the DNC's efforts on behalf of health care and the economic package provided an alternative means for policy promotion, they diminished the possibility that meaningful health care reform would pass. Additionally, the zealous fund-raising efforts placed the party organization in legal and financial jeopardy.

The War Room. The term *war room* refers to a tactic used during Bill Clinton's 1992 presidential campaign that centralized command and communication within a single office. During the presidential campaign, James Carville and George Stephanopoulos commandeered the war room with reputed success. The source of the success was thought to be the war room's ability to overcome the physical separation of staff members working on the same issue. Bringing together policy, political, and communications staff enabled the campaign, and later the White House, to formulate a coherent strategy facilitating the delivery of a unified administration message.[60]

Initially, White House staff members adopted the tactic during the promotion of the health care reform effort. But with the battle of the economic package heating up, senior staff members abolished the health care war room and replaced it with the "pit" or the "rec [reconciliation] room"—the new home for staff members involved in promoting the president's economic package.[61] Staff members lobbied Capitol Hill, courted the press, arranged cabinet appearances across the country, scheduled publicity events, coordinated with other allies, and bused supporters into the city. Those activities were not very different from ones that took place in the Little Rock war room several months before the battle over the economic package. One news account reported:

> Now the operation is up and running, coordinating a daily barrage of media events; radio, television, and print ads paid for by the Democratic National Committee; talking points for White House surrogates and supporters on

Capitol Hill; party-generated phone calls to members of Congress; and all the other ammunition available to the high-tech pol.[62]

That is but one instance of a more general phenomenon. Behind-the-scenes efforts to gain support for a presidential initiative are not uncommon, but the publicity surrounding the war-room tactic during the 1992 campaign and its subsequent adoption convinced observers that the White House did, indeed, operate in a campaign-like atmosphere.

Of course, adopting a campaign-like tactic to govern has its share of complications. First and foremost is that the war-room mentality ignores fundamental aspects of the legislative process that require deliberation, policy knowledge, compromise, and negotiation. A conflict-oriented pursuit of policy, particularly in an era of divided government, is unlikely to facilitate agreement. The war-room mentality reflects a single-minded quest for victory, not a bipartisan attempt to work with the opposition. Finally, the war room's pivotal role on health care and the economic package suggested that a new war room be formed for every major policy goal. Such a strategy would, in practice, be unworkable, given the multiple demands on White House staff members. Staffers cannot remain fixed on a single issue without dropping the other eight balls that they are juggling; their skill lies in the ability to accomplish multiple tasks simultaneously. The war room, on the other hand, requires a single-minded focus that seeks victory in the midst of conflict and hostility—an environment clearly unsuited for good governance. To assume that a tactic that worked well in the campaign would do the same in government fails to acknowledge important differences between the two tasks.

Line of the Day. The line-of-the-day strategy was designed to focus media attention on a single issue. It emerged during Nixon's 1968 campaign, when author Joe McGinniss labeled that effort to manage the news "the selling of the president."[63] At the time, observers were surprised to see that campaign tactic incorporated into President Nixon's press operation.[64] Nevertheless, its dual purpose of unifying communication across the administration while forcing the media to follow the line of the day proved to be a valuable strategy.

Used in various forms by subsequent presidents, it was mastered by the Reagan administration:

> Never before in any administration had the line of the day been so well choreographed. In part, the Reagan administration was aided by the advent of new technology. . . . [O]fficials could find out what the line was just by punching a few keys on their office terminals.[65]

What was once a mainstay of political campaigns has become a prominent feature of modern White House communications.

Like the other campaign tactics used in the governing arena, the line of the day has its shortcomings. For one, the simplification of complex policy matters to a pithy sound bite, while soothing to the press, may stifle debate and discussion. Imposing limits on the White House message may be frustrating to those both inside and outside the White House. In the early days of an administration, the opportunity for implementing or introducing new policy initiatives is greatest, and a religious adherence to a communications strategy might limit an aggressive presidency. Furthermore, the line of the day is something with which journalists are quite familiar, and they no doubt are looking for the story behind the story. The White House is thus simply making an already adversarial relationship all the more difficult. The press knows that it is being "fed" a line, so it is constantly on the hunt. Why not give the press a real story to chew on, something of policy significance that affects voters? Even with the understanding that presidents are merely responding to the political game being played at the moment, the "dumbing down" of presidential news so that it is tailor-made for the nightly news programs is less than desirable. In campaign mode, when candidates are hurling mud and rapid response is the rule, the line of the day is appropriate, but governing is another story, one that deserves to be taken more seriously. The use of campaign tactics for governing is not surprising, but one should not ignore the consequences of such behavior.

Conclusion

By this point, it should be quite clear that the American presidency has adapted to the permanent campaign. It was inescapable. The multiple forces creating such a political environment, particularly the unstoppable technological advances, left no choice for the president but to adapt. The issue at hand was *how* to adapt. President Nixon developed the presidency's capacity to survive in the permanent campaign era, and his successors maintained, and in some cases expanded upon, that ability. But presidents do have choices. Indeed, across administrations, the president's willingness to engage in the permanent campaign has varied. For instance, the amount of money spent by the Bush administration on polling was much less than the amount spent by either the Reagan or the Clinton administration. For good or ill, President Bush was simply less interested in polling. It was not that he was a Luddite, but merely that he was not convinced of polling's purported virtues. At the same time, President Bush maintained vigorous communications, public liaison, and political affairs offices and thus showed that he recognized the importance of constituency outreach, one of the key elements of the permanent campaign.

Given the inexorable nature of that trend, it is worthwhile to consider what it means for governing. Difficult questions elicit complicated answers, and this one is no exception. The permanent campaign has potential advantages as surely as it has serious drawbacks. But given that it is here to stay, presidents must adapt to it. On the positive side, the permanent campaign mentality may heighten accountability. If presidents are continuously campaigning while in office, it is easier for the public to hold them accountable for their promises. Additionally, the continuous feedback from public opinion polls creates a more informed president with a better sense of the electorate's policy preferences. As such, the permanent campaign is likely to enhance representation by bringing the president closer to the people. The continuous connection with key constituencies through the specialized White House offices may also enhance accountability inasmuch as those groups have an access point in the White House and can pressure the administration. Finally, a president in permanent campaign mode is constantly thinking and rethinking his positions. Might not such an exercise improve civil discourse by emphasizing policy options? By extension, might the more open debate enhance public dialogue and knowledge on key issues of the day? Contributions such as those are noteworthy, particularly given today's high level of public cynicism and alienation among the electorate.

Such benefits are, however, offset by the various difficulties that arise in maintaining a campaign-mode White House whose first priority should be good governance. As scholar Karen Hult suggested, the increased permeability resulting from the outreach offices within the White House might jeopardize policy coherence and effectiveness as well as the presidency's institutional capacity for policy analysis. The president's increased responsiveness to a multitude of constituencies "may well also reduce the attention, energy, and incentive for decisionmaking focused on more substantive issues."[66] So, while openness is often tied to the positive concept of "democratization," excessive openness jeopardizes effective governance. Future presidents would be wise to consider the consequences of catering to so many special interests. At a certain point, the costs of specialization outweigh the benefits as staff members become overburdened by the multiple groups seeking the administration's assistance. With a White House that reaches out to every conceivable political interest, expectations rise to unreasonable levels. In the end, catering to all means serving none.

And while polling is certainly a useful tool in discerning public attitudes, at what point does leadership become followership? The Founding Fathers never intended that our constitutional system would create a direct democracy, but rather a representative, deliberative democracy. Excessive reliance on polls thwarts a long-lasting American tradition of leadership, not to mention the fact that polling is not as scientific as we might like to think. The myriad methodological pitfalls in polling suggest that we should read all polls with a grain of salt. The good news is that recent history indicates that presidents since Nixon have not uniformly relied on poll results. Some use them to assist in forming a policy agenda or to advise on how to sell a policy. Presidents like Bush, Carter, and at times Reagan have chosen to ignore the polls. While polling data certainly have a place at the debate table, excessive reliance on polling can be problematic.

The integration of external pollsters and consultants with the White House staff also creates a special challenge. The tension between White House staff members and the external consultants has been palpable, particularly in the days of Dick Morris during the Clinton administration. White House staff members resented the input of a campaign expert who was unfamiliar with presidential constraints. While staff members worked twelve-hour days, seven days a week, in the White House, the independent consultant would flit in for a meeting, unload a barrage of policy ideas that dazzled the president, and be on his or her merry way. Meanwhile, the frustrated staff would be left to determine how such policy initiatives could be implemented and whether they were even feasible in the first place. Consultants respond to such criticism by pointing out that their "outside the beltway" connections coupled with mounds of polling data fully support their policy proposals. After all, they have been running House and Senate races throughout the country and are much more familiar than the staff with the problems affecting "real" people. Certainly, both points have validity. It would be helpful if consultants were more aware of the constraints on the president so that they would be less likely to suggest grandiose proposals that might endanger the president's standing with the cabinet or with allies on Capitol Hill. On the other hand, White House staff members can become so myopic that they lose touch with political reality. One cannot easily overestimate the effects of the insular environment and the stress staffers endure when working in the White House. Nevertheless, it would be useful for future occupants of the White House to consider how to integrate the external consultants into the White House staff mechanism so as to minimize tension.

The tide cannot be turned. The permanent campaign is and will remain with us. Future presidents would be wise to follow their predecessors' lead by maintaining the constituency-related offices within the White House, consulting external pollsters and political consultants, and utilizing campaign tactics with full recognition of their shortcomings. So while the permanent campaign poses serious challenges, presidents must accept the current environment and make choices about the degree to which they will be drawn into campaign mode.

Notes

1. Although my goal is not to determine the source of this growth, a number of interesting perspectives exist on this development. One argument claims that presidents are attempting to cope with an expectations gap. As Richard Waterman noted, "All modern presidents have been confronted with a common dilemma: expectations of presidential performance are continuously expanding, but resources and capacity are limited." The increasing specialization and expansion would then be an inevitable development. See Joseph Pika, "Reaching Out to Organized Interests: Public Liaison in the Modern White House," in *The Presidency Reconsidered,* edited by Richard Waterman (Itasca, Ill.: Peacock Press, 1993), 149.

2. Much has been written about this subject. See, for example, Charles E. Walcott and Karen M. Hult, *Governing the White House: From Hoover through LBJ* (Lawrence: University Press of Kansas, 1995); John Burke, *The Institutional Presidency* (Baltimore: Johns Hopkins University Press, 1992); Lyn Ragsdale, "The Institutionalization of the American Presidency 1924–92," *American Journal of Political Science* 41, no. 4 (October 1997): 1280–1318; Stephen Hess, *Organizing the Presidency,* rev. ed. (Washington, D.C.: Brookings Institution, 1988); and John Hart, *The Presidential Branch: From Washington to Clinton,* 2d ed. (Chatham, N.J.: Chatham House Press, 1994).

3. Note that some of these efforts and campaign-like tactics existed in administrations before Nixon. For example, Presidents Roosevelt, Truman, and Eisenhower all utilized group liaisons to advance the administration's policy and political goals. Nixon, however, formally established the Office of Public Liaison.

4. See Karen Hult, "Strengthening Presidential Decisionmaking Capacity," paper presented at the Conference on Reinventing the Presidency, Texas A&M University, October 1–2, 1999. Beginning on page five, she discussed recent presidents' "preoccupation with public relations," such that "growing presidential permeability to external publics has contributed to rather poor performance" (p. 6).

5. Bradley Patterson provided an overview of each of these offices in *The White House Staff* (Washington, D.C.: Brookings Institution Press, 2000).

6. While a valid reason certainly exists to create such offices, constituency groups no doubt see the offices as points of contact that enable them to make their plea directly to a presidential staff member. Therefore, while the White House thinks it is good politics to reach out to those groups, they, in turn, take full advantage of the outreach.

7. John Anthony Maltese, *Spin Control: The White House Office of Communications and the Management of Presidential News,* 2d ed. (Chapel Hill: University of North Carolina Press, 1994), 28.

8. Ibid., 27.

9. See Samuel Kernell, *Going Public: New Strategies of Presidential Leadership,* 3d ed. (Washington, D.C.: Congressional Quarterly, 1997).

10. See Hart, *The Presidential Branch,* 127.

11. See Pika, "Reaching Out to Organized Interests," and Mark A. Peterson, "The Presidency and Organized Interests: White House Patterns of Interest Group Liaison," *American Political Science Review* 86, no. 3 (1992): 612–25.

12. For a comprehensive examination of the White House role in reelection planning, see Kathryn Dunn Tenpas, *Presidents as Candidates: Inside the White House for the Presidential Campaign* (New York: Garland Press, 1997).

13. See Kathryn Dunn Tenpas, "Institutionalized Politics: The White House Office of Political Affairs," *Presidential Studies Quarterly* 26, no. 2 (Spring 1996): 511.

14. Sidney Blumenthal, *The Permanent Campaign* (New York: Simon and Schuster, 1982), 7.

15. Notably, the increasing capacity to reach out to key constituencies is part of the larger phenomenon of the increasing centralization and politicization within the White House. See Terry Moe, "The Politicized Presidency," in *The New Direction in American Politics,* edited by John E. Chubb and Paul E. Peterson (Washington, D.C.: Brookings Institution, 1985), 235–72.

16. Lawrence Jacobs and Robert Shapiro, "The Rise of Presidential Polling: The Nixon White House in Historical Perspective," *Public Opinion Quarterly* 50 (1995): 174.

17. Note that Lawrence Jacobs and Robert Shapiro have conducted extensive research about the Nixon polling operation. My approach is unique in that it examines those pollsters as quasi–White House staff members by paying close attention to the nature of their advice as well as their relationship with the president and staff instead of explaining the institutionalization of the presidential polling operation. See ibid.

18. Note that Paul Begala eventually became a White House staff member in the aftermath of the Lewinsky scandal. That position, however, was distinct from his prior role as external political consultant.

19. The list of consultants is based on a comprehensive examination of major news sources, interviews, and archival materials. These presidential political consultants are distinctive for two basic reasons: a long-term, direct association with a sitting president and evidence of a client relationship (for example, citations in numerous periodicals and secondary sources as the president's political consultant and party or campaign expenditures to the political consultant). The relationship refers to a scenario in which the president serves as one of the political consultants' many clients.

20. See Kathryn Dunn Tenpas, "Campaigning to Govern: Political Consultants as Presidential Advisers," paper presented at the annual meeting of the American Political Science Association, Boston, September 3–6, 1998.

21. Jacobs and Shapiro, "The Rise of Presidential Polling," 172, 180.

22. Note that during the Clinton administration, the polling firm of Penn and Schoen largely superseded Stanley Greenberg, campaign-pollster-turned-

administration-pollster, during the reelection campaign of 1996. He never-theless maintained his contract with the DNC and continued polling for the party.

23. Elizabeth Drew, *On the Edge* (New York: Simon and Schuster, 1994), 124.

24. Charles O. Jones, "Campaigning to Govern: The Clinton Style," in *The Clinton Presidency: First Appraisals*, edited by Colin Campbell and Bert A. Rockman (Chatham, N.J.: Chatham House Publishers, 1996), 45.

25. Republican National Committee expenditure records from the Nixon administration, initially housed at the General Accounting Office, are avail-able from 1972 through the remainder of his term. Note that passage of the Federal Election Campaign Act occurred in 1971. As a result, only incom-plete records are available for the Nixon administration.

26. See, for example, Jerry Hagstrom, "The Souls of a New Machine," *National Journal* (June 18, 1994): 1497; John Harris, "Latest Additions to Staff May Add Spice to White House Stew," *Washington Post,* June 29, 1997; Russell Tisinger, "Health Care Reform's Hidden Persuader," *National Journal* (October 30, 1993): 2604; and William Safire, "The Guru behind Clinton's Centrist Leap," *Denver Post,* June 21, 1995.

27. The data come from research conducted at the Federal Election Commission in Washington, D.C., in July and December of 1998, with the assistance of graduate assistant Karina Shields. Obtaining the figures requires reviewing party expenditure reports and identifying the consult-ants' specific payments on a quarterly basis. In some cases the party organ-ization alphabetizes their expenditures, while in others they reported expenditures in a random manner. The process is also complicated by the fact that Bush pollster Robert Teeter's firm had three names over the course of the four years in which he worked for the president. The firm was orig-inally named Market Opinion Research, then the Coldwater Corporation, and finally Market Strategies. Nevertheless, these preliminary findings, which are subject to revision, provide a rough gauge of how much money was spent on presidential political consultants.

28. See Ann Devroy, "Keeping a Campaign Pledge to Rein in Costs," *Washington Post,* July 3, 1995. Note that Ann Devroy identifies the salaries for "top offi-cials," a category that includes thirty-seven individuals. I extracted the salaries of fifteen of those members who possessed the most senior positions on the White House staff. The titles included counselor to the president (two), assistant to the president, communications coordinator, director of legislative affairs, director for public liaison, director of Oval Office opera-tions, cabinet secretary, national security adviser, press secretary, chief of staff, director of political affairs, National Economic Council director, director of scheduling and advance, and chief of staff to the first lady.

29. Mandy Grunwald was part of the firm Grunwald, Eskew, and Donilon.

30. Mark Penn was part of the two-man polling firm Penn and Schoen.

31. Note that these expenditures include the costs of actual polling and media buys as well as consulting, travel, and other expenses incurred by the con-

sultants. FEC records provide a brief entry on the disbursement form that identifies the "purpose" of the expenditure. Examples of purposes include polling, car rental, travel expenses, and the like.

32. The exceptions include Mandy Grunwald, Paul Begala, and James Carville, whose input gradually declined after the midterm elections. Similarly, as mentioned above, Stanley Greenberg remained the DNC pollster but was superseded by Mark Penn as the president's reelection campaign pollster. For a cogent explanation of Pat Caddell's reelection advice to Carter, see Theodore White, *America in Search of Itself* (New York: Harper and Row, 1982), 379–82.

33. "Is PFC a 1976 CREEP?" *National Journal* (January 24, 1976): 107.

34. In the case of the Clinton administration, two campaigners from the 1992 campaign, Paul Begala (who moved back to Texas) and Mandy Grunwald, had all but lost their political consulting positions to Dick Morris by the time preparation for the 1996 reelection campaign began. As Morris noted in his memoirs, however, Clinton "never really fired any of the consultants who helped him win in 1992. Mandy Grunwald, his former media adviser, was shifted over to the First Lady's staff, to give Hillary advice on TV appearances." Dick Morris, *Behind the Oval Office* (New York: Random House, 1997), 27. Interestingly, well after the reelection campaign, at the height of the Monica Lewinsky scandal, Bill Clinton rehired Paul Begala as a White House staff member to help "control" the fallout.

35. This information is based on extensive document review conducted at the Jimmy Carter Center in Atlanta, Georgia, in March 1998.

36. This evidence was gleaned in interviews conducted with Press Secretary Jody Powell, Assistant to the President for Congressional Liaison Frank Moore, and Assistant to the President for Communications Jerry Rafshoon.

37. See Box 1, PR Public Relations, PR015 Public Relations: Opinion Polls (044601–050000), Ronald Reagan Presidential Library, Simi Valley, California.

38. I am hesitant to state conclusively that there were more issue surveys than performance surveys since it is not clear that I have seen all the D/M/I Wirthlin surveys at the Ronald Reagan Presidential Library, Simi Valley, California. It may be the case that the archivists have not opened all the polling-related documents or that no single staff member kept an entire eight-year record of Wirthlin surveys. I therefore find it necessary to inform the reader in a somewhat tentative manner.

39. This information was obtained from document review at the Ronald Reagan Presidential Library, Simi Valley, California, in June 1998. See also Diane Heith, "Staffing the White House Public Opinion Apparatus 1969–1988," paper presented at the 1996 annual meeting of the American Political Science Association, San Francisco, August 28–September 1, 1996.

40. See David Maraniss, "Clinton's Elusive Adviser," *Washington Post,* June 23, 1995.

41. See Lou Cannon, *Ronald Reagan: The Role of a Lifetime* (New York: Simon and Schuster, 1991), 508–9, 451.

42. See #043822, WHORM: Subject File, PR015, Ronald Reagan Presidential Library, Simi Valley, California.

43. Morris, *Behind the Oval Office,* 246.

44. Robert A. Strong, "Recapturing Leadership: The Carter Administration and the Crisis of Confidence," *Presidential Studies Quarterly* 16 (Fall 1986), 639–42. See especially p. 642.

45. This statement was made in an off-the-record interview.

46. Papers of the Staff Secretary, #139, Folder Title 7/16/79, Jimmy Carter Library, Atlanta, Georgia.

47. Morris, *Behind the Oval Office,* 83.

48. WHORM: Subject File, #36621855, PR015, "Analysis of the February 4, 1986 State of the Union," Ronald Reagan Presidential Library, Simi Valley, California.

49. Ibid.

50. White, *America in Search of Itself,* 378.

51. Jeffrey Birnbaum, *Madhouse* (New York: Random House, 1996), 225.

52. Bob Woodward, *The Agenda* (New York: Simon and Schuster, 1994), 239.

53. Jacobs and Shapiro, "The Rise of Presidential Polling," 183.

54. See Dick Kirschten, "Around the White House Bunker," *National Journal* (December 6, 1986): 2950.

55. Interview with Stuart Spencer, June 5, 1998.

56. Interview with Tad Devine, Schrum, Devine, and Donilon, March 24, 1998.

57. See Kathryn Dunn Tenpas, "Promoting President Clinton's Policy Agenda: DNC as Presidential Lobbyist," *American Review of Politics* 17 (Fall/Winter 1996): 287–93.

58. Ibid., 292.

59. See Anthony Corrado, "Giving, Spending, and 'Soft Money,'" *Journal of Law and Policy* 6, no. 1 (1997): 51–52.

60. This strategy is not very different from the "task force" that presidents often employ to examine a key policy issue.

61. Woodward, *The Agenda,* 255, 259–61. The term *war room* was forbidden for fear of associating a campaign tactic with governing.

62. Lloyd Grove, "All Noisy on the Budget Front; A Visit to the 'Rec Room,' Clinton's Command Center," *Washington Post,* July 31, 1993.

63. Maltese, *Spin Control,* 3.

64. Ibid.

65. Ibid.

66. See Hult, "Strengthening Presidential Decisionmaking Capacity," 8.

6

Congress in the Era of the Permanent Campaign
David Brady and Morris Fiorina

Congress is the most electorally sensitive of our national institutions. Consequently, it is not surprising that the effects of the permanent campaign appear to be widely evident in its recent evolution and current operation. We use the cautious locution "appear to be" in the preceding sentence, however, because systematic empirical research on the manifestations of the permanent campaign in Congress lags behind both theoretical arguments and impressionistic observations. This chapter surveys changes taking place at the same time as the arrival of the permanent campaign and invites the reader to speculate with us about the possible causal connections.

The Susceptibility of Congress to the Permanent Campaign

Scholars have long assumed (we think correctly) that most members of Congress are, if not "single-minded seekers of reelection," at least highly interested in reelection.[1] Because of that interest, Congress operates according to a two-year electoral rhythm. Members of the House function in a campaign mode more or less all the time, and while senators serve six-year terms, the needs of the one-third standing for reelection every two years exert a strong influence on the actions of the larger body. As Anthony King noted, Congress's two-year electoral cycle is very short by world

134

standards.[2] It is short even by U.S. standards, as only members of the lower houses of state legislatures and other subnational legislative bodies typically serve terms of fewer than four years.

The effects of the short congressional term are reinforced by the occurrence of primaries, which begin as early as March of election year and shorten the period during which members might be expected to be in a governing as opposed to a campaigning mode. In 1996, for example, Representative Greg Laughlin (R-Texas) was defeated in a primary on April 9, scarcely fifteen months after taking the oath of office.

Since the advent of the permanent campaign, the number of members defeated in primaries has not increased.[3] But congressional observers have the impression that the number of primaries and the number of serious primaries have increased. Surprisingly, we have not been able to find any time series on House primaries. In figure 6-1 we present some data gathered at selected intervals that indicate an increase in Democratic primaries into the mid-1970s, followed by a decrease, and a sudden upsurge in Republican primaries in the 1990s. Clearly, more detailed research is needed on temporal variation in the susceptibility of members to primary threats.

In addition to shortening the effective length of a member's term, primaries have a second effect that has received academic attention. Primaries create representational incentives that often are at odds with those created by general elections. The standard theory of political science holds that in two-way elections in single-member districts candidates move toward the center.[4] But primary electorates are small and unrepresentative, so that, to protect their flanks, members of Congress may be forced to play to noncentrist elements of their constituencies. Research demonstrates that this is a problem for Republicans on issues such as abortion, and in general, evidence exists that candidates diverge from centrist positions in part because of their primary electorates.[5] Thus, the polarization of Congress that we discuss below might be partly rooted in the hypothesized increased importance of primaries.

In sum, take a body of elected officials who are highly interested in staying elected, make them stand for election every two years—

Figure 6-1 Number of House Primaries, Excluding Runoffs

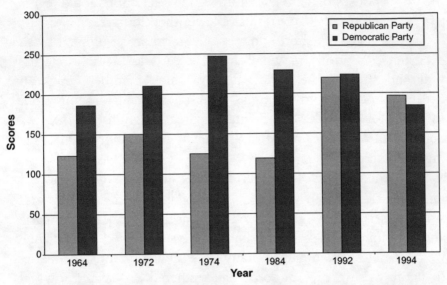

Source: Richard M. Scammon, Alice V. McGillivray, and Rhodes Cook, *America Votes* (Washington, D.C.: Congressional Quarterly, various years).

sooner if they face a serious primary—and we have a recipe for maximizing the effects of the permanent campaign. Members of Congress should have a continuous interest in constructing, maintaining, and reconstructing electoral coalitions, guaranteeing an adequate supply of electoral resources, and preempting possible challenges. Mayhew argued a quarter century ago that members of Congress of that era had structured the institution to maximize its electoral usefulness.[6] Are there indications that the arrival of the permanent campaign has led to further changes in internal organization, rules and procedures, norms and practices, behavior, and policy outputs?

Internal Organization

Throughout the 1970s, students of Congress discussed and critiqued the ongoing decentralization of power in Congress.[7] To earlier eras of "party government" and "committee government" some added the "era of subcommittee government" as the total number of committees and subcommittees and member assignments surged.[8] (See figures 6-2 and 6-3.) Pressures for decentralization generally

Figure 6-2 Total Number of Committees

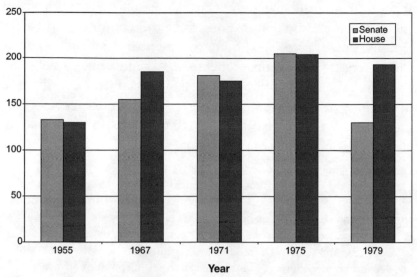

Source: Norman J. Ornstein, Thomas E. Mann, and Michael J. Malbin, *Vital Statistics on Congress 1999–2000* (Washington, D.C.: AEI Press, 2000).

Figure 6-3 Mean Number of Committee Assignments

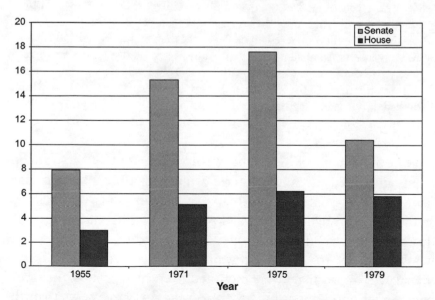

Source: Norman J. Ornstein, Thomas E. Mann, and Michael J. Malbin, *Vital Statistics on Congress 1999–2000* (Washington, D.C.: AEI Press, 2000).

were viewed as reflections of two related changes. First, an influx of younger and more liberal Democrats increased the contingent of members frustrated by domination of the full committees by older and more conservative (and southern) members. Second, whether liberal or conservative, younger members were more interested than their elders in making public policy. Hence, they were unwilling to wait patiently for an eventual turn as a committee chair—they wanted to make an impact right away. We can do no better than to quote James Sundquist at some length:

> The typical member produced by an old-style pre-Progressive party organization—whether Republican or Democratic, liberal or conservative, urban or rural—had been trained to be deferential. Coming from a political apprenticeship in which leadership and hierarchy were normal and accepted, he accepted them in the Congress, too. His views on political issues were compatible with those of his organization. . . . His career did not depend on any showing of brilliance in the conception or advocacy of legislative measures, and he was not likely to mount a challenge to the way the Congress was organized or run.
>
> The new-style member contrasts with the old in political manners, political vocabulary, interests, and conception of the proper nature of the institution in which he serves. As a congressional candidate, he was self-chosen. Nobody handed him the nomination; he won it in open competition, usually by the vote of the party rank and file in a direct primary. He won it by identifying and articulating the issues better than his competitors. . . . His background is likely to be less in party service than in intellectual and advocacy organizations, of all kinds. . . . His absorbing interest is governmental policy. He came to the Congress with a sense of mission, even a mandate, to have an impact on the legislative process. He is impatient, for those who backed him expect legislative results. An upstart as a candidate—self-selected, self-organized, self-propelled, self-reliant—he will be an upstart in the House or Senate, too.[9]

With the benefit of hindsight, we now can see that the developments identified by Sundquist were manifestations of the permanent campaign. The decline of party organizations that selected candidates for qualities such as loyalty and electability left a void that was filled by interest groups that selected the candidates they would back on the basis of the purity of their views. Candidates themselves increasingly were recruited from such groups; they were people with more intensely held and more extreme views than the generations of party loyalists who preceded them.[10] They were quick to take advantage of new technologies, and the spread of polling gave them more information about their electoral standing than ever before. The politics they practiced soon came to be called "candidate-centered" or "entrepreneurial" politics.[11]

The new breed of member greatly changed Congress. At first, some of the changes seemed to work at cross-purposes. In the House, for example, the internal distribution of influence was broadened and flattened, particularly by the subcommittee reforms—at the height of House committee decentralization, half the Democratic members were subcommittee chairs. On the other hand, the caucus and the party leadership were strengthened relative to the committees. The Speaker gained new assignment powers, and the caucus gained the right to approve committee chairs and some subcommittee chairs. Seemingly, the new members were supporting decentralization and centralization at the same time. Over time, the scholarly consensus has concluded that the centralizing reforms were more important than the decentralizing ones.[12]

In the Senate, internal organization had always been more fluid and less formal than in the House.[13] But there, too, senior members began to share power more generously with junior members. And although an individual senator's ability to stymie legislation increased—a point discussed below—those individualistic senators allowed modern leaders like George Mitchell and Robert Dole to take a more active part in managing the Senate than leaders like Mike Mansfield and Hugh Scott, who preceded the advent of the permanent campaign.

With hindsight, the apparent conflict between trends in internal organization is not so puzzling. Decentralizing the committee system and otherwise distributing power more broadly gave more members a piece of the action—more opportunities to stake out positions and claim credit for legislative activities. That helped their reelections. On the other hand, a totally decentralized Congress was incapable of acting—of satisfying the members' personal policy preferences or delivering for the interest groups that supported them. Thus, stronger parties were a means to satisfy policy goals. Moreover, as realignment in the South and other factors made the parties internally more homogeneous, the potential costs of ceding power to party leaders fell, because members had less reason to fear that party power would be used in ways inimical to their electoral interests.[14]

While we think that the preceding brief overview accurately summarizes the views of congressional scholars, we hasten to add that important points of disagreement exist. Most important, in a series of contributions Keith Krehbiel has argued persuasively that much of the evidence cited in support of the strengthening of the congressional parties is ambiguous.[15] On the one hand, there is little evidence of tangible punishing and rewarding by party leaders, and on the other hand, frequently cited measures of rising intraparty cohesion and interparty differences might simply reflect the aforementioned trends in member preferences—more homogeneous parties whose centers of gravity are farther apart.

In sum, while the arrival of the permanent campaign is clearly associated with changes in the internal organization of Congress, the interpretation of those changes is not so clear, and the evaluation of those changes is less clear still. In and of itself, we think that it is hard to make a case that the organization of Congress today is less optimal than a generation ago. Critics have a tendency to confuse what a Dick Gephardt or a Newt Gingrich and their troops do within today's congressional structure with the structure itself. If we were to ask instead what a Sam Rayburn or a Joe Martin and their troops might have done within today's structure, we might evaluate it differently. Our own view is that from the standpoint of governing, Congress probably is better organized today than a generation ago. Of course, that is not to say that Congress actually makes more of a positive contribution today. There is more to the picture than formal organization.

Rules and Procedures

At least four types of changes in formal rules and procedures in the House and Senate are temporally associated with the permanent campaign's candidate-centered politics. Whether they are causally associated in all cases is less certain.

First came a series of rules changes in the House designed to "open up" Congress and expose its decisionmaking to public view.

After 1971 it became relatively easy to demand a recorded vote on amendments, and anonymous voting via tellers ceased to be an important part of the congressional process after electronic voting was implemented in 1973. As figure 6-4 shows, the number of roll call votes taken rose sharply in the wake of such rules changes. Of course, public voting conformed to the ethos of the time (recall "government in the sunshine"), and some members believed that public voting would have favorable (that is, liberal) policy consequences because conservative chairmen would no longer be able to coerce the votes of the rank and file on critical but unrecorded votes on amendments.

But such rules changes have complicated the lives of members and reinforced some of the more troubling aspects of the permanent campaign as well. Opposition researchers pore over members' voting records in an attempt to find a vote contrary to—or a vote that can be (mis)construed as contrary to—the preferences of their constituents. Every vote a member casts must be considered a potential campaign issue. Indeed, some bills and amendments are offered only as a vehicle for forcing a vote that will provide a campaign

Figure 6-4 Recorded Votes in the House

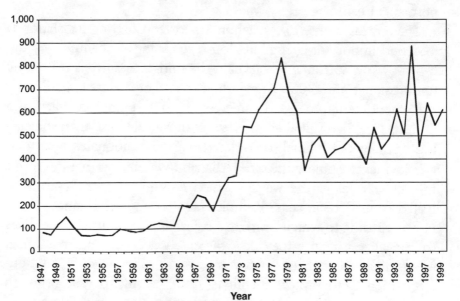

Source: *Congressional Record, Daily Digest.*

Figure 6-5 Percentage of Rules Considered Open

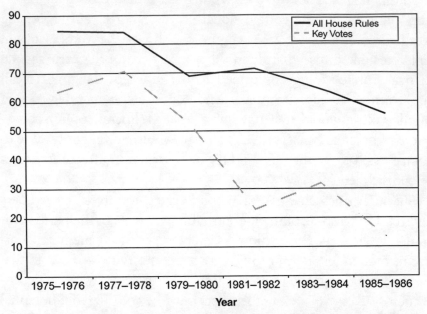

Source: Steven Smith, *Call to Order* (Washington, D.C.: Brookings Institution,1989).

issue. Thus, this rules change fosters the kind of posturing for electoral purposes that is at the heart of concerns about the effects of the permanent campaign.

The increasing use of special orders for considering legislation is a second important change in House rules and procedures. Figure 6-5 shows how, from a low level in the mid-1970s, rules restricting the substance and order of amendments and otherwise constraining the amendment process became increasingly common. Bach and Smith provided a valuable overview of those rules and their increasing use, and Krehbiel considered various rationales for their employment.[16] One is the older "distributive theory" that interprets restrictive rules as the way in which committee logrolls are protected from floor attacks. Krehbiel favored an "informational theory" according to which restrictive rules give committees incentives to specialize and give the floor reasonably accurate information. It seems likely to us that restrictive rules can also have a third rationale, which is to protect members from having to cast votes on amendments that would damage or embarrass them in the eyes of constituents, an increasingly important function if the opposition is increasingly offering amendments for just that purpose.

Of course, restrictive rules can also have the opposite function— to permit members to take positions that will make them look good in the eyes of their supporters. Of considerable interest is the "King-of-the-Hill" rule that came into frequent usage after 1982. Under that rule a number of amendments to a bill, or different versions of a bill, are voted on sequentially, with the last one getting a majority being adopted. The rule gives members the opportunity to cast votes for proposals favored by constituents and interest groups— however irresponsible—while members are secure in the knowledge that such proposals will never be implemented. Instead, the last proposal slated by the Rules Committee, the arm of the party leadership, is the one that carries. Often a number of different budget resolutions were in order (Democratic, Republican, Blue Dog Democrat, Black Caucus, Brown) and enabled members to vote for very liberal or conservative budgets, while members were secure in the knowledge that the majority party budget would be the outcome.

It may be that the rise of restrictive rules is partly a consequence of the first set of rules changes that made congressional operations more visible. Members may have found that such reforms made life more dangerous for them.[17] In particular, putting so many votes on record may have provided challengers with excessive ammunition. Hence, restrictive rules may serve somewhat the same protective function as the nonrecorded vote procedures members did away with in the 1970s.

A third category of changes in congressional procedures is represented by multiple referrals, leadership task forces, and so forth. The old civics book diagram, wherein a bill is referred to a single committee, marked up, then reported out, became increasingly outdated in the 1980s as more and more bills were referred to more than one committee, divided among several committees, or handled by special ad hoc committees and task forces. The House changed its rules to permit multiple referral in 1975, and in a decade the proportion of multiple referrals rose to one-quarter of all bills. The Senate, too, liberalized its rules regarding multiple referral, but actual usage did not increase as it did in the House.[18] Although we doubt that procedural innovations like these are directly related to electoral considerations—certainly, the rise of complex issues such as energy and the environment must have had a lot to do with that—they may be indirect reflections of the arrival of the permanent campaign. The earlier decentralization of internal organization increased the need for coordinating mechanisms that would put back together what the subcommittee reforms had taken apart.

A fourth notable change in congressional rules and procedures consists of the informal Senate practices concerning the use of filibusters and "holds." The roots of the filibuster run deep in Senate history, of course, but beginning in the 1960s the filibuster began to be used more frequently, a trend that continued through the 1970s. (See figures 6-6 and 6-7.) Today, the filibuster is considered such a normal feature of Senate procedure that observers commonly think of sixty votes (the number required to cut off a filibuster) as the size of a winning coalition. Binder and Smith trace the increasing use of the filibuster to factors previously discussed as part of the perma-

Figure 6-6 Filibusters per Congress

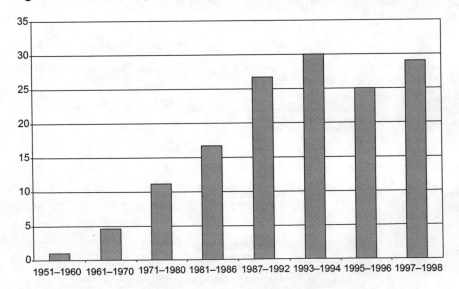

Source: Barbara Sinclair, "Individualism, Partisanship, and Cooperation in the Senate," paper for Civility and Deliberation in the United States Senate Conference, Washington, D.C., July 16, 1999.

Figure 6-7   Percentage of Major Measures Subject to Filibuster, Selected Congresses

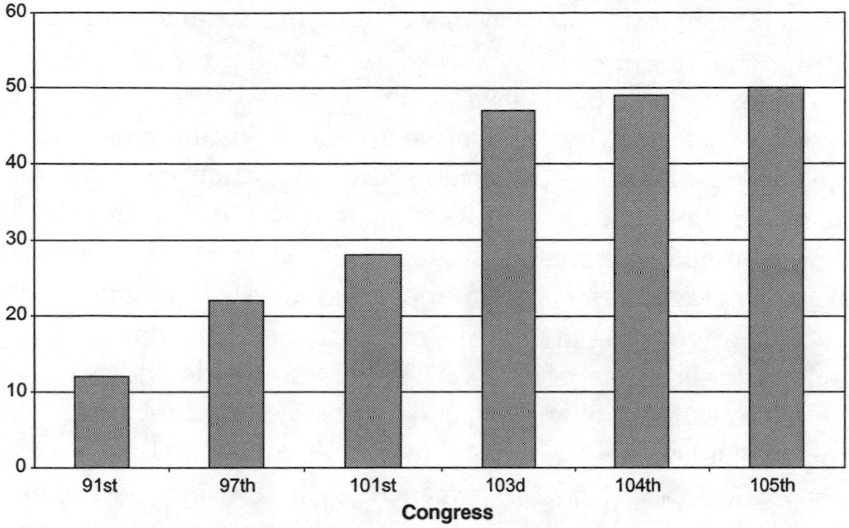

Source: Barbara Sinclair, "Individualism, Partisanship, and Cooperation in the Senate," paper for Civility and Deliberation in the United States Senate Conference, Washington, D.C., July 16, 1999.

nent campaign.[19] In particular, a more open legislative process coupled with the proliferation of interest groups easily able to monitor the process subjects senators to greater pressure to accommodate special-interest demands. In addition, if today's senators attach relatively more importance to their personal policy goals than did the senators of past generations, their personal willingness to stymie legislation would reinforce that of their interest-group constituents.

Much the same argument applies to anonymous holds, although they have received less study, for obvious reasons. The ability of one senator to prevent the body from taking up a proposal or nomination (because of the implied threat of a filibuster) is the ultimate expression of placing one individual's or interest's policy preferences above those of the entire body, even if only temporarily. That senators can do so anonymously is particularly troubling, if we can step outside the academic mode for a moment. At least a filibuster is out in the open; countervailing pressure can be brought to bear on the filibusterers.

Norms and Practices

According to descriptions of the "textbook Congress" of the prereform era, congressional behavior was governed as much by internal norms and practices as by formal rules and procedures.[20] Like members of an exclusive men's club, senators adhered to a set of norms—courtesy, reciprocity, apprenticeship, institutional patriotism, and hard work—that made social interaction congenial and facilitated the work of the institution.[21] In the House, at least on some committees, representatives served an apprenticeship, learned the value of courtesy, specialization, and reciprocity, and otherwise learned to "go along in order to get along."[22] Those days are long gone, according to most observers. Asher found little evidence of an apprenticeship norm by 1970, and Loomis found further deterioration of that and other norms by the late 1980s.[23] In 1982 Senator Joseph Biden (D-Delaware) remarked, "There's much less civility than when I came here ten years ago. There aren't as many nice people as there were before. . . . Ten years ago you didn't have people calling each other sons of bitches and vowing to get each other."[24] Table 6-1 compares findings over time, although, given differences in wording the questions, we must be cautious about interpreting the results.

Not everyone accepted that generally harmonious portrait of the textbook Congress, to be sure. Huitt pointed out that senators who violated the purported norms did not seem to be sanctioned in any observable ways; indeed, he identified senators who seemed to violate the norms regularly but nevertheless were held in high regard within the institution.[25] Fenno found the "norms" framework less applicable when he later published his larger committee study.[26] More recently, Hall has raised questions about the accuracy of the portrait of internal life in the preform Congress. Focusing on observable measures rather than interview reports, Hall proposed that actual behavior across the two periods differed less than the scholarly portraits of congressional life based on interviews suggested.[27] It may be that some members have always held expectations about behavior that were ignored by others—or even themselves. Consider these reminiscences of Senator Shelby Cullom (R-Illinois), writing in 1911:

**Table 6-1 Weakening of Congressional Norms: Norm Acceptance
among House Freshmen**

Norm	1969	1976	1980
Personal cordiality	100	63	37
Ability to compromise	72	50	49
Specialization	73	54	44
Expertise	90	77	72
Apprenticeship	57	19	8
Seniority	–	21	26
Hard work	–	–	74
Institutional patriotism	–	–	5

Note: In 1969 *personal cordiality* was defined as "friendly relations important." *Ability to compromise* was defined as "likely to trade votes." *Expertise* was "important work done in committees."

Sources: Eric Uslaner, *The Decline of Comity in Congress* (Ann Arbor: University of Michigan Press, 1993), 25. Original data from Herbert Asher, "The Learning of Legislative Norms," *American Political Science Review* 67 (1973): 503; Burdett Loomis, *The New American Politician* (New York: Basic Books, 1988), 48.

That fine old term "senatorial courtesy" has lost much of its meaning as a result of the brusque and breezy manner of the time. No longer is it said that the young Senator must be seen rather than heard. Indeed, while formerly the spectacle of a Senator rising to make a speech before the close of his second year in the Senate was regarded as unusual, it recently has come to be remarked upon if a new man remains in his seat for two months before undertaking to enlighten the Senate as to its duties towards itself and the world.[28]

Amusingly, earlier in his memoir, Cullom reported that he made his first "extended address" in the Senate a month after taking office![29]

So, have congressional norms eroded, or were they never more than wishful thinking on the part of some members? Whatever the ultimate resolution of this scholarly discussion, we think it difficult to deny that, at a minimum, there is less civility, or to use Uslaner's term, less *comity* in the contemporary Congress than in the Congresses of a generation ago.[30] Our recollection is that some of the decline in civility began during the intense policy disagreements surrounding the Vietnam War in the late 1960s, but a more systematic component exists as well. Uslaner suggested that changes in the perspectives of the American people, especially trust, are at the

root of the decline in comity. While that may be part of the explanation, we think that the arrival of the permanent campaign should
be considered a significant part of the explanation.

In a context in which members themselves have stronger and
more distinct policy preferences, where they scarcely know each
other personally because every spare moment is spent fund-raising
or cultivating constituents, where interest groups monitor every
word a member speaks and levy harsh attacks upon the slightest
deviation from group orthodoxy, where the media provide coverage
in direct proportion to the negativity and conflict contained in one's
messages, where money is desperately needed and is best raised by
scaring the bejesus out of people, is it any wonder that comity and
courtesy are among the first casualties? If the norm-guided portrait
of the textbook Congress was accurate, surely it owed much to the
fact that both Congress and its members were different in those
days. As Sundquist remarked in the passage previously quoted,
members had undergone a different sort of political socialization.
They lived in Washington for much of the year and socialized
together. A few large established interests dominated the interest-
group universe and worked in concert with long-standing allies
among the committee and party leadership. The media found
Congress relatively uninteresting. Campaigning was cheap, and
some of it was done by the local parties. In that context "to get
along, go along" made good sense to the members.

Congressional Behavior

While there may be some disagreement about the extent to which
the permanent campaign has altered congressional norms, there is
more of a consensus that it has changed congressional behavior in
significant other respects. Members of Congress travel home much
more frequently than at midcentury, they vote with their party in
opposition to the other party much more frequently, and they
choose different sorts of leaders to coordinate their behavior and
present a collective face to the outside world.

Travel. Representative Clem Miller (D-California) penned a delight-
ful series of letters to constituents in 1959–1961. Scanning them
today gives one the sense of reading about a bygone time. In one let-

ter he wrote: "I have just returned to Washington after two months in the district, meeting with friends, strangers, and even a foe or two. It was an exhilarating experience."[31] Miller noted that even then congressional sessions had stretched out to nine or ten months, lengths that seem short by today's standards. He described the full days in Washington and at home, but the descriptions seem placid compared with the frenetic pace maintained by today's members:

> Evenings I spend at home as much as possible. . . . At night, after supper I read another district paper as well as the reports, speeches, and magazines that have accumulated during the day. . . . About 11:00 or 12:00 P.M. the day is at an end. I like to top it off with a chapter from a book.[32]

Miller was writing as Congress was changing. Before the jet plane made rapid coast-to-coast travel possible, before session lengths stretched out to eleven or twelve months, and before the permanent campaign arrived on the scene, members spent long periods of time in Washington, typically moving their families and maintaining two residences.[33] A subset of members from East Coast districts were known somewhat pejoratively as the "Tuesday to Thursday club" because they lived sufficiently close to Washington to make weekly car trips home feasible. Such a term is inapplicable today as Congress mostly runs on a Tuesday to Thursday schedule. Glenn Parker has documented how time spent in home districts and states skyrocketed beginning in the mid-1960s.[34]

A huge academic literature described the growth of the incumbency advantage during the late 1960s.[35] Part of the growth generally was attributed to the increasingly close attention new members paid to their districts. Going home weekly, meeting people, servicing the district, raising money, and so forth certainly helped incumbents to secure their reelections, but the cost was a change in the rhythm of congressional life—less time spent personally interacting with colleagues, a greater role for the greatly expanded congressional staffs, and probably less of a sense of a collective "we."

Voting. One of the most studied forms of congressional behavior is roll call voting. And two of the most remarked-on features of contemporary roll call voting are the resurgence of party cohesion and the increasing polarization of the parties.

Party cohesion reached a nadir in the 1960s and bottomed out around that end of that decade.[36] As figures 6-8 and 6-9 show, however, in the late 1970s and 1980s the parties became internally more cohesive. Increasingly, they took stands against each other, as well—party differences grew.[37] The literature identified several factors underlying those trends: the waning of divisive issues like Vietnam, the decline of the conservative wing of the Democratic Party, and increasingly active leadership.[38]

The increase in party cohesion and party voting is closely associated with the increased polarization of the parties in Congress, which likely has a significant relation to the permanent campaign. Both in the House and in the Senate a variety of voting indexes show that moderates have declined in numbers so that Democrats and Republicans are much farther apart today than a generation ago.[39] Much confusion attends discussions of polarization in Congress. Arguments about polarization of the parties within Congress get mixed up with polarization of the candidates within districts, and ambiguity reigns on the theoretical level.[40] Even the basic claim itself—that Democrats and Republicans are much farther apart than a generation ago—has some skeptics. Apparently, diverging roll call records could theoretically be the result of the extremity of proposals brought to the floor, rather than diverging member preferences.[41] On the basis of the totality of the evidence, however, we are satisfied that figure 6-10 has the story about right: the average Republican and Democrat are farther apart than they were during the era of the textbook Congress.

Part of that increased divergence arises from political change in the South. Conservative Democrats have been replaced by conservative Republicans, a result that leaves the Democrats a more liberal party and reinforces the conservatism of the Republican Party. But even outside the South, Democrats and Republicans are increasingly polarized.[42] While the precise relationships have not been worked out, we have reason to suspect that the permanent campaign is associated with increased polarization. As noted above, many observers believe that members of Congress themselves have stronger and more extreme preferences today. Their personal organizations rely heavily on policy activists. The contemporary political landscape abounds with strident interest groups. The media search

Figure 6-8 House Average Party Cohesion Scores

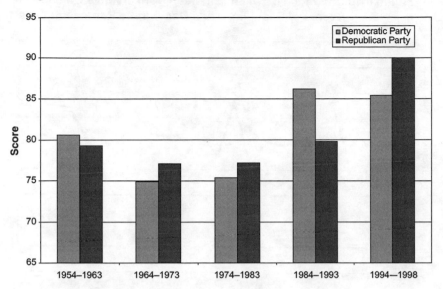

Source: *Congressional Quarterly*, various *Weekly Reports*.

Figure 6-9 Senate Average Party Cohesion Scores

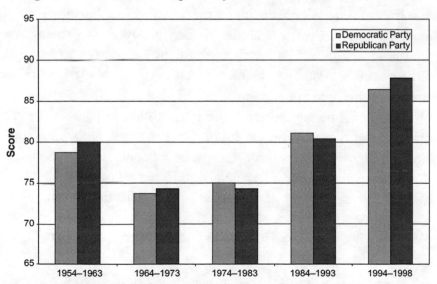

Source: *Congressional Quarterly*, various *Weekly Reports*.

Figure 6-10 Difference between American Conservative Union Scores of Republican and Democratic Representatives

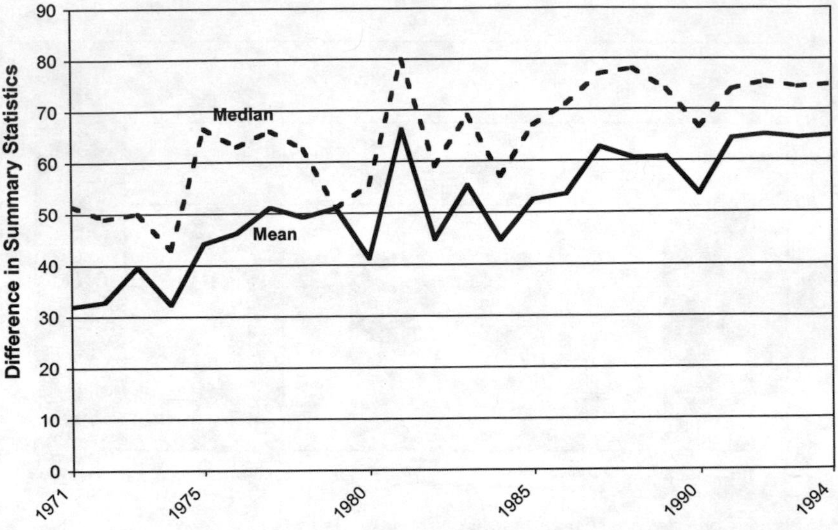

Source: Melissa P. Collie and John Lyman Mason,"The Electoral Connection between Party and Constituency Reconsidered: Evidence from the U.S. House of Representatives, 1972–1994," *Congressional Elections in the Post WWII Era: Continuity and Change*, edited by David W. Brady and John F. Cogan (Stanford: Standford University Press, 2000).

for conflict. Campaigns utilize negative advertising. Fund-raisers use fear appeals. All of that likely produces a cumulative sense that political opponents are enemies to be destroyed and their views heresies to be buried. It bears emphasizing, we hasten to add, that little evidence exists that the mass electorate has polarized since the arrival of the permanent campaign.[43] There is conflicting evidence that the constituency bases of the parties have become more distinct, with Collie and Mason finding in the negative for the House and Abramowitz finding more positive evidence for the Senate.[44] But no one argues that voter polarization has caused elite polarization. If it exists at all, voter polarization is a reflection of elite polarization. And as elites fight wars that ordinary voters find uninteresting, voters feel increasingly distant from both parties, and trust in government declines.[45]

Choosing Leaders. Here is one of the most striking passages in Clem Miller's letters:

Joe Martin rises. . . . [H]is words are slow and full, deep affection showing through their formality. The chamber is silent, each of us pondering what is between these two, while Martin talks throatily of long, long ago. . . .

> Mr. Speaker and my colleagues, it is a great privilege to have the opportunity, even for a few moments, to pay my respects to a dear friend, an old friend and a Member whose friendship has lasted over 35 years without a jarring note. It has been my privilege to know Sam Rayburn all these years, and I can testify, as few men can testify, to his rugged Americanism, his loyalty to country, and his intense desire above everything else to maintain the high honor and integrity of the House of Representatives. . . .

Rayburn's face never flinches, but he shifts his weight heavily from one side to the other, cups his jaw in one and then the other hand, as he looks unblinkingly at his friend Joe Martin.[46]

Substitute "Newt Gingrich" for "Joe Martin" and "Dick Gephardt" for "Sam Rayburn" and try to read this passage without laughing. It just "does not compute," our students might say.

As the congressional parties enjoyed a resurgence, the character of leadership changed. Conditions that favored selection of a Carl Albert over a Richard Bolling in the early 1960s evidently had changed by the 1980s, as relatively passive "insiders" like House Speakers John McCormack (D-Massachusetts) and Carl Albert (D-Oklahoma) and Senate Leader Mike Mansfield (D-Montana) gave way to aggressive leaders like Speakers Jim Wright (D-Texas) and Newt Gingrich (R-Georgia) and Senate leaders George Mitchell (D-Maine) and Trent Lott (R-Mississippi).[47]

And activity was not the only dimension on which the new leaders differed from the old. At one time congressional floor leaders were viewed as political tacticians whose principal goal was facilitating the business of the chamber. The most effective ones were pragmatists who had no strong policy views of their own, or at least suppressed those views for the sake of building coalitions behind legislation. Rayburn in the House and Lyndon Johnson in the Senate were prototypical.[48] Leaders today are of a different type. As Terry Sullivan noted, "Congressional leadership has slipped from the hands of the majority party's moderates and compromisers into the hands of those on the party's message edge, further blurring the distinction between campaigning and governing."[49] Using quantitative data, it is difficult to make a case that today's leaders are any more extreme—relative to their parties—than those of a generation ago, but stylistically, they seem quite different.[50]

Sullivan remarked that polarized leadership is part of the permanent campaign. When campaign commercials in the early 1980s featured a Tip O'Neill (D-Massachusetts) look-alike irresponsibly driving a car until it ran out of gas, it was a new departure. Since that time ads regularly feature congressional leaders. According to the ads, the malevolence of Wright, Gephardt, Gingrich, or Lott threatens the country, and candidates of their party morph into those malevolent leaders. Imagine a 1972 attack ad featuring then-Speaker Carl Albert or then–minority leader Gerald Ford! Political scientists will remember Newt Gingrich for a number of contributions to American politics, but surely elevating congressional leaders to national symbols of their parties is one of the more noteworthy ones. Ultimately, for him it was a politically fatal accomplishment.

Elections today have become more "nationalized."[51] Members of both parties—themselves increasingly extreme—believe it necessary to have a leader who can help the party electorally—to raise money, to fire up the activists, and to get out the message. Such leaders have less interest in legislative accomplishment—a festering issue may be more useful than a completed compromise. And election results increasingly are the test of their leadership.

Policy Outputs

One thing we know now is that U.S. policy processes are remarkably resilient in the face of influences political scientists might think would bring government to a standstill.[52] Divided party control of Congress and the presidency, for example, seems to have an unexpectedly small impact on what government produces, at least quantitatively.[53] Thus, it comes as no surprise that the arrival of the permanent campaign has not paralyzed the government. Its effects, if any, must be found by analyzing more subtle measures.

As a starting point it seems to us that the permanent campaign is least consequential when voters are satisfied with the status quo. In the summer of 1999, for example, a mammoth government surplus loomed on the horizon. Republicans proposed to return it to citizens via a large tax cut, while Democrats proposed to invest much of it in what they believed were needed government programs. Meanwhile, polls consistently showed that once Social Security and Medicare were secure, most voters preferred to use the surplus to pay down the national debt. In the end neither party could impose its position on the other nor reach an acceptable compromise. So, as we write, voters are getting what they want. That is a default option, of course, and not one to endear either party to the electorate, however satisfactory the outcome may be.

In contrast, when voters see a problem and believe that government should take some action to alleviate the problem, the permanent campaign is probably a hindrance. The parties calculate whether they have more to gain by reaching an acceptable compromise and claiming bipartisan credit, or by accepting—or even creating—a stalemate and trying to lay the blame on the other party. Such calculations, moreover, may well be biased by the members' own extreme positions and those of the activists with whom they most frequently interact.

If those suppositions are correct, the corrosive effects of the permanent campaign on policymaking have been partly masked by the historically unprecedented economic expansion of the 1990s. Contemporary voters demand relatively little from government, save that it do nothing to end the good times. If the country once again were to endure the kinds of social problems that troubled it during the 1960s or the kinds of economic problems that plagued it during the 1970s (let alone the 1930s), we might find our government even less able to act in the general interest than it has been historically.

Discussion

The arrival of the permanent campaign has affected Congress in a myriad of ways. On the whole, our discussion suggests that the net impact has been negative, although we emphasize the verb *suggests*. Evidence in support of the arguments and hypotheses developed in the literature and in this survey is circumstantial in some cases, and much of the evidence consists of impressions and examples. The research community has a rich agenda to pursue.

We do not believe that every aspect of the permanent campaign has had a negative impact on Congress. As we noted earlier, given different motives on the part of members and leaders, changes in congressional organization might have worked to make Congress more efficient and more majoritarian. Developments in party organization might have had similar effects—again, given different motives. Too often, however, the motives of today's members revolve around destroying their enemies rather than developing a legislative product broadly acceptable to the electorate. As a result, in the contemporary Congress the tendency is for civility to lose out to conflict, compromise to deadlock, deliberation to sound bites, and legislative product to campaign issues.

Those developments will not ruin the U.S. Congress as we know it. One of the factors that contribute to the intensity of the permanent campaign is the competitive national situation. In the present context control of the House and the presidency are up for grabs, and control of the Senate is only a bit less so. With control of national institutions at risk in each election, it is no wonder that every move Congress or the president makes is evaluated through electoral lenses. There have been other eras like this. In the late nineteenth century "era of no decision," institutional control was similarly at risk, and majorities were fleeting. Nevertheless, the politicians of the day managed to push through the Interstate Commerce Act, the Sherman Act, important tariff and veterans' legislation and otherwise to facilitate the country's transition to the new industrial order. One important difference we see between that era and today is that the politicians of a century ago operated in a context of full mobilization of the electorate. There were no primaries that gave advantages to the "wing nuts" of the two parties.[54] Even the off-year electorate consisted of 70 percent of those eligible to vote, not 35 percent. Congressional leaders calculating how to maintain or win control had more reason to believe that reasonable compromises would be more electorally productive than strident speeches laced with ideological symbols.

That brings us to our final point. If the harmful effects of the permanent campaign on Congress are to be alleviated, we doubt that the solutions lie within Congress. No organizational or procedural reforms internal to the institution are likely to redraw a bright line between campaigning and governing. Rather, we think that the reasons for the unsavory character of contemporary politics lie not within our institutions but within the political stratum that operates them. The increasingly participatory nature of American politics coupled with the unrepresentative nature of the few who choose to participate are at the root of the excesses of the permanent campaign.[55] In our view, curbing those excesses would require changes like these: higher levels of participation—voting and otherwise—on the part of the moderate middle, open primaries, public financing, free media time for candidates, a deemphasis of rights-justifications for policies, and other proposals, the effects of which are to dilute extreme points of view with substantial doses of moderation. Of course, many people might prefer to live with the devil that we know rather than to adopt reforms like those.

Notes

We wish to thank Keith Krehbiel, Thomas E. Mann, and Kenneth Shepsle for helpful comments and Jeremy Pope for able research assistance.

1. David Mayhew, *Congress: The Electoral Connection* (New Haven: Yale University Press, 1974), 5.
2. Anthony King, *Running Scared: Why America's Politicians Campaign Too Much and Govern Too Little* (New York: Free Press, 1996).
3. Norman J. Ornstein, Thomas E. Mann, and Michael J. Malbin, *Vital Statistics on Congress 1999–2000* (Washington, D.C.: AEI Press), tables 2-7 and 2-8.
4. The *locus classicus* is Anthony Downs, *An Economic Theory of Democracy* (New York: Harper and Row, 1957), chap. 8.
5. David Brady and Edward Schwartz, "Ideology and Interests in Congressional Voting: The Politics of Abortion in the U.S. Senate," *Public Choice* 84 (1995): 25–48; Wayne Francis, Lawrence Kenny, Rebecca Morton, and Amy Schmidt, "Retrospective Voting and Political Mobility," *American Journal of Political Science* 38 (1994): 999–1024.
6. *Congress: The Electoral Connection*, 81–82.
7. Norman J. Ornstein, ed., *Congress in Change: Evolution and Reform* (New York: Praeger, 1975); Roger Davidson and Walter Oleszek, *Congress against Itself* (Bloomington: Indiana University Press, 1977).
8. Larry Dodd and Richard Schott, *Congress and the Administrative State* (New York: John Wiley, 1979), 124.
9. James Sundquist, *The Decline and Resurgence of Congress* (Washington, D.C.: Brookings Institution, 1981), 371.

10. Earlier in this project we made a serious effort to document that hypothesis. Unfortunately, we were unable to come up with systematic data on the interest-group backgrounds and associations of congressional candidates in the 1950s before the relevant changes began. As in many areas of American politics research, it is difficult here to execute the "before" stage of a "before-after" research design.

11. Martin Wattenberg, *The Decline of American Political Parties, 1952–1984* (Cambridge: Harvard University Press, 1984); Burdett Loomis, *The New American Politician* (New York: Basic Books, 1988).

12. David Rohde, *Parties and Leaders in the Postreform House* (Chicago: University of Chicago Press, 1991).

13. Richard Fenno, "The Internal Distribution of Influence: The House," in *The Congress and America's Future,* edited by David Truman (Englewood Cliffs, N.J.: Prentice-Hall, 1965); Ralph Huitt, "The Internal Distribution of Influence: The Senate," in *The Congress and America's Future.*

14. Gary Cox and Mathew McCubbins, *Legislative Leviathan: Party Government in the House* (Berkeley: University of California Press, 1993).

15. Keith Krehbiel, "Where's the Party?" *British Journal of Political Science* 23 (1993): 235–66; Krehbiel, "Paradoxes of Parties in Congress," *Legislative Studies Quarterly* 24 (1999): 31–64.

16. Stanley Bach and Steven Smith, *Managing Uncertainty in the House of Representatives* (Washington, D.C.: Brookings Institution, 1988); Keith Krehbiel, *Information and Legislative Organization* (Ann Arbor: University of Michigan Press, 1991).

17. Robert Van Houweling, "Legislators' Personal Policy Preferences and Partisan Legislative Organization," Ph.D. dissertation, Harvard University, in progress.

18. Roger Davidson, Walter Oleszek, and Thomas Kephart, "One Bill, Many Committees: Multiple Referrals in the U.S. House of Representatives," *Legislative Studies Quarterly* 13 (1988): 3–28; Roger Davidson, "Multiple Referral of Legislation in the U.S. Senate," *Legislative Studies Quarterly* 14 (1989): 375–92.

19. Sarah Binder and Steven Smith, *Politics or Principle? Filibustering in the United States Senate* (Washington, D.C.: Brookings Institution, 1996).

20. The term is due to Kenneth Shepsle, "The Changing Textbook Congress," in *Can the Government Govern?* edited by John Chubb and Paul Peterson (Washington, D.C.: Brookings Institution, 1989), 238–66.

21. Donald Matthews, *U.S. Senators and Their World* (Chapel Hill: University of North Carolina Press, 1960).

22. Richard Fenno, "The Appropriations Committee as a Political System: The Problem of Integration," *American Political Science Review* 56 (1962): 310–24. Other committees seemed "normless," however. See Richard Fenno, "The House of Representatives and Federal Aid to Education," in *New Perspectives on the House of Representatives,* 2d ed., edited by Robert Peabody and Nelson Polsby (Chicago: Rand McNally, 1969), 283–323.

23. Herbert Asher, "The Learning of Legislative Norms," *American Political Science Review* 67 (1973): 499–513; Loomis, *New American Politician.*

24. Quoted in Alan Ehrenhalt, "In the Senate of the '80s Team Spirit Has Given Way to the Rule of Individuals," *Congressional Quarterly Weekly Report* (September 4, 1982): 2176.

25. Ralph Huitt, "The Outsider in the Senate: An Alternative Role," *American Political Science Review* 55 (1961): 566–75.

26. Richard Fenno, *Congressmen in Committees* (Boston: Little, Brown, 1973).

27. Richard Hall, *Participation in Congress* (New Haven: Yale University Press, 1996), chap. 6.

28. Shelby Cullom, *Fifty Years of Public Service* (Chicago: A. C. McClurg, 1911), 422.

29. Ibid., 222.

30. Eric Uslaner, *The Decline of Comity in Congress* (Ann Arbor: University of Michigan Press, 1993).

31. Clem Miller, *Member of the House,* edited by John Baker (New York: Scribner, 1962), 134.

32. Ibid., 67–68.

33. Charles Clapp, *The Congressman: His Work as He Sees It* (New York: Doubleday, 1963), chap. 9.

34. Glenn Parker, *Homeward Bound* (Pittsburgh: University of Pittsburgh Press, 1986): 16–18.

35. For a survey and discussion, see Morris Fiorina, *Congress—Keystone of the Washington Establishment,* 2d ed. (New Haven: Yale University Press, 1989).

36. David Brady, Joseph Cooper, and Patricia Hurley, "The Decline of Party in the U.S. House of Representatives: 1887–1968," *Legislative Studies Quarterly* 4 (1979): 381–407.

37. Rohde, *Parties and Leaders,* chap. 1.

38. Cox and McCubbins, *Legislative Leviathan.*

39. Sarah Binder, "The Disappearing Political Center," *Brookings Review* 14 (1996): 36–39.

40. Morris Fiorina, "Whatever Happened to the Median Voter?" manuscript, Stanford University, 1999.

41. James Snyder, "Artificial Extremism in Interest Group Ratings," *Legislative Studies Quarterly* 17 (1992): 338–39. Snyder reports that the possibility of such artifact is unlikely in the case of the Poole-Rosenthal scores or other measures that use all roll calls rather than selected subsets (personal communication, January 12, 2000).

42. Analyzing Senate data up to the mid-1980s, Poole and Rosenthal concluded that the transformation of southern politics accounts for about half the trend toward partisan polarization up to that time. Keith Poole and Howard Rosenthal, "The Polarization of American Politics," *Journal of Politics* 46 (1984): 1074.

43. Fiorina, "Median Voter."

44. Melissa Collie and John Mason, "The Electoral Connection between Party and Constituency Reconsidered: Evidence from the U.S. House of Representatives, 1972–94," in *Continuity and Change in House Elections,* edited by David Brady, John Cogan, and Morris Fiorina (Stanford: Stanford University Press, 2000). Alan Abramowitz, "Party Realignment, Ideological Polarization, and Voting Behavior in U.S. Senate Elections," paper prepared for the Norman Thomas Conference on Senate Exceptionalism, Vanderbilt University, October 1999.

45. David King, "The Polarization of American Parties and Mistrust of Government," in *Why People Don't Trust Government,* edited by Joseph Nye, Philip Zelikow, and David King (Cambridge: Harvard University Press, 1997), 155–78.

46. Miller, *Letters,* 82.

47. Nelson Polsby, "Two Strategies of Influence: Choosing a Majority Leader, 1962," in *New Perspectives on the House of Representatives,* edited by Robert Peabody and Nelson Polsby (Chicago: Rand McNally, 1969), 325–58.

48. D. B. Hardeman and Donald Bacon, *Rayburn: A Biography* (Austin: Texas Monthly Press, 1987), xx; Rowland Evans and Robert Novak, *Lyndon B. Johnson: The Exercise of Power* (New York: Signet, 1966), 84.

49. Terry Sullivan, "Impeachment Practice in the Era of Lethal Conflict," *Congress and the Presidency* 25 (1998): 117–28.

50. While today's leaders are more extreme than those of the 1970s and 1980s, they are less extreme than those of earlier decades. Tim Groseclose found that contrary to the classic "middleman" argument of David Truman, party leaders from the 56th to the 102d Congresses were more extreme than the median member of the party caucus: on average in Congress, before first election to the leadership, a leader was more extreme than 63 percent of his party (Poole-Rosenthal nominate scores). Contrary to casual impressions, 33 percent of the Republican caucus was more extreme than Gingrich, whereas only 19 percent was more extreme than Michel. Similarly, 59 percent of the Democratic caucus was more extreme than Wright, but only 24 percent was more extreme than O'Neill. Both Rayburn and Martin were more extreme than any of the above. Evidently, the widespread belief that today's leaders are different reflects behavior and activities not captured by roll call voting scores, as well as failure to account for the fact that the parties themselves are more extreme than in earlier decades. Tim Groseclose, personal communication, January 20, 1999.

51. Gary Jacobson, "Reversal of Fortune: The Transformation of House Elections in the 1990s," in *Continuity and Change in House Elections;* David Brady, Robert D'Onofrio, and Morris Fiorina, "The Nationalization of Electoral Forces Revisited," in *Continuity and Change in House Elections.*

52. Charles O. Jones, *The Presidency in a Separated System* (Washington, D.C.: Brookings Institution, 1994).

53. David Mayhew, *Divided We Govern: Party Control, Lawmaking, and Investigations, 1946–1990* (New Haven: Yale University Press, 1991). For a

more recent analysis that surveys reactions to Mayhew and offers qualifications of earlier findings, see John Coleman, "Unified Government, Divided Government, and Party Responsiveness," *American Political Science Review* 93 (1999): 821–35. In particular, Coleman finds that unified governments are more responsive to public mood.

54. David King was the first one we heard use this apt term.
55. Morris Fiorina, "Extreme Voices: A Dark Side of Civic Engagement," in *Civic Engagement and American Democracy,* edited by Theda Skocpol and Morris Fiorina (Washington, D.C.: Brookings Institution Press, 1999), 395–425.

7

The Never Ending Story: Campaigns without Elections

Burdett A. Loomis

Every good writer and every effective politician understand the power of a good story, the right anecdote, the telling metaphor. As Bill Buford, the *New Yorker*'s fiction editor, put it, "Strong narrative writing is, at its most elementary, an act of seduction."[1] In most seductions, emotion trumps logic, even as the story line may emphasize the logical and the believable. A campaign is nothing if not a series of seductions, from fund-raising to advertisements to last-minute solicitations for the votes of undecided voters.

The permanent campaign has made an industry of inventing, honing, and selling narratives. The campaign process is continual (if not continuous), with fund-raising for the next election requiring a new, or renewed, story line to extract contributions from the same old pockets. Even in the early months of a new Congress, political positioning often overwhelms the dynamics of deliberation and compromise. And those who govern adopt campaign techniques to sell their agendas and issues, which is part of what we mean by *the permanent campaign*. In the 1990s, with narrow congressional majorities and a series of competitive presidential elections, the permanent campaign, as other studies in this volume have shown, has come to dominate the politics of policymaking. At the same time, the permanent campaign has spread far beyond the confines of electoral politics. Interests of all shapes and sizes seek to set the policy agenda, in Washington and, increasingly, in state capitals. At first blush, that element of the permanent campaign may seem to reflect the public posturing of advocacy groups (the National Rifle Association and Handgun Control, for example)[2] or of moneyed interests[3] that seek to influence public opinion through advertising and public relations campaigns. To be sure, those interests do sometimes target public opinion as a whole. Much more common, however, are attempts to frame an issue or a controversy for elites—ranging from the attentive public to a handful of members of a congressional committee. Just as electoral campaigns send a series of coordinated, but distinct, messages to a variety of overlapping constituencies (as, for example, all Latinos, Cubans in Miami, or the ten wealthiest Cuban Americans in Florida), organized interests do much the same, as they construct narratives that can shape discourse in various venues, ranging from a private meeting with a key senator to Cable News Network advertisements to a set of "grass-roots" messages crafted in a K Street office.

Most techniques of the permanent campaign are similar in and out of the electoral arena, with one major exception. Organized interests do attempt to influence electoral outcomes, which ordinarily require majorities to guarantee success, but they rarely seek to influence mass opinion, at least directly; to do so would be prohibitively expensive. For example, the Health Insurance Industry Association spent only $14 million on its "Harry and Louise" ads that opposed the Clinton health care proposal in 1993–1994. Such an expenditure could not—and did not—move public opinion in any significant way, but it did influence any number of elites, from lawmakers to reporters.[4] The best analogy to influencing general public opinion may be the introduction of a new consumer product, which can cost $250 million. Although a Microsoft or a General Electric might have the resources to embark upon that kind of issue-oriented campaign, such corporations have shied away from such an expense for a single message to a single mass audience. In 1998 Microsoft did embark upon a major public relations campaign to make its case in the Internet browser wars, but most of its attention was directed at elites, not the public at large. And the firm proved unsuccessful in stopping aggressive antitrust efforts by both the federal government and the states.

In their pursuit of policy advantage, organized interests use survey research, focus groups, advertising, public relations, grass-roots lobbying (often of the astroturf variety), the commissioning of think tank studies, and other techniques, and they certainly invest heavily in electoral politics. For them, the permanent campaign encompasses both elections and governing, of course, but more than that, their continuing focus remains on the issues they define as most important. Allies may be transitory, elected officials may be "here today, gone tomorrow," but the groups' campaigns will continue because their core interests remain in play. Consider the telecommunications industry in the 1990s. That diverse set of interests has weathered immense technological change and the first rewrite of basic communications laws since the 1930s, a time well before the invention of many contemporary technologies. Although the industry's conventional political spending has increased dramatically over the decade, it has been dwarfed by the issue-based advertising and campaigning that began in the mid-1990s and has continued in the wake of the Telecommunications Act of 1996, which moved the industry's lobbying away from Congress and toward the Federal Communications Commission and the states.[5] Other issue areas (defense, retailing) may not reflect quite the same levels of uncertainty and change as telecommunications, but the relevant interests have invested more heavily in issue campaigns, such as saving the F-22 and enacting bankruptcy reforms, than they have in traditional electoral politics. Even in a highly partisan age, important issues, such as reform of health maintenance organizations, are often defined beyond the bounds of party and party majorities within Congress.

What follows will offer a framework for understanding how interests of all sorts seek to shape the issues that mean the most to them. Although their tactics usually include ordinary lobbying and participating in electoral politics (as, for example, through political action committees), the focus here will be on the politics of issues and agendas. The argument—that issue-based initiatives and politicking make up the core of the permanent campaign for most interests—draws on literature in several areas.

Winner-Takes-All Economics. Even as the distributive power of the federal government declines in a balanced-budget era, the stakes grow higher as Congress, the executive, and the bureaucracy use tax and regulatory tools to effect policy change.[6] Many interests conclude that large expenditures are justified by the high stakes involved in the decisions.

The Glut of Information. Even before the Internet placed countless information sources at everyone's electronic doorstep, the glut of information on many important issues produced a "data smog" that overwhelmed the capacity to deal with it.[7] Equally important, legislators and other policymakers often see themselves as receiving information that precludes active discussion and deliberation. Christopher Lasch has reminded us that Walter Lippmann made that point in the 1920s, another era of information explosion. With skepticism, Lippmann observed that "information precluded argument, made argument unnecessary. Arguments were what took place in the absence of reliable information."[8] All interests thus seek to make their information "reliable."

The Dominance of Narrative(s). Information begs for structure, and narratives offer perhaps the most universal and most human means for constructing a framework for understanding. Setting the agenda, defining problems, assigning causality—all are integral to the narrative form.[9] A simple table or trend line contains the seeds of narrative, as does a photograph. The narrative notion overlaps with the "framing" perspective of psychology and communications,[10] but the concern here lies more with constructing narratives for various elites than with framing issues for the public at large.

The Scope of Conflict. As Schattschneider famously noted, the extent of a conflict, as well as who is involved, often determines its outcome.[11] Interests have always sought to expand or restrict the scope of conflict, with the assumption that broadening the conflict would help the prospective losers, who could benefit when more players and many citizens entered the fray. That remains the strategy of environmentalists, public-interest advocates, and consumer organizations, and they often benefit from such "socialization of conflict." Conversely, with immense resources that can purchase the political expertise to play the outside game, moneyed interests can develop a permanent campaign to frame issues in the public arena. Thus, banking interests, technology companies, and the defense industry, among others, can hammer home narratives with advertising and public relations strategies that consumer organizations and environmental groups cannot ordinarily match.[12]

Even as interests generally emphasize their own issue-oriented aspects of the permanent campaign, they ordinarily attend to the more conventional elements of that phenomenon. That is, they form political action committees, they encourage individual contributions to candidates, they make soft-money contributions to political parties, and they sometimes spend funds independently on behalf of a favored candidate. Moreover, interests lobby in all the conventional ways. Embarking upon a highly public, issue-oriented strategy does not preclude participating in regular electoral politics or in conventional lobbying: quite the reverse. Those interests that develop extensive permanent campaign strategies on issues are likely to be veteran participants in the continuing politics of elections and lobbying, played out across the entire election cycle.

At some point, interests that act in heavily politicized ways and regularly employ a raft of techniques to affect policy and electoral outcomes become something qualitatively different from organizations that confine themselves to lobbying and participating in electoral politics. Everything ends up being politicized; communications take on a political bent; and influencing the terms of the debate, as well as electoral and policy outcomes, requires substantial investment of time, effort, and, especially, money.

High-Stakes Decisions and the Calculus of Political Investment

The battles over such issues as the Clinton health care proposals, telecommunications restructuring, and financial services reform have generated incredible amounts of spending on lobbying public officials.[13] Any estimate of the funds expended to affect the outcomes of those broad sets of prospective policy changes—as with the $300 million-plus spent on financial services politicking in 1997 and 1998—is likely to be excessively low, largely because many corporate interests and trade associations devoted substantial parts of their nonlobbying budgets to affecting the terms of the final legislation.[14] Although neither financial services reform, nor health care reform, nor telecommunications deregulation fell wholly into the category of "winner-takes-all" decisions, all did propose to affect about one-seventh of the national economy (roughly speaking, $1 trillion). All sides rightly perceived the stakes as immense, and in some instances the policy options did constitute an actual "winner-takes-all" choice, as with medium-sized health insurers, who viewed their very survival at risk. Nor were those policy changes especially unusual; trade policies such as the North American Free Trade Agreement, tort reform, and bankruptcy legislation all represent high-stakes policy decisions, as do deregulatory measures in the electric utility industry.[15]

As Jeffrey Birnbaum observed, the growth of corporate—and trade association—lobbying makes good economic sense:

> [Even] in relatively small changes to larger pieces of legislation . . . big money is made and lost. Careful *investment* in a Washington lobbyist can yield enormous returns in the form of taxes avoided or regulations curbed—an odd negative sort of calculation, but one that forms the basis of the economics of lobbying.[16]

The nature of high-stakes decisions makes such investment almost mandatory, given the potential for tremendous gains and staggering losses. In addition, the usual cost-benefit logic that applies to most managerial decisions—lobbying extensively versus building a new plant or embarking on an ambitious new research project—does not apply when the stakes are high, because the potential benefits or costs—or both—are so great that virtually any expenditure can be justified, even if its chance to affect the outcome is minuscule. The need to establish a clear link between a certain lobbying tactic or strategy and some bit of subsequent policy success is not very important, in that such linkages are difficult to demonstrate in the best of circumstances. In addition, a single general strategy may include a large number of tactical initiatives, to the point where objectively assessing the success of individual actions becomes impossible.

Two implications flow directly from that state of affairs. First, firms and their representatives enter the lobbying fray with high hopes and low expectations. As one lobbyist put it, referring to a major issue, "If I throw in a million here or a million there, I may get a hundred million back. And there are probably enough cases like that so [my clients] keep throwing money in."[17] Second, lobbyists and corporate strategists find such circumstances extremely attractive because there is virtually no accountability for the way immense amounts are spent. One veteran Washington representative described such high-stakes maneuvers: "Lots of money is spent externally for internal reasons—to cover your ass."[18] Moreover, spending on issue-oriented permanent campaigns and electorally oriented permanent campaigns often overlaps, as advocacy groups, corporations, and trade associations "invest" in parties, candidates, and policies.[19]

It is a mistake to make an excessively precise distinction between spending on candidates through contributions and providing information to elected officials with lobbying, advertising, or public relations campaigns. Nevertheless, information exchanges between interest groups and legislators may well differ from the seeking of influence through contributions or favors. Interest-group scholar Jack Wright noted that interests

> achieve influence in the legislative process not by applying electoral or financial pressure, but by developing expertise about politics and policy and by strategically sharing this expertise with legislators through normal lobbying activities. . . . [Organized interests] can and do exercise substantial influence even without making campaign contributions[,] and . . . contributions and other material gifts or favors are not the primary sources of interest group influence in the legislative process.[20]

Even if information, and not favors or contributions, reflects the basis for interest-group influence, does that mean that money is unimportant? Or that all information is equal? Hardly. Inevitably, some interests possess many more resources to develop information that shapes policy debates. For that reason, a disproportionate share of the policy and political information that flows toward decisionmakers reflects the views of well-heeled interests that subsidize think tanks, pay for surveys, and engage public relations firms. High-stakes decisions generate rising levels of investment, and the most affluent interests are best positioned to participate.[21] That said, those interests do not always win, as the tobacco and firearms industries have discovered in the 1990s.

Many Voices, Many Messages

Never has more information been more easily available to policymakers than at the present. On all but the most arcane issues, no member of Congress, staffer, bureaucrat, or lobbyist can sensibly argue that he or she desperately needs more policy information or additional data—at least in terms of the state of knowledge at a given moment. Although some information remains closely held and is thus valuable, in most instances the problem for policymakers is excessive, not insufficient, information. As political scientist John Kingdon and would-be reformer Ross Perot noted, Washington is awash with any number of solutions for any number of problems—from tax rates to saving Medicare to military preparedness.[22] District and national sources bombard legislators with information that they have no time to digest.

David Shenk, in his aptly titled *Data Smog,* argued that more than just the *volume* of data, the *sources* of information reduce its coherence.[23] Nor is it just any information that muddies the waters. Rather, "with the widening pool of elaborate studies and arguments on every side of every question, *more expert knowledge has, paradoxically, led to less clarity.*"[24] And everyone can play. As Hugh Heclo noted, "Information about politics and public affairs now flows continuously into the public forum. . . . But the complexity of public problems usually gets lost in the dramatic factoids and disconnected commentaries." In the welter of information, coming from a multitude of sources (and through a variety of media), "data seldom speak loudly for themselves."[25]

Not only do we have *hyperdemocracy* (Heclo's term), but we also have *hyperpolitics,* with almost every interest having a voice and some kind of claim on public policymakers.[26] What makes democracy and politics "hyper" is the constancy of communication, coupled with the number of interests making their claims. The cable-Internet–driven notion of "all news, all the time," fostered by cable television and the Internet, meshes firmly with the notion of "all-directional advocacy," in which groups lobby citizens, decisionmakers, and the media by sending out campaign-like messages to anyone who might be an audience.[27]

In that context, the quantity of information often affects its quality—both the quality of the information itself and the capacity for its coherent interpretation. Either we get niches of information, communicated by specialists and enthusiasts to each other,[28] or we get campaign-like sound bites, slogans, and symbols, even when the subjects at hand (budget politics, health care, test-ban treaties) and the related decisionmaking processes are complex. The public can turn away from many controversies, but policymakers cannot. So, to entice the public and to cater to the needs of legislators and other policy elites, interests strive to place their information in context. They seek themes and story lines that will connect—narratives that will convince the public and provide the possibility of explanation for legislators.

Narratives as Explanations

For elected officials, audiences come in all shapes and sizes. For example, a legislator may pay attention to a few local notables, the district's constituents, a single important organized interest, or a set of political action committee managers.[29] In virtually every instance, the linkage is cemented through a common understanding, based on a narrative that ties the actor to the audience. Rarely does one dominant narrative or a single given story dictate a legislator's position. Rather, a good tale will include the fodder for a set of acceptable explanations, constructed to fit various groups of voters and interests. As Richard Fenno pointed out, a legislator must stockpile many explanations for a whole range of actions, especially votes. "There isn't one voter in 20,000 who knows my voting record," he quoted one House member, "except on the one thing that affects him."[30]

In a related vein, Grant Reeher found that legislators use stories as ways to think through difficult issues that confront them. Even sophisticated policymakers employ stories to process information. Cognitive psychologists would predict as much in their characterization of individuals as "cognitive misers."[31] Narrative, Reeher noted, supplies cognitive shortcuts, provides an organization for the other, more specific organizations of attitudes, and places them in a familiar context. It tells us what items of information are to be treated as evidence and what items are irrelevant. It also invests the information with both meaning and purpose.[32]

Organized interests of all stripes take seriously the task of providing material for congressional explanations. On some issues the narratives come to dominate the discourse, as with the legions of HMO horror stories that defined the playing field on patients' bill of rights legislation.[33] Lobbyists and grass-roots advocates offer up stories that members can incorporate in their communications with constituents. Or legislators and their staffers may draw upon public themes articulated by interests through advertisements and public relations campaigns: to the extent that their stories are adopted, interests tend to claim credit—both internally and externally—for influencing the policy discourse.

Lawmakers and lobbyists share the desire to reduce uncertainty as they make policy. In an era when most "iron triangles"—linking Congress, the bureaucracy, and organized interests—have disintegrated, to be replaced by much looser and more inclusive issue networks, alternative means of organizing the policymaking process have grown in importance. As Deborah Stone observed, to cut through the multitude of voices and rhetoric, "causal stories" play increasingly important roles in shaping agendas and particular decisions.[34] Such stories are usually more specific than the narratives put forward to organize the discourse—and structure the conflict—within broad policy communities. Indeed, many causal stories are spun out in relatively private settings of congressional subcommittees or executive agencies, where sophisticated, complicated arguments can be made and understood.

If narratives are powerful, what is the nature of that power? Literary scholar Jay Clayton saw the strength of narrative as "not individual but neither . . . precisely collective; it arises from one's participation in established networks of expertise."[35] But many actors and interests participate within dozens, even hundreds, of distinct networks. Participation merely allows an individual or interest the chance to employ narrative powerfully. All messages are not created—or delivered—in an equal fashion. Resources are crucial in developing and conveying meaningful communication. Survey research and focus groups help determine what message is most palatable or most powerful; political consultants, public relations firms, and advertising professionals craft themes that appeal to policymakers, partisans, and the public audiences, though rarely to all simultaneously.

In terms of shaping the policymaking process, two types of competition among narratives come into play. First are the competing "causal stories" that imply very different policy choices on such issues as welfare, violence, and trade. Second, and equally important, are those narratives that socialize (expand) or privatize (limit) the scope of conflict. Narratives are important on both those dimensions (causality and socialization of conflict) because they ordinarily mix together empirical and normative elements. Thus, causal stories both "purport to demonstrate the mechanism by which one set of people brings about harms to another set" and "blame one set of people for causing the suffering of others."[36] It is no wonder that so many narratives flow from Washington think tanks with distinct ideological leanings—for example, the conservative Heritage Foundation, the libertarian Cato Institute, or the "New Democrat" Progressive Policy Institute. Stripped bare, however, the analyses are both stories in themselves and the grist for many other stories—as with Charles Murray's welfare studies presented in *Losing Ground* and *The Bell Curve* and the many responses inspired by those works.

Still, many different kinds of narrative are possible. An extended, complex story spun out at length and in private for a congressional staffer would not work when presented to most average citizens. In those instances, narratives are ordinarily truncated, left with little more than metaphors or symbolic appeals.[37] (See table 7-1.) As Murray Edelman observed, "Unless their audience is receptive to the depiction of a condition as a problem, leaders and interest groups cannot use it to their advantage."[38] A complex, detailed narrative may, by definition, restrict the receptivity of a mass audience. What remains to be seen, then, is how various audiences are addressed in constructing problems and posing solutions. Interested narratives can be spun around either problems (global warming), solutions (tax credits for emissions), or both, depending on the audience. And the

Table 7-1 Narratives, Interests, and the Scope of Conflict

Number of Individuals and Interests Affected	Scope of Conflict	
	Narrow	Broad
	Niche Politics	**Symbolic Politics**
Few	Detailed private narratives	Truncated narratives
	Sketchy public narratives	Highly public reliance on symbol and myth
	Pure political "muscle"	
	Policy Community Politics	**Public Confrontation Politics**
Many	Detailed narratives, available to public, but not widely disseminated	Combination of detailed narratives (personal lobbying, including local elites) and truncated narratives (public relations, ads, astroturf)
	Coalitions unified around agreed-upon narratives	Highly visible coalitions

storytelling may well have more of an impact outside ordinary electoral politics, a venue in which claims are more likely to be subject to both enhanced scrutiny and counterclaims. Interests may well prefer to "campaign" beyond the bounds of electoral politics, where competition may be less vigorous.

The Scope of Conflict and the Reach of Policy

In hopes of shaping the policy thoughts and political considerations of political elites, organized interests fashion their narratives to suit particular audiences. As the scope of the conflict broadens, narratives become less complex, and meaning is more frequently conveyed by metaphor and symbol. What this means is that different policy arenas, as framed by the scope of the conflict and the number of individuals ultimately affected by policy decisions, will encourage distinctive communication patterns. (See table 7-1.) The policy and political information conveyed by interests (among other actors) to the multiple audiences varies greatly from quadrant to quadrant; at the same time, the general themes of the messages remain at least roughly consistent.

In the symbolic and public confrontation arenas, the audiences are extensive, although only occasionally would the great majority of all citizens be included within the audience—as, for example, during the Great Depression or the Second World War. Still, for interests—and leaders—to influence those audiences, they must tap into well-developed social myths. As John Nelson observed, "[P]olitical myth-making provides crucial requirements for the virtuous practice of mass persuasion."[39] But tapping into myths does not mean that they cannot be changed. In fact, constructing arguments around myths and metaphors may well encourage changes in meaning.

In the end, however, politicians usually employ metaphors that reinforce social stereotypes or those of dominant interests within a policy community.[40] Audiences responded to such characterizations as Ronald Reagan's description of the Soviet Union as an "evil empire" and his desire to protect us with "Star Wars" technologies. Presidents possess great advantages in employing such symbols and metaphors, when compared with legislators or lobbyists. On occasion, however, an individual legislator, such as Newt Gingrich with the Contract with America or Bill Bradley with tax reform, can succeed in shaping the nature of a policy debate, as can an interest group, such as the health insurers on health care reform or the AFL-CIO on NAFTA (and later "fast track" procedures for trade bills), especially when the news media elevate and repeat their narratives into positions of prominence.

Interests have often employed narratives to attempt to change the scope of conflict, usually because they are losing the battle within a policy community, but sometimes because they enthusiastically seek a wider and more decisive victory.[41] In an era of zero-sum budget politics, reduced governmental spending (as a percentage of the total GDP), and divided government, the temptation to change the scope of conflict is great. Indeed, the incentives are at least as great to use the resources of the permanent campaign to privatize conflicts as to socialize them. Devolution of responsibilities to the states is one way to move a conflict away from broad public attention and allow the states, with their own balance of forces, to decide matters, often largely out of sight. Likewise, the resources of the permanent campaign can move a conflict into the open at the national level (as, for example, electricity deregulation), so that it can be implemented, usually in more private regulatory venues in the states. Thus, the group Americans for Affordable Electricity, chaired by former congressman and current top lobbyist Bill Paxon, argues in a full-color, inside-cover advertisement in the *New Republic* that "electricity doesn't stop at the state line" and that "only Congress can guarantee all Americans the freedom to choose and save."[42]

In a different vein, interests frequently alter their focus away from policies that will affect large numbers of individuals (the "public confrontation" sector in table 7-1) and develop story lines that are essentially symbolic. Thus, the high-profile fight over late-term, "partial-birth" abortions remains highly emotional and extremely visible, even if few individuals directly feel its impact. Rather, the efforts to ban "partial-birth" abortion procedures have taken on the elements of an extended, symbolic campaign on the grisly details of the procedure that stands for a much broader social conflict.

Interest groups have always known that choice of venue and scope of conflict can make a huge difference in determining policy outcomes. With great resources and sophisticated strategies, many organized interests have embraced long-term, expensive issue campaigns that relate to, but remain separate from, the regular cycle of electoral politics. In recent years, many such efforts have come into existence; they have ranged from deregulation of electricity to bankruptcy reform to defense of the "right to bear arms." That does not imply that the traditional means of influence inside lobbying and election-based efforts have been superseded. But the wars of influence in the capital have opened another front: one for which lobbyists, campaign firms, pollsters, and public relations experts seem to be all too willing to volunteer. Thus, not only does the "permanent campaign" become more entrenched over time, but it expands its reach beyond the realm of candidates and elections.

Financial Services, Telecommunications, and Health Care: The Core of the Permanent Campaign

Given the emphasis on the term *permanent campaign*, the temptation is great to focus on elections or at the least on election-like activities such as polling, focus groups, advertising, and the like. To be sure, the interest-group campaigns described here do have many of those elements. For the most part, however, they do not have the ultimate goal of electoral campaigns to win a popular election. Rather, the constituents in the campaigns are mostly elites of various stripes, and the legislative votes that conclude the campaigns are often anticlimactic.

In large part, the politics of high-stakes interest-group campaigning takes place within the "policy communities" that encompass such complex issues as health care, telecommunications, and financial services. Even if an issue becomes highly public, such as the "choice of physicians" in the Clinton health care package or cable television rates in the telecommunications bill, the complexity and interrelatedness of the nest of major issues make it almost impossible to keep the scope of conflict socialized. Any "public confrontation" victory (see table 7-1) will likely be transitory, in that dozens of important and highly connected decisions still need to be made, and only the policy community members can work through their complex nature.

Although individual firms such as Merrill Lynch and Mobil have long spent considerable amounts of money to influence the policy debate, the nature of the permanent campaign can best be viewed by examining the three largest interest-group concentrations of spending on total lobbying and campaigning. (See table 7-2.) The financial services–insurance–real estate sector, the communications-electronics sector, and the health sector combined to generate $268 million in campaign contributions in the 1997–1998 cycle, a figure that pales in comparison with their lobbying expenditures of *$1.042 billion* over that same time.[43] Moreover, many expenditures go undercounted or uncounted in the collection of lobbying data.[44] As Baumgartner and Leech pointed out, those data are part of a pattern that demonstrates a tremendous bias toward the business sector.[45]

The absolute amount of funding is certainly important, but perhaps more significant is the capacity for interests to spend enough money to tell their stories in any number of overlapping and highly sophisticated ways. Thus, in 1999 health insurers planned to spend more than $20 million in attacking the specter of rising health costs

Table 7-2 Lobbying and Campaign Expenditures, 1997–1998

Sector	1997–1998 Campaign Contributions	1997–1998 Lobbying Expenditures	Lobbying as a Percentage of Total Expenditures
Finance, Insurance & Real Estate	$154,414,056	$378,159,242	71%
Lawyers & Lobbyists	$69,790,807	$32,560,725	32%
Labor	$60,777,724	$44,379,999	42%
Health	$58,803,092	$326,415,297	85%
Communications/ Electronics	$54,553,753	$338,453,610	86%
Agribusiness	$43,262,232	$205,117,793	83%
Ideological/ Single-Issue	$42,428,534	$149,438,607	78%
Energy & Natural Resources	$41,146,858	$282,602,274	87%
Transportation	$35,531,510	$227,324,383	86%
Construction	$32,857,600	$39,336,892	54%
Defense	$11,431,320	$96,640,555	89%

Source: "Money in Politics Alert, The Big Picture: Campaign Contributions and the 1998 Elections," Center for Responsive Politics, October 18,1999.

in an attempt to ward off (or at least modify) so-called patients' bill of rights legislation.[46] The advertisements combined direct-issue advocacy with campaign-based advertising, as some were run in Iowa and New Hampshire, while others were broadcast in Washington, D.C, and still others were directed at Republican senators in several states.[47] Indeed, in 1999, the patients' bill of rights legislation became part of the extended warfare over medical expenses and responsibilities. "It's a permanent campaign," observed Mark Merritt, the major strategist for managed care providers.[48] At the core of the lobbying effort was a combination of extensive survey research, done by Bill McInturff of Public Opinion Strategies, which in turn tested arguments based on economists' studies that higher health insurance costs will result in larger numbers of uninsured individuals. Then, the campaign, sponsored by the Business Roundtable, framed the issue on a state-by-state basis. "We found that when we argued the big [national] numbers . . .

people were kind of unimpressed, but when we started breaking things down into the impact on *individual states and individual districts*, we had much more impact," a Roundtable spokesperson stated.[49] Just as there are only a few swing districts in contemporary House elections, which receive immense infusions of resources and outside advertisements, so too are there a handful of key legislators to be targeted in issues-based campaigns.

If health care conflicts remain highly public, the struggles over telecommunications policy, while well reported, continue to be fought out within the extremely complex, even inchoate, policy community that includes media giants and combinations that defy easy categorization.[50] In fact, the outcome of one Oregon court case hinges on the definition of AT&T as a telephone company rather than as a cable firm. As with the health care industry, telecommunications lobbying expenditures make up more than 85 percent of the industry's combined totals for lobbying and campaign contributions. For every dollar contributed to campaigns or spent on elections, firms in the telecommunications industry spent six dollars on lobbying—and additional funds on litigation, another interest-group activity.

Even those figures may seriously understate the amount of resources dedicated to crafting and presenting narratives designed to sway a relatively small number of decisionmakers. Microsoft, whose first full-time Washington lobbyist was hired in 1995 (and worked in a Chevy Chase office, far from K Street or Capitol Hill), greatly expanded its operations in the contentious late 1990s, as it came under fire for antitrust violations.[51] Using a combination of advertising, grass-roots organization of its business partners, retailers, and shareholders, think tank studies, and public relations campaigning, Microsoft embarked upon, then publicly backed away from, a $40 million campaign to "create a political climate that discourages the Justice Department from seeking aggressive sanctions in the [antitrust] lawsuit."[52] If the campaign was disowned, the overall strategy and tactics remained largely dedicated to framing the Microsoft perspective. The *Washington Post* reported:

> Microsoft has a simple story to tell lawmakers on Capitol Hill: It would be unfair to penalize a company for success that helped set off the company's

economic boom. [Lobbyists] carry a poll by the firm of Democrat Peter Hart and Republican Robert Teeter showing that two-thirds of Americans believe that Microsoft benefits consumers and that the suit is wrong-headed.[53]

Microsoft's mushrooming efforts to influence policies and mitigate outcomes may be exceptional, but the entire telecommunications-electronics-computer industry has just begun to have its weight felt. Internet lobbying groups have sprung up, including one headed by a former Netscape general counsel, and their members have the financial strength to tell and retell simple stories about complex processes.[54]

The last of the three major lobbying groups, which represents the financial services, insurance, and real estate industries, has long played the combination of inside and outside games that character-ize the issue-oriented permanent campaign. Even more than on fluid and difficult-to-predict communications issues, the banking reform stakes were huge. John Yingling, chief lobbyist of the American Bankers Association, argued, "The way we saw it, if we didn't get this legislation, we were going to disappear."[55] A bit of hyperbole, perhaps, but his sentiments were close to those expressed by many insurance companies in the Clinton health care battles—and echoed by them on this issue. Although the bankers—and insurance companies and brokerages—did make major contri-butions, tilted 60 to 40 percent in recent years toward the ruling Republicans in Congress, their major campaign over the years focused on antiquated rules in an age of electronic transfers and global competition. Ironically, the 1999 legislation did not change much in the financial services sector, in that many of the corporate players had already crossed from banking to brokerage to insurance, through merger or court rulings. As with telecommunications pol-icy in 1999, the major interests wanted to tell one story—modern-ization and competition—while seeking to restrain other actors, such as Wal-Mart, from entering the marketplace.[56]

Interests, Issues, and the Permanent Campaign

The outlines of the permanent campaign as practiced by organized interests in American politics offer few surprises. In many ways the public is inured to the claims and counterclaims of myriad interests, as waves of information wash over a mostly uninterested citizenry. Still, the stories—of environmental degradation, of HMO indifference, of the glorious choices available to telecommunications consumers—gush forth, based on individual experiences, focus groups, and survey research. Issues are frequently condensed into catch phrases and symbols. Moreover, in the wake of the campaign rhetoric, the framing techniques, and the attempts to manipulate information, important decisions are made: to deregulate cable television rates, to allow patients to sue their employers over HMO decisions, and to permit banks and brokerage firms to enter each others' markets. As Murray Edelman has long reminded us, symbols and substance are wrapped around each other, and the decisions made in the wake of the permanent campaign over issues have substantive results.[57] The stakes are high.

At least three implications of the permanent campaigning on issues deserve attention. First, and not to belabor the point, organized interests often campaign a lot more on issues than on electoral politics. The magnitudes of spending offer some general insights into what interests see as important and how they seek to achieve their goals. Money in politics can make a difference, but we may want to reconsider how that is so.

Second, and more concretely, the infusion of permanent campaign tactics and funding into interest-group politics contributes to the decline of deliberation in Congress. If the stakes are high, and interests have "invested" a great deal in both politicians and the framing of issues, why would they encourage deliberation? As Lasch argued, "Argument is risky and unpredictable, therefore educational." Going further, argument "carries the risk . . . that we may adopt [our opponents'] point of view."[58] That is scarcely the goal of issues-based campaigning. After investing millions of dollars, interests are rarely open to actual deliberation, which may change the shape of the issue under discussion. Compromise is possible, because it carries little risk and falls within the range of acceptable outcomes. But to engage in actual deliberation on free trade, health care, or telecommunications policies could lead to unanticipated policy outcomes, however beneficial their total effects might be.

Better to reduce the possibility for surprise by constructing narratives that lead to safe positions for legislators and predictable outcomes for interests.

Finally, the permanent campaign on issues favors those interests that can bring the most resources to bear in a context where the disparity in resources is usually immense. Citizens' groups can, of course, make a difference, as Jeff Berry has argued and as losses by the tobacco industry have attested.[59] The very power of constructed narratives allows moneyed interests to make the case that they are acting to benefit citizens and consumers as part of their overall argument on a given policy. Thus, health insurers advertised that they were protecting the "right to choose," when in fact they were complicit in reducing the choices available as they encouraged HMO restrictions. The regional Bell companies and the long-distance providers fought a battle as to who was most in favor of competition (to benefit consumers, of course) at the very time they were trying to maintain control over the markets they dominated.

In 1998 telephone utilities and lobbyists for telecommunications and electronics firms spent $93 million, while the major citizens' group, the Consumer Federation of America, could muster no more than $420,000. Given such an imbalance, it would be foolish for long-distance coalitions, regional Bells, Intel, Microsoft, and dozens of other interests to place their fates in the hands of elected officials. Their permanent campaign on the issues gives them an overwhelming advantage, most of the time in most venues. As David Cohen, the codirector of the Advocacy Institute—a training ground for citizen groups—realistically conceded, "The whole effort of these campaigns is to prevent a second opinion from occurring."[60]

Notes

1. Bill Buford, "The Seduction of Storytelling," New Yorker, June 24–July 1, 1996, 12.
2. Hugh Heclo, "Hyperdemocracy," Wilson Quarterly 24, no. 1 (Winter 1999): 62–71.
3. Darrell M. West and Burdett A. Loomis, The Sound of Money (New York: Norton, 1999).
4. Darrell West, Diane Heith, and Chris Goodman, "Harry and Louise Go to Washington: Political Advertising and Health Care Reform," Journal of Health Politics, Policy, and Law 21, no. 2 (Spring 1996): 35–68.

5. West and Loomis, *The Sound of Money*, chap. 6.

6. Robert H. Frank and Philip J. Cook, *The Winner-Take-All Society* (New York: Basic Books, 1995); Pietro Nivola, "Regulation: The New Pork Barrel," *Brookings Review* 16, no. 1 (Winter 1998), 6–9.

7. David Shenk, *Data Smog* (New York: HarperCollins, 1997).

8. Christopher Lasch, *The Revolt of the Elites* (New York: W. W. Norton, 1997), 170.

9. David Rochefort and Roger Cobb, eds., *The Politics of Problem Definition* (Lawrence: University Press of Kansas, 1994); Deborah Stone, "Causal Stories and the Formation of Political Agendas," *Political Science Quarterly* 104, no. 2 (1989): 281–301.

10. See, for example, Robert M. Entman, "Framing: Toward Clarification of a Fractured Paradigm," *Journal of Communications* 42, no. 1 (1993), 51–58.

11. E. E. Schattschneider, *The Semisovereign People* (New York: Holt, Rinehart, and Winston, 1960).

12. Frank R. Baumgartner and Beth L. Leech, "Business Advantage in the Washington Lobbying Community: Evidence from the 1996 Lobby Disclosure Reports," paper delivered at the 1999 Midwest Political Science Association meetings, Chicago, April 14–16, 1999.

13. Theda Skocpol, *Boomerang* (New York: Norton, 1996).

14. J. Brinkley, "Surveying the Results, 20 Years and Millions of Dollars Later," *New York Times,* October 23, 1999.

15. The continuing battle over utility deregulation has regularly prompted large-scale advertising and public relations campaigns. For example, the electric utility industry paid for a ten-page color insert to the *New York Times* (October 18, 1999) to make its case to a broad, attentive public.

16. Jeffrey Birnbaum, *The Lobbyists* (New York: Times Books, 1993), 4 (emphasis added).

17. Quoted in Jonathan Rauch, "The Parasite Economy," *National Journal* (April 25, 1992): 981.

18. Personal interview, anonymity guaranteed.

19. On parties, see Thomas Ferguson, *Golden Rule: The Investment Theory of Party Competition and the Logic of Money-Driven Political Systems* (Chicago: University of Chicago Press, 1995).

20. John Wright, *Interest Groups and Congress* (Boston: Allyn and Bacon, 1996).

21. Robert G. Kaiser and Ira Chinoy, "The Right's Funding Father," *Washington Post*, May 17, 1999.

22. John Kingdon, *Agendas, Alternatives, and Public Policy*, 2d ed. (New York: HarperCollins, 1995).

23. Shenk, *Data Smog*, 91. Parts of the following paragraphs derive from this source.

24. Ibid., 91.

25. Heclo, "Hyperdemocracy," 66.

26. Allan J. Cigler and Burdett A. Loomis, "From Big Bird to Bill Gates: Organized Interests and the Emergence of Hyperpolitics," in *Interest Group*

Politics, 5th ed., edited by Allan J. Cigler and Burdett Loomis (Washington, D.C.: Congressional Quarterly, 1998), 389–403.

27. Heclo, "Hyperdemocracy," 65; William P. Browne, "Lobbying the Public: All-Directional Lobbying," in Cigler and Loomis, eds., *Interest Group Politics,* 343–64.

28. Shenk, *Data Smog,* 120.

29. The literature here is extensive, but an excellent starting point is William Browne's *Cultivating Congress* (Lawrence: University Press of Kansas, 1995).

30. Richard F. Fenno, Jr., *Home Style* (Boston: Little, Brown, 1978), 144.

31. Grant Reeher, *Narratives of Justice* (Ann Arbor: University of Michigan Press, 1996), 31.

32. Ibid.

33. See, among others, David E. Rosenbaum, "House Hears Grim Tales about Managed Care," *New York Times,* October 8, 1999.

34. Stone, "Causal Stories and the Formation of Political Agendas," 281–301.

35. Jay Clayton, *The Pleasures of Babel* (New York: Oxford University Press, 1993), 27.

36. Stone, "Causal Stories and the Formation of Political Agendas," 283.

37. George Lakoff, "The Contemporary Theory of Metaphor," in *Metaphor and Thought,* edited by Andrew Ortony (New York: Cambridge University Press, 1993), 202–51; Murray Edelman, *The Symbolic Uses of Politics* (Urbana: University of Illinois Press, 1964) and *Constructing the Political Spectacle* (Chicago: University of Chicago Press, 1988).

38. Edelman, *Constructing the Political Spectacle,* 33.

39. John S. Nelson, "What If the Government Was Never a Machine or a Man? Myth as Cognition and Communication in Politics," University of Iowa, no date.

40. Murray Edelman, *Political Language* (New York: Academic Press, 1977).

41. In *Agendas and Instability in American Politics* (Chicago: University of Chicago Press, 1993), Frank R. Baumgartner and Bryan D. Jones describe these as "Schattschneider" and "Downsian" mobilizations. The former seek to defeat policy oligarchies, while the latter seek to broaden support for new and popular initiatives.

42. *New Republic,* inside front cover, May 10, 1999.

43. "The Big Picture," Center for Responsive Politics press release, October 18, 1999 (www.opensecrets.org).

44. See Scott Furlong, "The Lobbying Disclosure Act and Interest Group Lobbying Data: Two Steps Forward and One Step Back," *Vox Pop Newsletter* 17, no. 3 (1999), 4–6; "Summary," *Influence, Inc.* (Washington, D.C.: Center for Responsive Politics, 1999), 5–6 (www.opensecrets.org).

45. Frank R. Baumgartner and Beth L. Leech, "Business Advantage in the Washington Lobbying Community: Evidence from the 1996 Lobby Disclosure Reports," paper delivered at the 1999 Midwest Political Science Association meetings, Chicago, April 14–16, 1999. See also, more generally, West and Loomis, *The Sound of Money.*

46. Eric Schmitt, "Ads Enter Skirmish over Health Care," *New York Times,* July 15, 1999.
47. Ibid.
48. Quoted in Alissa Rubin, "Business Joins Fight against Health Reform," *Los Angeles Times,* August 8, 1999.
49. Ibid.
50. See West and Loomis, chap. 6; Jeffrey M. Berry, *The Interest Group Society,* 3d ed. (New York: Longman, 1997), 210ff.
51. Rajiv Chandrasekaran and John Mintz, "Microsoft's Window of Influence: Intensive Lobbying Aims to Neutralize Antitrust Efforts," *Washington Post,* May 7, 1999.
52. Ibid.
53. Ibid.
54. J. Leffall, "Internet Firms Start Lobbying Group," *Richmond Times-Dispatch,* July 13, 1999; Charles Piller, "Roberta Katz Now Heads the Wealthy Lobbying Group That Is Likely to Be a Major Player in the 2000 Election," *Los Angeles Times,* June 14, 1999.
55. Quoted in Brinkley, "Surveying the Results."
56. Aaron Zitner, "Consumer Bank-Bill Impact Seen Minimal," *Boston Globe,* October 23, 1999.
57. Edelman, *The Symbolic Uses of Politics.*
58. Lasch, *The Revolt of the Elites,* 170.
59. Jeffrey M. Berry, *The New Liberalism: The Rising Power of Citizen Groups* (Washington, D.C.: Brookings Institution Press, 1997).
60. Quoted in Allison Mitchell, "A New Form of Lobbying Puts Public Face on Private Interest," *New York Times,* September 30, 1998.

8

Preparing to Govern in 2001: Lessons from the Clinton Presidency

Charles O. Jones

In a radio address broadcast during a six-day western trip, President Clinton announced a new federal rule for children's car seats. All new child seats will have three standard attachments for securing them to the vehicle, and new vehicles will have standard anchors. The president explained, "With this new rule and with these three simple attachments, we can save lives and prevent up to 3,000 injuries a year." In what had become a familiar style, he personalized the issue by referring to the fact that one member of the expert panel recommending the change had lost a young niece in a car crash. He also observed, "Anyone who has struggled to get a car seat to fit snugly into a back seat knows exactly what I mean."[1] And so the connection was made. Some listeners may have wondered why the president of the United States was announcing a policy on standards for children's car seats, but parents understood and related to the message.

Here was a prime example of the campaigning style of governing, practiced by a virtuoso. A lesser, yet well-recognized, issue was brought forward and sympathetically treated by the president. A favorable response by the listener was virtually ensured. No one would fault the president for worrying about, in his words, "our smallest and most vulnerable passengers."[2] Presidential expressions of concern regarding ordinary problems of modern living—discipline in the schools, longer hospital stays for new mothers, violence shown on television, reading deficiencies, deadbeat dads, teenage smoking—very likely had a cumulatively positive public effect. Political consultant Dick Morris explained it this way: "We really sought to redefine the job of president in such a way that he was uniquely qualified to fill it."[3] In fact, Morris claimed that he had advised Clinton of such a strategy when he first ran for governor of Arkansas. He recalled this conversation (Morris speaking first):

> "These days . . . we want to know where a candidate stands—the issues and just the issues. Don't ask us to fall in love; just tell us where you stand, and we'll vote for you. We won't bet our hearts on you, but we'll give you our votes until you screw up."
>
> Clinton probed: "So you use the issues you care about to show your personality. If you want to clean up nursing homes, that suggests you must be compassionate. If you are for schools, you might be a person who likes kids."
>
> "That's right." I elaborated: "But you can't go out there and say, 'I love children.' Voters sense that's baloney. You can't even say, 'I'm for education.' But if you say, 'I want to raise taxes to help schools,' then voters can believe you really care about kids because they see you're willing to take heat to help them."[4]

Morris discussed the application of those principles in the 1996 presidential election and explained how it was that they parlayed "small things" into positive results with the voters:

> This values agenda, which stretched over eight months, was the mainstay of Clinton's reelection campaign. Trivialized in the press as "small bore," it nevertheless showed voters what an activist president could do for the average person with the help of Congress and often without it. With each of these proposals, Clinton delivered a message of relevance to the lives of the people that had not really been offered in more than a decade.[5]

Issue discussion as reinforcement of personality, comprehension, and caring should produce positive feedback for the president, particularly if the job has been defined to suit those characteristics. For, if the American people come to believe that the job they are asked to rate is that which the president is doing, then they are likely to approve. The trick for Clinton's political advisers was to influence the way voters perceived the duties of the president and provide positive reinforcement of their man's performance.[6] Knowing the questions, Morris and others in the White House wanted to provide respondents with the right answers when the pollsters called. And as long as times were good, that strategy would work, as it did.

As a campaign consultant, Morris was centrally interested in reelecting Clinton—an enormous challenge following the 1994 election results. Election day is but one time of judgment, however. Nowadays, presidents want and need to win more often, as, for example, with each measure of job approval and every editorial or other media-based evaluation of performance. In fact, as Richard Davis and Diana Owen show in their book, *New Media and American Politics,* the 1990s experienced a burst of media in old and new formats: talk radio, television talk programs and news magazines, electronic town meetings, MTV, print and television tabloids, and computer networks.[7] For political consultants as presidential aides, the lesson was clear enough: those responding to polls and going to the polls were experiencing a quantum increase in alternative forms of communication. Those who wished to influence their thinking had to know what voters were watching and listening to.

For a scandal-prone president like Clinton, the performance measures in the media, most notably the job-approval scores, have had special significance. If the marks are strong, then the president can continue to be a major player in national politics and never have to declare his relevance. Clinton's style of "going public" is not limited to seeking influence or coercive power in regard to specific legislation, as suited to the formulation by Samuel Kernell.[8] Rather, the style is employed additionally to maintain status and credibility in the face of serious charges about fitness for office.[9] The latter must be achieved and sustained for the former to be realized.

One consequence of the attentiveness to measures of public support is the honing of issue articulation so that, when scandal stops, the president is prepared to move beyond agenda setting to a more active role in lawmaking. At the very least, respectable poll numbers for a scandalized presidency are likely to mystify political opponents and thus give the president an unforeseen advantage. The Clinton presidency is a case in point. His surprisingly strong job-approval ratings despite serious charges appeared to fluster congressional Republicans and to prevent Democratic defections. Those same ratings also encouraged the president to campaign continuously.[10] His contact with the public was never allowed to grow stale. The topics on the road were those related to public policy, not scandal. He was "doing his job" as he and his consultants had defined it, while others in Washington were absorbed in partisan politics. Therefore, a return to policy business following the Senate impeachment trial found the president prepared to participate actively, outwardly unfazed by scandal. He successfully implemented a scandal and impeachment survival strategy with a contemporary campaigning style.

Change and Transition

What is the relevance of President Clinton's campaigning style for an essay on "Preparing to Govern in 2001"? Simply this: The presidency is defined in part by expectations of the institution, as affected by the incumbent at any one time. It is a melding of the "then" and the "now." Judgments are rendered about the extent to which "the politics that presidents make," as Stephen Skowronek has put it, suits the politics history has made at any one time to shape the presidency.[11] And so it is pertinent to ask: To what extent will the Clinton experience influence future expectations of presidential style and management? The answer to that question may well depend on whether Clinton is just different from other presidents or whether he represents changes that are influencing national politics more generally. I argue that the latter is the case and acknowledge that the Clinton case is confounded by his having to campaign to restore his personal status, tarnished by scandal, so as to maintain influence on public policy. I turn first to the changes that will endure to affect future presidencies.

Each year, Beloit College in Wisconsin issues statements to acquaint the faculty with the incoming freshmen. Here is a sample for 1998 (the graduating class of 2002):

- They have no meaningful recollection of the Reagan era and did not know that he had been shot.
- They were prepubescent when the Persian Gulf War was waged.
- There has been only one pope. They can only really remember one president.

- Their lifetime has always included AIDS.
- They never had a polio shot and likely do not know what it is.
- Atari predated them, as did vinyl albums.
- The expression "you sound like a broken record" means nothing to them.
- The computer disk was introduced when they were a year old.
- They have always had an answering machine.
- Most have never seen a TV set with only thirteen channels, nor have they seen a black-and-white TV.
- They cannot fathom not having a remote control.
- They have no idea that Americans were ever held hostage in Iran.
- MTV has always existed.

Table 8-1 shows the number of newly eligible voters for 1996, with that group then carried forward to 2000 as supplemented by the cohort becoming eligible between the two elections. What is the significance of that group? It includes the Clinton-era eligible voters, those coming of political age from 1993 to 2000. As the Beloit College faculty was advised of the 1998 class, "They can only really remember one president." As shown, the numbers are notable— 14.4 million as newly eligible in 1996, another 15.1 million in 2000, for a total of nearly 30 million. Low turnout has been characteristic of that age cohort (eighteen to twenty-five)—typically

Table 8-1 Number of Newly Eligible Voters, 1996 and 2000

Age in 1996 (birth year)	No. Eligible in 1996 (millions)	No. Eligible in 2000 (millions)
21 (1975)	3.5	3.5
20 (1976)	3.5	3.5
19 (1977)	3.8	3.8
18 (1978)	3.6	3.6
17 (1979)	—	3.7
16 (1980)	—	3.8
15 (1981)	—	3.8
14 (1982)	—	3.8
Totals	14.4	29.5

Source: U.S. Bureau of the Census, *Statistical Abstract of the United States, 1997*, 117th ed. (Washington, D.C.: Government Printing Office, 1997), 16, table 16.

averaging about one-third of those eligible.[12] Still, 10 million is not an inconsiderable number of voters to have had their expectations of the presidency influenced by the Clinton administration (approximately 10 percent of the total voters in 1996). Nor is 30 million a small number for whom the personal computer is as common as the radio was for my generation.

That cohort of new or one-time voters has come to accept the following as part of ordinary living during the 1990s: multiple offerings of television channels; cellular phones; paging devices; telephone answering machines and services; Internet access; CD roms; limitless software packages; and electronic mail. More specialized but generally available soon are other communication services: digital satellite television; satellite location tracking; digital smart phones (combining cellular phone, two-way radio, paging, short-messaging, and Internet services); hand-held wireless computers; two-way paging; fixed wireless local phone service; wireless cable television; wireless computer modems; wireless local area computer networks; and infrared devices for data input and television remote control. And there is more to come soon: satellite data broadcasting and cellular phone service; satellite high-speed Internet service; digital television (providing high-resolution programming, a combination of Internet services and programming, or both); and wideband digital networks (capable of simultaneously providing television, cellular phone, data, paging, and Internet access). The personal computer has moved rapidly from the office to schools to the home. Today, a family room or den fixture for millions, the PC is a library, theater and music hall, game center, post office, travel office, shopping mall, stock broker, bank, tax accountant, weather station, and search and research center, to cite a few of the more common usages.[13]

As the Clinton class (the new voters, 1993–2001) moves into their thirties, can one expect that they will adapt to the new era of communication? The evidence strongly suggests that they will—joined by the next cohort of voters now being trained to live and work in the digital age. Here are statistics on the Internet provided in a report issued by the Department of Commerce:[14]

USAGE
- Number using the Internet: 1994 = 3 million worldwide; 1998 = 100 million; projection = 1 billion users by 2005.[15]
- Traffic on the Internet has been doubling every 100 days.
- Domain names registered: 1996 = 627,000; 1997 = 1.5 million; 1998 = 2.3 million.
- Growth of Internet hosts: 1993 = 1.8 million; 1997 = 20 million.
- Radio existed thirty-eight years before there were 50 million users; once opened, it took just four years for the Internet to reach that mark.

COMPUTING POWER AND COST
- Computing power has doubled every eighteen months for the past thirty years; the average price of a transistor has fallen by six orders of magnitude; the cost of microprocessor computing power has fallen from $230 to $3.42 per MIPS [million instructions per second] in six years.

ECONOMIC IMPACT
- Without the contribution of the information technology sector, overall inflation in 1997 would have been 3.1 percent instead of 2.0 percent.
- In recent years, the information technology sector has been responsible for more than one-quarter of real economic growth.
- Information technology equipment represented 3 percent of total business equipment in the 1960s and 45 percent in 1996.
- The collective market capitalizations of five major information technology companies increased from under $12 billion in 1987 to $588 billion in 1997.
- Cisco Systems booked just over $100 million in sales on the Internet in 1996 and $3.2 billion in 1997.
- Dell Computers sold less than $1 million of computers per day in January 1997 and reached daily sales of $6 million several times during the December 1997 holiday period, with annual sales from its Web site "now running at a pace of $5 billion a year."[16]
- "Internet generated about $30 billion in U.S. revenue in 1998—closing in on the automobile industry."[17]

VOLUME
- As late as 1980, copper wires carried less than one page of information per second; in 1998, a strand of optical fiber as thin as a human hair can transmit the equivalent of over 90,000 volumes of an encyclopedia in a single second.

The implications of those developments for ordinary Americans are staggering. As stated in the Department of Commerce's report, "With digital broadcasting, TV viewers will be able to interact with their televisions and surf the Web, pay bills, plan a weekend trip, or make dinner reservations."[18] The report continued:

> The wait for broadband Internet access to households is measured in years, not decades. Within the next five to ten years, the vast majority of Americans should be able to interact with the Internet from their television sets, watch television on their PCs, and make telephone calls from both devices. Those combined services will be brought to homes by satellite, wireless, microwave, television cable, and telephone lines, all interconnected in one system.
>
> People will also access the Internet away from their homes or offices. Cellular telephones and portable digital assistants have become very sophisticated devices capable of sending faxes, receiving e-mail and electronic pages, and now, accessing the Internet. Industry experts predict that users of cellular phones and digital personal communications devices will more than triple from 77 million to 251 million by 1999.[19]

Speaking at Nuffield College, Oxford, in November 1998, Sir John Birt, then–director general of the British Broadcasting Corporation, made reference to the "democratization of expression" as one characteristic effect of the digital age. Other effects included a move from scarcity to plenty with an infinite number of channels, globalization and the need for controls, and a quantum increase in memory technology by which all BBC programs for a week would be available on a small disk in five years, and if still available, all BBC programs ever made on that same disk in ten years. He spoke of providing services as much as preparing programs. And he emphasized the importance of who or what would control the memory.[20] In fact, regulating digital commerce will surely be a major issue, one poorly defined at present.[21]

The political implications of those developments have yet to be fully analyzed or appreciated, although the argument here is that the Clinton White House has been sensitive to the political uses of the emerging information technology. Davis and Owen offer an interesting and useful analysis of the effects of the new media on traditional media, the presidential campaign, and public policy. Their conclusion is: "The effects . . . are not as large as either the proponents promote or the critics fear."[22] Their emphasis, however, is on the media more than on their political use. Theirs is not a study of how politicians are adapting to the new media.

One recent article in the *American Political Science Review* offered a systematic analysis of the effects of cable television on the president's audience for major television appearances. Matthew A. Baum and Samuel Kernell found:

> [A]s the number of television households receiving cable has swelled, as have the programming alternatives it offers, the percentage of viewers who stay tuned to the president has steadily declined. . . . Gone are the days when a president could "appear simultaneously on all national radio and television networks at prime, large-audience evening hours, virtually whenever and however the president wishes."[23]

The article appeared in March 1999, whereas the data on network audience share and households with cable television show the two trends crossing in 1985, fourteen years earlier. The Internet as a programmatic alternative is not mentioned, although events analyzed by Baum and Kernell are well into the period of its heavy and growing use. That fact alone suggests that research on political implications lags far behind developments in information technology, as well as politicians' adaptations to those changes. At such a pace, we cannot expect analysis in our major journals of current Internet and other integrative communication instruments for another decade, by which time projections suggest that any conclusions will be primarily of historical interest.

Government agencies, political parties, campaign organizations, candidates, and elected public officials have adapted swiftly to developments in information technology. As expected, Web sites abound, given the golden opportunity to beam information about one's record directly into the homes of constituents. Most representatives and senators have home pages that tout the members' records and invite feedback from constituents. Members have used newsletters in the past for those purposes but were restricted in their use near an election. Significant increases in personal staff during the 1970s permitted more direct in-state and in-district services to constituents and generated a permanent home presence. Now that contact is enhanced by the capability of reaching into homes and offices, all in the service of effective representation. Some sites even provide a count of visitors: for example, at the time of my visits, 10,403 for Representative Phil English (R-Pennsylvania), 183,471 for Senator Dianne Feinstein (D-California), and 30,701 for Senator Ted Stevens (R-Alaska).

Members of Congress are barred from using public funds for lobbying purposes. But no one yet has established a clear distinction between lobbying and education. "Now that Web sites are standard elements of election campaigns, the practice of building support for legislation online could prove to be a natural progression for politicians using the Internet."[24] Both House floor leaders, Dick Armey (R-Texas) and Dick Gephardt (D-Missouri), have tax-plan home pages that describe their proposals and show how much taxpayers would save. Armey's press secretary reported that 140,000 people visited their site in January 1999. "Armey promotes the site in radio interviews, and the e-mail updates help keep the Web traffic coming."[25]

Suitably, both major political parties have Web sites, as do thirty-six other political parties. The Democratic and Republican party sites provide basic organizational information along with briefing materials on issues. The White House site offers a full menu of information on the activities of the president and vice president, along with access to federal services. Like the others, the White House site is a well-designed campaign document. Visitors can tour the building, learn of its history and previous occupants, e-mail the president and vice president, read a White House newsletter for kids, print out the latest presidential speech, and browse through White House press releases and briefings. All that is required for the distribution of such campaign-style literature is a reminder to encourage visits to the site, a prospect enhanced by President Clinton's fielding questions over the Internet in November 1999.

Web sites are created even before candidates make announcements that they are running and certainly thereafter (with prominent instructions for contributing or volunteering). "'In the last campaign [1996], the Web was not even a line item in the budget,' said Bill Dal Col, campaign manager for Malcolm S. 'Steve' Forbes. 'This time it is its own section with its own line items.'"[26] Jesse Ventura, the surprise Reform Party winner for governor of Minnesota in 1998, made effective use of this low-cost means of communication. Others are emulating his application of the technology. By April 1999, a dozen potential presidential candidates had active Web sites, with innovative uses proliferating:

Aides to several campaigns said they plan to use digital cameras to record events and download them onto their Web sites so viewers can follow them in almost real time. . . . The Internet will not replace traditional tools, such as television and radio, but will augment them in ways never before seen on such a broad scale. Candidates are planning, for instance, to promote their Web addresses in commercials. Once viewers are there, the candidate might ask them to submit questions for an online chat or for biographical data that will be used to build a database of supporters.[27]

Aristotle, a California-based political software company, has matched public information on voters with Internet subscriber information. So candidates, for the first time, can restrict who sees their Internet ads to targeted voters. For instance, a candidate could design ads that only Democrats over thirty who have voted in three of the past five elections in the Third Congressional District of Maryland would see.[28]

What remains to be analyzed is the extent to which such efforts influence the sender and the receiver. Consider, for example, the fact that information is available that formerly was brokered by government, legislators and other elected officials, political parties, and interest groups. How, then, do those entities preserve or redefine a role in information distribution? As Sir John Birt pointed out, much will depend on who controls the buildup of memory and thus the availability and form of information.

Clinton and Change

It is, I believe, reasonable to observe that had President George Bush been reelected in 1992, much less attention now would be paid to the permanent campaign. His pollster, Robert Teeter, would have stayed on, to be sure. And President Bush would have continued to travel extensively, perhaps more internationally than domestically. Much less likely, however, is that he would have launched campaign-style treks or advertising blitzes on issues. Yet the developments in information technology just described would have proceeded apace, perhaps then to be exploited by the winner in 1996.

As it was, however, President Bush was defeated in 1992 by new-age candidate Bill Clinton, the first president born after World War II. As a member of the baby-boom generation, Clinton grew into adulthood with television. He embodied the campaign experiences of the 1980s and 1990s, as candidates adapted to modern forms of communicating. By the time of his unsuccessful bid for a House seat in 1974, television was in common use in campaigns. From that time forward, Clinton campaigned as a candidate as much as or more than anyone in the nation. He ran successfully for attorney general of Arkansas in 1976 and six times for governor (five successfully) before running twice for president, for a total of ten general election campaigns (eight of which he won). Add to those his primary wins in Arkansas and the state-by-state nominating campaigns for convention delegates in 1992 (he was unopposed for the nomination in 1996, in part because of early campaigning and fund-raising), and the grand total is at least forty. Whatever happened by way of campaigning techniques and refinements during that period was known about or practiced and pioneered by Bill Clinton and his advisers.

But it is not only the time line of Clinton's political life that is relevant to the continuity of campaigning from election through to governing. It is also his skill at and devotion to communicating. Not all baby boomers have the verbal proficiency and dexterity of Bill Clinton. Thus, for example, neither of the two most recent vice presidents, Dan Quayle or Al Gore, is judged to be so skilled, yet both are of Clinton's generation (Quayle five and one-half months younger, Gore nineteen months younger).

Clinton's penchant for talking is renowned. He is a functional talker. George Stephanopoulos observed: "Bill Clinton . . . liked to shroud conflict in soft language and shape his thoughts by hearing how they sounded out loud."[29] Seemingly, the very acts of forming and expressing words serve a decisional purpose for him, involving as they do a gamelike process featuring the exploration of ideas and options. Words are a means, not necessarily an end. They are also a fascination for talkers as they search for and inspect multiple meanings either to clarify or to obscure an intent or argument. In his detailed biography of Clinton, David Maraniss recorded many instances of his subject's talkativeness as a young man—in school, at Georgetown, Oxford, and Yale, and during campaigns.[30] Utilitarian process-oriented talkers, as distinct from bores, are also listeners, for listening can produce topics and perspectives for more talk, feedback for the endless seminar of the mind.

If the talker's chosen profession is that of public service, there is a perpetual rationale for expression. The declared purpose of the public servant is to resolve public problems. By their nature, problems require interactive definition and explication. Therefore, the talker-listener always has work. New problems persistently emerge, and old problems are constantly undergoing change. The agenda for expression is regularly full.

Just as Franklin D. Roosevelt's talents were well suited for the political use of radio, and John F. Kennedy's talents qualified him to take advantage of television, so did Bill Clinton's verbal dexterity, intellect, and physical energy prepare him to exploit the rapid developments in information technology and distribution. Supply the instinctive talker with new and captivating forms of communication, place that person in a position of political power, and expect then to witness a campaigning style of governing. In that sense, Bill Clinton has been a president for our time and his, one whose very presence marks crucial changes and technological developments. He did not have to invent the permanent campaign: he is a permanent campaigner who worked in and from the White House, that place to which the media and the world look for talk.

Other conditions also accommodated a campaigning style. Apart from natural disasters, two terrorist bombings (at the World Trade Center, New York City, 1993, and the Murrah Federal Building, Oklahoma City, 1995), and the NATO-led war against Serbia, the Clinton administration has been mostly a noncrisis presidency. Good economic times and a lack of crisis provide somewhat greater options in agenda setting and decisionmaking. Absent an emergency, the president has time to choose issues and build support and even take to the road. A crisis structures priority setting and decisionmaking. Ordinarily, time is limited for conducting a public campaign, and the event itself—war, catastrophe, or severe economic disruption—demands orderly, sometimes routine, sequences and hierarchical responses.

In that sense, the Clinton presidency in its first seven years (1993–2000) has had a more leisurely pace, if bedeviled by scandal, with the president free to make substantive and stylistic choices.[31] Interestingly, that was the case even during 1998, when a robust economy and congressional preoccupation with the Lewinsky scandal and the Starr report left the president free to design a campaign for personal support and policy status. Good times allowed for an absence of ambitious policy leadership by either the president or congressional leaders during 1998.

The Republican takeover of Congress in 1995 was a second condition facilitating a campaigning style of governing. Judged at the time to be a serious blow to Clinton's chances for reelection, in fact, the Republican win reduced expectations to such an extent that the president at one point was moved to declare his relevance:

> The Constitution gives me relevance. The power of our ideas gives me relevance. The record we have built over the last two years, and the things we're trying to do to implement it, give it relevance. The president is relevant here, especially an activist president.[32]

It was precisely that self-proclaimed activism that moved Stanley A. Renshon to view the Republican win as a "great service to Clinton":

> It may help him to truly define himself. Clinton's pre-1994 political identity can be described as a "yes and" identity. Clinton was for many things: labor, business, environmentalists, growth and development, and so on. Except at the polar extremes, it was hard to find something Clinton was really against.
>
> The Republicans have provided Clinton with an enormous personal and political opportunity in this regard. Freed from the need to scramble constantly to make sense to the public of how he can endorse so many seemingly incompatible positions, he can now directly, honestly, and more clearly find where he really stands. He no longer has to be for many things; he can now be for and against specific things.[33]

Renshon also judged that the Republican win could well produce a defining debate on the political center: "This would not be the somewhat artificial political center manufactured by Clinton, but rather the concrete center that is located through real debate and compromise on specific policy issues."[34] That debate, however, was unlikely to take place in Washington in 1995. President Clinton was all but excluded from the lawmaking process until late in the first session of the 104th Congress. Congressional Republicans, particularly those in the House, confidently proceeded as though the separated powers had been suddenly joined on Capitol Hill. On more than one occasion, Speaker Newt Gingrich declared that the president would be forced to accept Republican budget and fiscal policy or suffer the consequences of thwarting the will of the American people: "I'm not sure the President will want to be in the position of shutting down the government in order to block something that most of the people in the country want."[35]

That statement by Speaker Gingrich reveals a third condition facilitating of constant campaigning: the nature of the agenda. The Contract with America was itself a campaign document, one that was virtually canonized by the Republicans and unconditionally demonized by the Democrats. It received much more media attention than is common for a party platform because of the surprise win by the House Republicans and the heralding of the document that accompanied the passage of each item during the first hundred days of the 104th Congress.

Yet serious doubts existed about whether the 1994 election results could be interpreted as having endorsed the Contract's agenda. One poll showed that just before the election 71 percent of respondents had never heard of the document, 15 percent had heard of it but it made no difference to them, and only 12 percent judged that it did make a difference—7 percent positively, 5 percent negatively, for an insignificant plus 2 percent.[36]

Here then was an invitation for the president to engage in serious political calculation. What was the meaning of the 1994 election? Was it a certification of a conservative revolution, as claimed by Gingrich? Or was it a rebuke of the president and his party's record during the first two years? If it was the first, then there was little Clinton could do of a more positive nature. If it was the second, he could seek to reposition himself so as to regain political advantages. He estimated correctly that it was some of each. Voters favored change, but not revolution. And they had doubts about the Democrats' ability to govern effectively. In a postelection statement, the president provided a shrewd interpretation that stressed the voters' restlessness with the pace of change and their belief that the Democrats had not done enough to satisfy their wishes. One reporter then asked: "Are you essentially saying that the electorate was agreeing with you?" The president responded:

> I think they were agreeing with me, but they don't think we produced. . . . I agree with much of what the electorate said yesterday. . . . They sent us a clear message. I got it, and I'm going to try to redouble my efforts to get there. I think that the Republican congressional leadership will at least have the chance to work with us. I'm going to do my dead-level best to do that and to be less partisan. Most Americans are not strongly partisan and they don't want us to be.[37]

Implicit in the president's analysis was a need to campaign so as to clarify the policy meaning of the election (as well as his intention to neutralize partisanship in a manner that would stigmatize Republicans). But there was something else. Most of the issues being debated were domestic, even personal in nature, associated as they were with who was getting and paying for what.[38] "Reform" was, perhaps, the most common label for legislation—welfare reform, tax-code reform, budget reform, regulatory reform, tort reform, Social Security reform, and health care reform. Making changes in existing programs was potentially threatening to various clienteles. If those reforms bore the stamp of voter approval, no further campaigning was necessary. Speaker Gingrich seemingly believed that the 1994 election had conveyed that consent: "This is a genuine revolution. We're going to rethink every element of the federal government."[39] It was that confidence that led Gingrich to believe that the president would not risk interfering with Republican legislative plans in 1995.

Here then was a challenge for a president who specialized in campaigning. Was the House-passed contract what the public wanted? It was worth finding out and, in the discovery, establishing exactly what it was the public did want to happen. Reforming the distribution of benefits can be very threatening to recipients, even those not wholly satisfied with existing formulas and their application. Often, in fact, those who go first in making proposals are at a disadvantage owing to the uncertainty of effects. Republicans were characterized as supporting extreme measures that would harm the poor and the aged so as to provide tax relief for the rich. The president was able to posture in favor of change, but not the change being proposed on Capitol Hill. Stephanopoulos reported that the president was anxious to agree to a budget deal even quite late in the congressional session. And, in fact, he believed that this possibility had the effect of a "disinformation campaign": "It lulled the Republicans into believing Clinton would cave, if only they waited long enough."[40]

Bolstered by what he learned on the road, as confirmed by more favorable poll results, the president positioned himself to veto Republican proposals and to bargain from strength in the second session of the 104th Congress. He campaigned both to govern and to win reelection. By late fall 1995 he had gained a substantial edge in public approval, with respondents' favoring his position in the budget fight over that of the congressional Republicans by a margin of 56 percent to 36 percent.[41] It was an advantage he would retain through the 1996 election.

How were those goals accomplished? Working with Dick Morris, the political consultant instrumental in Clinton's political recovery in Arkansas in 1982, the president accepted a "triangulation" design by which he would position himself between the extremes of the two parties.[42] Dubbed "third way" leadership by Stephen Skowronek, the technique is "to reach beyond the president's traditional party base toward some new and largely inchoate combination." Skowronek explained: "Leaders of the 'third way' are neither great repudiators nor orthodox-innovators; they are not out to establish or uphold any orthodoxy. Theirs is an unabashedly mongrel politics."[43]

The specifics of the "third way," as practiced in 1995, appeared to include the following guidelines:

1. Associate the president with the changes seemingly demanded by the voters in the 1994 election.
2. Remind the public that many of the proposals in the Contract with America were offered by him in less extreme form during the 1992 presidential campaign (tax cuts, family values, welfare reform, balancing the budget).
3. Argue that the Republicans proposed to go too far. Be the voice of reason against the extremist Republicans.
4. Identify high-profile issues subject to presidential actions that do not require congressional approval, that is, those that can

be treated by issuing executive orders or relying on existing discretionary authority.

5. Spot small matters (school uniforms, emergency numbers, hospital stays) that may serve as gateways to larger issues.

6. Employ a soft veto strategy that poses general threats but preserves flexibility on the major issues, all the while imploring Republicans to negotiate and rise above partisan politics.

7. Take advantage of the bully pulpit, posturing as the voice of reason and the legitimate interpreter of change.

8. Don't muscle the president into the lawmaking process, where he is unwelcome anyway. The passage of time and the sequence of lawmaking are a campaigning president's allies. Await the passage of the Republican budget proposals, then act in the public arena where the president excels.

9. Take full advantage of the uniquely presidential status in natural disasters, terrorists' acts, and national security issues.[44]

The components for implementing that strategy were travel, carefully crafted speeches, announcements on mini-issues, political advertisements, and polls.[45] The effort had all the characteristics of a full-scale presidential campaign. There were, however, several interlocking purposes. Surely reelection was a primary goal. But the president's status in lawmaking and governing had to be reestablished, almost relegitimized. His campaigning style of locating the center thus came to have more immediate policy and political effects. Campaigning for election has the proximate purpose of winning. Campaigning for policy, governing, or lawmaking status has the proximate purpose of creating advantages for negotiating, bargaining, and command. President Clinton had been all but excluded from a lawmaking process in 1995 that was pursuing quite radical goals, as announced by the House Republicans. There were institutional, perhaps even constitutional, reasons to reclaim standing, separate from (though related to) the presidential election in 1996.

To summarize, the Clinton years very likely witnessed acceleration in the unfolding and maturation of the permanent campaign. A communicating and traveling president took advantage of information technology and favorable conditions to interact constantly with the public.[46] So talented was the man and so accommodating were the times, that Bill Clinton was reelected and survived serious and credible charges about his fitness for office.

Transitions and Change

The conventional perspective for presidential transitions distinguishes between campaigning and governing. As Richard E. Neustadt admiringly explained about the Kennedy staff during the transition period: "Part of the brilliance was that those people could not wait to start governing. They were so glad the campaign was over. Within three hours they were getting ready to do what they wanted to do. . . . The season of governing was real for those people."[47] Bill Clinton was judged to have failed those tests in entering office. He did not cease campaigning, nor has he through his presidency. The transition in 1992–1993 was judged by seasoned Washington observers to be awkward, unprofessional, and indistinct. Consequently, the Clinton White House was not able to capitalize fully on the advantages usually available to a new president and a fresh crew.

No amount of revisionism will alter those critical reviews of how the Clinton team managed affairs from election day through the formative weeks of the new administration. The president-elect and his spirited and youthful aides may have just won an election against all the odds, but collectively they probably had less governing experience in Washington than the man they defeated, George Bush. And so, working from their basic talents in campaigning, they had much to learn.

I have argued that changes in information technology and various facilitative conditions were taken advantage of by an instinctive campaigner to produce and advance a campaigning style of governing. Earlier I questioned the extent to which the Clinton experience will influence future presidencies, pondering whether Bill Clinton might be a special case of a president extraordinarily devoted to going, even staying, public. Three observations are relevant for thinking ahead to the next presidency. First, comparisons will inevitably be made between the new president in 2001 and his predecessor, Bill Clinton. Second, and relatedly, power holders in

Washington will make adaptations to a president that are often brought forward to challenge the successor, who will have his own style. Third, developments in information technology are unlikely to vanish. They will persist and propagate. The questions then to be considered are these: What are the effects of those realities on the presidential transition in 2000–2001? How should the president-elect prepare for governing in 2001? Should the developments in constant campaigning be welcomed or resisted?

Effects. In regard to his decision to run for president in 1968, Richard M. Nixon wrote in his memoirs: "I wanted to run for President in 1968, but I wanted to leave open, until the last possible moment, the option of deciding *not* to run."[48] It is not clear in the era of permanent campaigning that prospective candidates can preserve that option, though candidates in 1999 sought to use the formation of an exploratory committee as a means to that end. Pleading the need to concentrate on his agenda while the Texas legislature was in session, Texas Governor George W. Bush was the most determined to preserve his noncandidate-candidate status. Meanwhile, many in the media and in politics declared his candidacy for him.

Here, then, is the first important effect of the developments outlined in this chapter: Permanent campaigns lack convenient starts and stops. Candidates fit themselves into a continuous flow of very public events. They compete with the incumbent president for media and voter attention. Thus, in their travels in 1999, prospective candidates were as likely to encounter Bill Clinton as to encounter their fellow aspirants. In the era of the permanent campaign, the "lame duck" flies. He is likely to be motivated by a perceived need to maintain high approval scores, a favorable judgment on legacy, and a wish to preserve continuity in the White House. Bill Clinton was even moved to provide unsolicited campaign advice to his vice president. Telephoning Richard L. Berke of the *New York Times*, Clinton unwittingly reinforced the criticism of Al Gore's campaign as too stiff by stating: "It is true that I have urged him to go out there and enjoy this. I have told him to go out and have a good time. I want people to know him the way I know him. I want people to see him the way I see him."[49] The president clarified that vision by emphasizing Gore's record, which, of course, was that of the president with whom he served. On the one hand, Clinton said that Gore's maintaining his distance was "smart." On the other hand, he should not retreat from boasting about his accomplishments in the Clinton-Gore administration:

> "He's got a lot to be proud of in his record," the President said. . . . Asked if he was hurt that Gore, in his campaign appearances, usually did not mention him, the President said, "Oh, goodness no. I think he should be very proud of what we accomplished together because he played a big role in a lot of the economic progress we made and a whole range of issues. We should be proud of that."
>
> "But," he continued, "people need to look at him when he's out there campaigning as the person who would be the next President. I would advise him to spend most of his time on that."[50]

Clearly, the signal given in those remarks was that a Gore candidacy was forever associated with a record in which "we" should have pride. And so a major effect is that campaigning to win office will run parallel with, and also intersect, campaigning to govern. The candidate for the president's party will compete for time with his or her incumbent; the opposing party candidates may expect to encounter the parallel campaigns of the new candidate and the incumbent president. The problems posed for the president's party candidate may be different only in degree from what has happened in the past. It has never been easy for succeeding candidates to establish their identity separate from their incumbent predecessor. In fact, there have been but three cases in the twentieth century of party succession by election (Roosevelt to Taft, 1908; Coolidge to Hoover, 1928; and Reagan to Bush, 1988).[51] Still, there can be no doubt that the problem for the successor is amplified by an activist incumbent campaigner.

Parallel or intersecting campaigns by the incumbent (for governing) and his putative successor (for election) may usually be expected to provide an advantage to the out-party candidate, notably so if the incumbent president and his party's candidate show signs of disharmony. The exception would be if unusually good times encourage voters to support a third term for the incumbent by electing his successor, judged by some to be the case in 1988 with Bush's succeeding Reagan. An activist campaigner-in-office like Bill Clinton, however, may well be more competitive with than complementary to his party's candidate. Ceci Connolly of the *Washington Post* reported on such a case, actually an instance where, presumably, President Clinton was intending to boost the vice president's campaign. Both were appearing on the same stage in south Texas at a conference on empowerment zones. According to Connolly, the event "was intended to generate support for Gore among key urban and minority voters and offer a showcase for him in rival George W. Bush's state." The effect, however, was to accent the differences in campaigning style between them, to Gore's disadvantage:

> Clinton and Gore were a study in contrasts. To the strains of "Hail to the Chief," Clinton strode on stage, waved to the crowd and draped his arm over the shoulders of Agriculture Secretary Dan Glickman. Gore, meanwhile, stood erect on the other side of the stage briefly waving. During Clinton's introduction, Gore studied his note cards and gazed out at the group of community leaders gathered at the University of Texas–Pan American. When it was Gore's time to speak, Clinton patted the vice president on the back; then, from his seat, waved and grinned at familiar faces in the gymnasium.[52]

No doubt, the awkwardness was in part attributable to a reversal in roles, with the president introducing the vice president and emphasizing his leadership on a national issue. The point is, however, that comparisons are inevitably made, and the vice president inevitably has less stylistic flexibility than the president, even when the script calls for role reversal. Put otherwise, it is difficult for the vice president to upstage the president, yet not in the least difficult for the opposite to occur. Connolly observed: "Gore's stylistic weaknesses are magnified by Clinton's strengths." She might have added that Gore's institutional status confirms, perhaps contributes to, his disadvantage.[53]

The vice president seeking election as president will not be the only candidate faced with matching the campaigning skills of Bill Clinton. Others, too, will inevitably be tested by his standard while he continues to work the public, all the while reiterating how free he is as a term-limited president to be less partisan. The comparisons will not be contemplative; they will be direct—the president campaigning for status and legacy from *Air Force One,* the candidates campaigning for election from whatever mode of transportation the campaign budget allows. An associated effect will be the impact on the agenda. Campaigning to govern features efforts to control the agenda. Whereas presidents in the past might accept a lesser role in agenda setting as their term expires (for example, Eisenhower, 1959–1960, and Reagan, 1987–1988), the permanent campaigner is unlikely to forgo that initiative. Election campaigns typically serve as issue searches, with candidates' taking inventory throughout as a means both to challenge their opponents and to form the policy basis of governing. The era of the permanent campaign should find the incumbent president actively involved in publicizing issues in potential rivalry to those proposed by the candidates. He may, in fact, set the terms of candidate debates. "I don't feel I'm on a victory lap, or a final lap," stated Bill Clinton. "I still show up." And, as reported by John M. Broder of the *New York Times:*

> In the past six days, he has given a major domestic policy speech laying out his priorities for the next year, conducted a 75-minute endurance test of a news conference and announced that his budget team had found an additional trillion dollars in Federal surpluses over the next 15 years.
>
> He also unveiled the most sweeping set of proposals for remaking Medicare in the program's 34-year history, which he pitched to senior citizens here today.[54]

Yet another related effect may be that candidates are pressed to take stands on the activist agenda of the permanent-campaigning president. Stealth candidacies will be difficult to conduct. With the president so actively involved in building support, candidates from both parties will be canvassed for their positions. That effect, too, is one of degree. Candidates have always been asked about their reactions to contemporary events. When the sitting president is such a commanding public presence, however, candidates may find themselves more reactive than proactive in regard to issues. For example, President Clinton offered the usual long list of proposals in his 2000 State of the Union Address. As was his practice, he followed up with campaign-style travel to boost the prospects of enactment. Candidates, including the vice president, are expected to respond to those initiatives, whatever else they are proposing at the time.

One possible consequence of constant campaigning may be a

celebrity effect. Presidents are, by definition, celebrities. That status is, however, typically associated with their constitutional or institutional position. In Clinton's case, which one might hope is unique, multiple scandals and his devotion to campaigning fabricated a notoriety of a different sort—one based more on personal than on public or institutional qualities. Thus, as with celebrities from the entertainment industry, Clinton generated a kind of popularity that is not prestige. And, in fact, innumerable polls show the low regard respondents have of the president's personal qualities.[55] Whereas the Clinton experience with personal scandal is unlikely to be repeated anytime soon, still the effect, especially in an era of the permanent campaign, may be detailed inquiries into the personal lives of candidates to an even greater extent than in the past. A related effect could easily be the need for legal counsel early in the campaign for purposes other than conformance to election and campaign finance laws.

Preparations. I believe that a campaigning style of governing is likely to persist beyond Bill Clinton's manner of conducting his presidency. The developments in information technology and distribution and the effects of Clinton's methods of managing his presidency, just discussed, virtually guarantee public and participatory governing styles. As I cannot imagine canceling the information revolution, altering Clinton's style, or ignoring the effects of either, I am moved to consider the way that candidates should prepare for effective campaign-mode governing.

Given that campaigning carries over into governing, readiness must begin as early as possible. If it is clear from the start that the campaign to win the presidency will influence the *who, how,* and *what* of governing, then it is crucial that the candidate manage a bi- or trifocal approach. It has ever been true that campaigning has lessons for governing, as, for example, in terms of contacts with candidates for other offices, management of a large staff, articulation of an agenda, and relationships with the press. Normally, however, experience in the national government is needed to recognize and absorb those lessons. Candidates lacking Washington-based experience—for example, Carter in 1976, Reagan in 1980, and Clinton in 1992—face a special problem in that regard. It may well be that one's candidacy is explained in part by that lack of familiarity; that is, conditions favor a candidate from out of town. But outsider candidates may attract staff who likewise lack a perspective that permits learning lessons about governing from the campaign. Under those circumstances, the candidate will find it beneficial to compensate in some way. Thus, for example, the Reagan campaign in 1980 retained Washington-wise James Baker III, who was then made chief of staff in the new administration.

Related is an attitude of governing during campaigning. It is often said that neither candidates nor their staffs can think ahead to governing. For some it is a matter of superstition, as related to the Thomas E. Dewey campaign in 1948. They do not want to be seen as planning beyond election day, essentially defying the logic of trying to win so as to govern. On a more practical or less obsessive level, it is thought that planning diverts staff from the campaign effort and, further, encourages them to pick out their offices before the candidate has won tenancy. Still, all candidates plan to some degree. And the impact of the permanent campaign may be to conceptualize governing more as seamless with campaigning than as separated from it. In that way, the candidate and his staff can adopt an attitude of governing while campaigning, one in which thought and planning are directed toward what is to be done by way of forming an administration.

What that conceptualization suggests is that the candidate will have thought ahead to what he or she wants to accomplish and have in mind those persons likely to be of positive assistance. President Clinton offered that advice to the first lady (in regard to her decision to run for the Senate in New York):

> You have to know, you need to know, why you want the job. You have to be able to tell somebody in 30 seconds, you have to be able to tell somebody in five minutes, you have to be able to give a 30-minute talk. . . . The most important thing is that you know why you want to serve.[56]

The fuller expression of that conceptualization adds a "they" to the "you." Others must know and understand why you want the job to such a degree that they can then act in your name. This process of goal setting and identity should begin during the campaign. Those who will be appointed later should be given strong signals during the campaign that they will be involved in governing in some way.

Associated with that corporate or holistic conceptualization of seeking and serving is the demand that the campaign technicians themselves have governing sensibilities. It has been conventional wisdom that campaign consultants and political pollsters should step aside once the campaign is over and the election won. "I think the damn pollsters should be put out to pasture," is how one seasoned staff aide put it. "You don't need to have somebody take a new pulse every two days in transition. You've already won the thing."[57] Whether the staff is ready or not, however, the "damn pollsters" will play an active part in the new administration, as will the other political consultants. They are a vital part of the campaigning-as-governing style. Therefore, the candidate is well advised to hire second-generation political consultants—those trained for and interested in campaigning for policy as well as for election.

Least clear, perhaps, is how candidates should prepare to govern with Congress. A campaigning-to-govern style is, by definition, competitive with the declared purposes of a representative legislature. A president commissioning and reading polls, promoting policies within congressional constituencies, communicating policy facts and figures into homes through the Internet, announcing positions on microissues, and dominating news coverage is a surrogate for representatives and senators. He or she seeks to measure, anticipate, and influence public opinion so legislators doing their job will be persuaded, if not compelled, to agree. The frequency of split-party government complicates that endeavor. Candidates cannot assume in advance that their party will be in majority control of Congress. Therefore, their preparations will often have to accommodate cross-partisan coalition building. Triangulation may have to be practiced in the campaign, with candidates' poaching from the more centrist of the opposite party's policy offerings.

Does that approach suggest that exceptional or extravagant policy positions are not allowable? Not necessarily. But any such forays by candidates are risky if the positions fall outside the range of current public acceptance. Campaigning to govern as practiced by the Clinton White House has been sensitive to those limits. The purpose is to discover what is ordinarily acceptable, then either to design proposals suited to those limits or to prepare the public for measures that exceed those limits. Much was learned from the experience with the national health care proposals, which were demonstrated by a countercampaign to have been excessive. The president did not make that mistake again, certainly not in the 1996 presidential campaign.

Evaluation

Has the campaigning style of governing enhanced the role and function of the presidency in the separated system? How is the Clinton experience to be evaluated? Is constant campaigning now an inevitability? If so, is that good or bad?

Answers to those questions are properly based on judgments about the institution of the presidency itself. My own perspective is set forth in *The Presidency in a Separated System*. It stresses separationism as suited to a constitutional order in which the presidency and Congress, as separated institutions, compete for shares of powers. I conclude: "The preferred institutional interaction is that of balanced participation, with both branches actively involved in the policy process."[58] By that formulation, the president has to be resourceful enough to maintain his advantages, as, for example, those postulated by Neustadt (position, reputation, and prestige).[59] The benefits of the separated system are lost if the president's status as a participant is seriously diminished, as is equally the case in Congress.

On the basis of study of post–World War II presidents before Clinton, I proposed several lessons as markers for evaluating the campaigning style, markers that can serve to rate the performance of the forty-second president. First, learn the job. Second, know who you are—your strengths and weaknesses. Third, understand change and how it affects you. Fourth, do not mistake approval for prestige. Fifth, beware the mandate. Sixth, others, too, are legitimate participants.[60] The test is whether perpetual campaigning enhances or impedes a president in absorbing and applying those guidelines. Thus, for example, a positive result may be achieved if the travel, speechmaking, polling, and advertising cause a president to be a more perceptive representative in policy and law making. What is learned may then be applied to each of the directions cited above. Even assuming that result to be the case, however, it is important that a president recognize that he is not a representative only. He listens but then must decide. He observes but then must lead. He appoints but then must supervise. He sets priorities but then must negotiate. And so the campaigning-to-govern style may aid a president in doing a part of the job without necessarily equipping him for the rest.

Therefore, a negative result may be realized if a president misconceives campaigning as the job itself. Misunderstanding the place and function of continuous campaigning can have a number of bad effects. In working outside the government, a president may fail to perform well inside the government. Accordingly, he may be misled about his strengths and weaknesses, that is, in knowing who he is in the government. While developing finely honed sensitivity to change outside, he may slight the changes occurring in Washington. Potentially most serious is a possible preoccupation with approval ratings as automatically enhancing prestige. That absorption may actually reduce his standing inside, with the collateral effect of bad marks for professional reputation. Closely related is the danger of interpreting either the ratings or the public response in travel as confirming a mandate. Conceiving of job-approval tests as a continuous series of election days may persuade a president and his (or her) team that they know what is right, yet that very concentration may prevent them from getting their way. Why? Because others, too, are legitimate participants (my sixth lesson) by reason of their continual testing of constituency attitudes. Time spent outside is time lost inside.

How, then, did Clinton perform by those tests? I offer general comments only since a full appraisal awaits completion of his presidency. We are unlikely to witness another pure case of the campaigner-as-president soon again. It is a fair judgment to state that Clinton did not learn the job well during his first two years in office. He knew his strengths and stressed those to the exclusion of bolstering his weaker areas. His lack of awareness of change in government was rooted in his unfamiliarity with Washington itself—

most notably Capitol Hill. Approval ratings became an obsession, particularly given the assaults on his character of a series of scandals. He fell victim to the mandate trap in his first term, largely because of high expectations associated with the return of one-party government. He would not have to cope with overblown anticipations for the rest of his term—the 1994 elections reshaped the politics of his presidency.

Assessing Clinton's performance by my sixth marker—acknowledging the legitimacy of others—is complicated. His limited experience in Washington prevented a full understanding of the workings of Congress, notably the role of the minority party. Yet he was force-fed the lesson of congressional status following the 1994 election, and it is fair to state that he applied it well in the 104th Congress. Bill Clinton learned to work with, even lead, a split-party government. In fact, his presidency from the final months of 1995 to the Monica Lewinsky scandal in January 1998 may come to be seen as the model for effective campaigning-style governing. The scandal interrupted that record. It is difficult, if not impossible, for there to be acknowledgment of interbranch legitimacy when impeachment and trial are underway.

Is constant campaigning now inevitable? I believe that it is. But future presidents and other public officials will vary in their skills as participants, as they do in regard to all political characteristics. Few will possess Bill Clinton's talent and zeal for public contact, though many will surpass his organizational and management competence. The comparison between the *then* and the *now* will be starkly portrayed if George W. Bush wins the presidency in 2000. To oversimplify in making the point, George H. W. Bush managed an inside presidency; George W. Bush will likely manage a blend between an inside and an outside presidency. On the Democratic side, should Al Gore win, he, too, will likely conduct an inside-outside administration in comparison with the more purely outside style of his predecessor.

Is constant campaigning good or bad? Though I lack data on the point, my impression is that most analysts judge that it is bad. And such an appraisal on their part is in a venerable tradition of criticism of politicians as crass seekers of reelection. We often reserve our harshest censure for those we need the most. But grades of "good" or "bad" should be related to effects as well as to behavior. The test should be based on something other than an expression of personal bias regarding political form and style. How does a president campaign and with what effect? Is the campaign itself educational for him and others? Is it substantive in support of proposals or merely negative? Is campaigning purposeful for the presidency and governing or merely personal? Those are a few of the questions to ask in a fair evaluation of a development that will not be canceled. The challenge is to ensure positive effects from a changing political environment.

Notes

This chapter was written during my year at Nuffield College, Oxford University, as John M. Olin Visiting Professor of American Government. I am grateful for the support provided by the Olin chair and Nuffield College. I am especially indebted to Byron E. Shafer, Andrew Mellon Professor of American Government, Nuffield College.

1. Associated Press, "Clinton Seeks New Child Seat Rules," *New York Times*, February 27, 1999. Vice President Al Gore has sought to emulate Clinton's style, with mixed success. For example, he identified lengthy commutes as a serious issue for working parents: "For people who don't think that it's a problem that parents are caught in traffic jams . . . I'll tell you, they haven't been in traffic jams and they don't know what it does to the desire to balance work and family." It was Gore's judgment that "[t]he person who deserves to be our next President is the one who understands how tired working parents are." Quoted in Katharine Q. Seelye, "Gore Offers a More 'Livable World' with Some Tinkering," *New York Times,* March 16, 1999.

2. Associated Press, "Clinton Seeks New Child Seat Rules."

3. Dick Morris, *Behind the Oval Office* (New York: Random House, 1997), 40. Note how this comment suits the principal theme of Stephen Skowronek's book, *The Politics That Presidents Make: Leadership from John Adams to George Bush* (Cambridge: Harvard University Press, 1993).

4. Morris, *Behind the Oval Office,* 47.

5. Ibid., 230.

6. Not all advisers, however, professed devotion to polling. George Stephanopoulos portrays himself and others as supporting issue positions, often in competition with Morris. See *All Too Human: A Political Education* (Boston: Little, Brown, 1999), especially chaps. 14 and 15.

7. Richard Davis and Diana Owen, *New Media and American Politics* (New York: Oxford University Press, 1998), chap. 1.

8. Samuel Kernell, *Going Public: New Strategies of Presidential Leadership*, 3d ed. (Washington, D.C.: Congressional Quarterly, 1997).

9. This is as described in detail in Stephanopoulos, *All Too Human*, even before the Lewinsky scandal.

10. That, no doubt, was stimulated too by low ratings of him as a person. Most such numbers were as low as they were high regarding his job performance. The many polls are consistent. For a sample, see Richard Benedetto, "Poll: Mixed Reviews for Clinton Continue," *USA Today*, February 15, 1999; Carol Morello and Robert Holguin, "Poll Reflects Disapproval of Bill Clinton, the Man," *USA Today*, February 23, 1999; and the trend data in "*Washington Post* Poll: Clinton Acquitted," *Washington Post*, February 15, 1999 (www.washingtonpost.com/wpsrv/politics/polls/vault/stories/data 021599.htm). Judging approval ratings is, itself, an important exercise. Thus, one might question why Clinton's ratings were not in the eighties, given the state of the economy.

11. Skowronek, *The Politics That Presidents Make*.

12. This is as reported in U.S. Bureau of the Census, *Statistical Abstract of the United States, 1997*, 117th ed. (Washington, D.C.: Government Printing Office, 1997), 288, table 462.

13. Survey data show that the most frequent activities for users are e-mail (88.4 percent), the World Wide Web (84.5 percent), search-engine sites (76.9 percent), visits to company or product sites (51.1 percent), research on products (46.6 percent), and obtaining weather information (46.1 percent). About a third of the users read newspapers or magazines; just over a fourth make purchases. Reported in Bruce Orwall and Lisa Bransten, "Caught in the Web," *Wall Street Journal*, March 22, 1999.

14. Lynn Margherio, project director, *The Emerging Digital Economy* (Washington, D.C.: U.S. Department of Commerce, 1998), especially chaps. 1 and 2.

15. Estimations of users vary. Davis and Owen, *New Media and American Politics*, p. 6, cite a source that reports 10 million to 11 million users in 1994 and 30 million to 40 million in 1996.

16. Steve Lohr and John Markoff, "Internet Fuels Revival of Centralized 'Big Iron' Computing," *New York Times*, May 19, 1999.

17. Mark Leibovich, Tim Smart, and Ianthe Jeanne Dugan, "Internet's E-conomy Gets Real," *Washington Post*, June 20, 1999.

18. Margherio, *The Emerging Digital Economy*, 10.

19. Ibid. I did, of course, get access to this report through the Internet.

20. Sir John Birt, "The Digital Age," lecture at Nuffield College, November 28, 1998. The matter of memory storage and control is relevant to the emergence of large "server farms" as a major component of a Web infrastructure industry. So-called megaservers will make it possible for "a person . . . to tap into a large central database via the Web to get e-mail, personal schedules, news, weather updates, and other information anywhere, anytime." Lohr and Markoff, "Internet Fuels Revival."

21. Robert E. Litan and William A. Niskanen, *Going Digital: A Guide to Policy in the Digital Age* (Washington, D.C.: Brookings Institution Press, 1999); "Digital Commerce," *Congressional Quarterly Outlook,* February 20, 1999; and Andrew L. Shapiro, "Internet's Gain, Society's Loss," *Washington Post,* June 27, 1999.

22. Davis and Owen, *New Media and American Politics,* 256.

23. Matthew A. Baum and Samuel Kernell, "Has Cable Ended the Golden Age of Presidential Television?" *American Political Science Review* 93, no. 1 (March 1999): 110.

24. Rebecca Fairley Raney, "Beyond Campaign Sites: Politicians Seek Support for Legislation Online," *New York Times,* April 18, 1999.

25. Ibid. Many state legislatures are ahead of Congress in their use of information technology. Thus, for example, laptop computers are prohibited on the House and Senate floors. Their use is encouraged in most state legislatures. Becky Neilson, "State Legislatures Are Leading the Way in the Use of Technology to Improve Lawmaking," *Hill,* July 21, 1999.

26. Quoted in Terry M. Neal, "Candidates Hit the Electronic Hustings," *Washington Post,* April 26, 1999.

27. Ibid.

28. Ibid.

29. Stephanopoulos, *All Too Human,* 158.

30. David Maraniss, *First in His Class: A Biography of Bill Clinton* (New York: Simon & Schuster, 1995). See examples on pp. 42, 91, 115, 139, and 240.

31. This observation will, no doubt, come as a surprise to many serving in the White House staff during this time. Thus, for example, George Stephanopoulos described an endless series of crises, which very nearly led to a nervous breakdown. As he conceded, however, many of the problems were self-induced. See *All Too Human.*

32. "Presidential News Conference," *Congressional Quarterly Weekly Report,* April 22, 1995, 1140.

33. Stanley A. Renshon, *High Hopes: The Clinton Presidency and the Politics of Ambition* (New York: Routledge, 1998), 302–3.

34. Ibid., 303.

35. Quoted in Michael Kelly, "You Ain't Seen Nothing Yet," *New Yorker,* April 24, 1995, 41.

36. As reported in Gary C. Jacobson, "The 1994 House Elections in Perspective," in *Midterm: Elections of 1994 in Context,* edited by Philip Klinkner (Boulder, Colo.: Westview Press, 1996), 6–7.

37. The text was printed in the *Washington Post,* November 10, 1994.

38. Byron E. Shafer pointed out that there are periods in which large issues dominate to an extent that an integrative program is possible, one susceptible to labels—for example, the New Deal, the Great Society. The present period lacks any such overriding set of issues—most rather are directed to refining those programs already set in place. See Byron E. Shafer and William J. M. Claggett, *The Two Majorities: The Issue Context of Modern*

American Politics (Baltimore: Johns Hopkins University Press, 1995), especially chap. 2.

39. Quoted in Karen Hosler, "GOP Gets a Glimpse of the Promised Land," *Baltimore Sun,* May 14, 1995.

40. Stephanopoulos, *All Too Human,* 398. Evidence for the Republican conclusion was Clinton's shift from a ten-year to a seven-year balanced budget, Dick Morris's contacts with Trent Lott, and Clinton's calls to Gingrich.

41. Richard Morin, "Public Sides with Clinton over GOP in Fiscal Fight, Poll Finds," *Washington Post*, November 21, 1995.

42. For details, see Morris, *Behind the Oval Office,* 80.

43. Stephen Skowronek, "President Clinton and the Risks of 'Third-Way' Politics," *Extensions* (Spring 1996), 11.

44. As outlined in Charles O. Jones, *Clinton and Congress, 1993–1996: Risk, Restoration, and Reelection* (Norman: University of Oklahoma Press, 1999), 143–44.

45. For details, see ibid., 144–65.

46. A Clinton cabinet secretary pointed out that "if an agency wants to sell the White House on something, they have to use the same techniques that the White House uses, including the use of polls to sell an issue, the use of focus groups, and the agencies themselves are developing more than an event management capacity, but a capacity to do policy development at a very sophisticated level that integrates the use of things that you would normally use in a campaign." Transcript, "Transitions to Governing," American Enterprise Institute, Washington, D.C., January 5, 1999, 22–23.

47. Remarks at the Woodrow Wilson International Center for Scholars, Smithsonian Institution, at a conference "Presidential Power Revisited," June 13, 1996.

48. Richard M. Nixon, *RN: The Memoirs of Richard Nixon* (New York: Grosset and Dunlap, 1978), 278. Emphasis in original.

49. Quoted in Richard L. Berke, "Clinton Admits to Concerns as Gore Campaign Stumbles," *New York Times*, May 14, 1999.

50. Richard L. Berke, "Clinton Calls Gore 'Smart' to Maintain His Distance," *New York Times,* May 14, 1999.

51. And these were troubled presidencies, with Taft and Bush finding it most difficult to establish independent identities. See the most interesting essay: Walter Dean Burnham, "The Legacy of George Bush: Travails of an Understudy," in *The Election of 1992: Reports and Interpretations,* edited by Gerald Pomper (Chatham, N.J.: Chatham House Publishers, 1993), chap. 1.

52. Ceci Connolly, "Clinton and Gore Are Awkward Texas Sidekicks," *Washington Post*, May 28, 1999.

53. Substantial anecdotal evidence supports the view that presidential candidates select running mates with contrasting styles that, by comparison, emphasize their strengths. That fact does not necessarily hamper the vice president in seeking the office himself if he can successfully elevate his own

strengths as suited to the job. Where the president is a constant campaigner, however, the vice president may have less opportunity to make the substitution or escape direct comparison.

54. John M. Broder, "Clinton Says He's Not Slowing Down," *New York Times*, July 1, 1999.

55. For example, the *USA Today*/CNN/Gallup poll following his acquittal by the Senate reported: 53 percent of respondents did not believe that acquittal vindicated him; 59 percent believed that he lowered the stature of the presidency; 57 percent had a negative opinion of him as a person; 62 percent believed that he is not honest and trustworthy. Richard Benedetto, "Poll: Mixed Reviews for Clinton Continue," *USA Today*, February 15, 1999. Similar results were reported in the *Washington Post* poll (summary provided on the Internet at www.washingtonpost.com/wp-srv/politics/polls).

56. Quoted in "President Gives First Lady Advice on Senate," *CNN: Interactive*, May 31, 1999.

57. Quoted in Charles O. Jones, *Passages to the Presidency: From Campaigning to Governing* (Washington: Brookings Institution Press, 1998), 109.

58. Charles O. Jones, *The Presidency in a Separated System* (Washington, D.C.: Brookings Institution Press, 1994), 297.

59. Richard E. Neustadt, *Presidential Power and the Modern Presidents: The Politics of Leadership from Roosevelt to Reagan* (New York: Free Press, 1990), 150.

60. Jones, *The Presidency in a Separated System*, 294–95.

9

Conclusion:
The Permanent Campaign and the
Future of American Democracy
Norman J. Ornstein and Thomas E. Mann

We live in the era of the permanent campaign. As Hugh Heclo's brief
history makes clear, even if campaigning and governing are inextri-
cably interlinked in American-style democracy, the process is dis-
tinctly different now from what it was some decades ago. Sidney
Blumenthal popularized the term *permanent campaign* in 1982, but
the change goes back further. Systematic and sophisticated polling
in presidential campaigns reached nearly its full bloom in 1960, but
the process of tracking public views, or of politicians' garnering
support from the public for their priorities, is not what we mean by
the *permanent campaign.* Rather, it is, as Heclo suggests, "a *nonstop*
process seeking to manipulate sources of public approval to engage
in the act of governing itself." In this era of the permanent campaign, the process of campaigning and the process of governing
have each lost their distinctiveness. Just as significant, the process
of campaigning has become in many ways the dominant partner of
the two.

As Charles O. Jones suggests, Bill Clinton is the epitome of a
politician governing via a continuous campaign—a process changed
not at all by his inability to run for a third term. In his eighth and
final year in the White House, Clinton remains in full campaign
mode. And many would argue that the 2000 presidential campaign
began not with the first formal contest for party delegates in Iowa in

January 2000, nor even at the conclusion of the last presidential election, but with the carefully showcased keynote speech of Vice President (and heir apparent) Al Gore at the Democratic convention that renominated Bill Clinton in August 1996—or even with Gore's selection in 1992.

The permanent campaign means that campaigns are nonstop and year-round, and governing/campaigning/governing/campaigning takes place in a continuous loop. Campaign consultants move without pause from the campaign trail to work for the victorious elected officials and help to shape their policy messages and frame issues for advantage in the next campaign. As described by Kathryn Dunn Tenpas, some consultants go directly on the White House or congressional payroll; others work via contract with the party national committees (at high rates of compensation via soft money). Yet others provide inside advice without direct charge and make their money by lobbying their former campaign clients on behalf of a wide range of new clients including corporations, foreign governments, labor unions, and wealthy individuals. When policy and political aides leave White House, Senate, or House staffs, they regularly join campaign consulting shops or lobbying operations.

Legislative proposals, routinely subjected to intense polling and focus groups before they are launched, are thereafter monitored by tracking polls. Outside groups complement their inside lobbying with advertising campaigns designed to shape the policy agenda and define the terms of debate—a practice well documented in the chapter by Burdett Loomis. As elections approach, many of those groups run "issue" advertising campaigns, indistinguishable from electioneering, that target candidates directly—often with less issue content than any other kind of advertising, including that of the candidates. More recently, political parties have become the biggest players in the sham-issue-advocacy game. Funded in substantial part with soft (unregulated) money, their broadcast ads make no pretense of discussing issues or promoting parties—they are overwhelmingly attack ads against specific candidates run only in the relevant electoral jurisdictions.

The permanent campaign takes place on the campaign trail, on the airwaves, on the floors of the House and Senate, in the Oval

Office—and increasingly in the courts and in law offices. Private groups now almost routinely orchestrate legal challenges to laws they oppose, sue government and their adversaries, and use the discovery process to troll for politically embarrassing revelations about their opponents. Meanwhile, as Anthony Corrado makes crystal clear, congressional leaders devote more and more of their time and energies to building campaign war chests, for themselves and their parties, an activity that distracts from (or shapes) their governing responsibilities. Many legislators turn their attention to amassing extra campaign funds, via leadership PACs, to distribute to party colleagues to build chits for possible runs for congressional leadership posts in parties or committees and thus further interconnect campaigns and legislative activities. Elected officials, including high-ranking leaders in Congress, also now are often willing to campaign directly against their colleagues on the other side of the aisle and thus violate an unwritten norm that persisted for decades and damage the bipartisan comity of the legislature.

The press is also involved. For decades, critics of campaign journalists decried the excessive media focus on the "horse race," on who was up or down, and on the strategies and tactics of the contenders, as opposed to a focus on what the candidates stood for or how they would implement their plans if elected. Reporters now increasingly cover policy battles in Congress and the White House as campaigns, with the focus on who is winning and losing and on the motives and machinations of the players, not on the stakes or the choices involved.

The Good Old Days?

As Heclo, David Brady and Morris Fiorina, and Jones suggest, earlier eras in American political history were not halcyon periods of warmth, comity, and studious nonpartisan debate about important policy challenges. Through most of American history, politics and campaigns were frequently rough-and-tumble, rowdy, even harsh, and occasionally physically dangerous. Rhetoric could be scorching between the White House and Capitol Hill and in the House and the Senate.

But distinct differences exist between earlier eras and today. For most of American history, campaigns generally were confined to the latter half of election years, and when the campaign ended, the governing began—after a lengthy transition interval of more than four months. Political actors accepted as a matter of course that once the campaigns were over, erstwhile adversaries would often become allies. With rare exceptions, campaign bitterness was generally confined to one's opponent, not directed at all members of his or her party. The day after the election, campaign materials were put away, as Christmas lights are boxed and returned to the attic after the holidays, and the tools and personnel for governing emerged.

So what changed? Heclo suggests six trends that brought us a pattern of campaigning to govern and governing to campaign. First are the changing roles of political parties. They are weaker in organization, candidate recruitment, and mobilization and stronger in ideology, social distinctiveness, and attack politics. Second is the expansion of an open and extensive system of interest-group politics. Third is the new communications technology of modern politics. Fourth are new political technologies, especially public relations and polling. Fifth is the ever growing need for political money. Last are the higher stakes, for all actors, in activist government.

Those factors are, of course, interrelated. The rise of the modern interest-group system was shaped in large part by the growth of the federal government and the collapse of the parties as vital and consequential umbrella organizations that could act as interest-group surrogates at both the national and, in machine areas, the local levels. The new communications technologies led to the advent of modern polling techniques, modern commercial advertising approaches that could be applied to politics and policy battles, and modern fund-raising (such as direct mail). The telecommunications revolution also led to vast expansion of the avenues of communication and made it more difficult and costly to get a message across to a broad audience and to cut through the cacophony of hundreds of competing "narrowcast" messages—hence the need for more money by candidates and parties to communicate with voters.

It is a fundamental reality that America is not going to return to the earlier era in which campaigning and governing had a distinct separation. Even if one or two of the factors Heclo outlines were to change or reverse their modern trends—if, for example, parties became stronger in organization and mobilization, or the need for political money diminished via reform—the other factors and their interrelationship mean that some version of a permanent campaign is, well, permanent.

Modern telecommunications are not going to disappear or slow down in innovation or breadth. Campaign consultants, public relations firms engaged in politics, political pollsters, issue-advocacy organizations, party campaign committees, and congressional leadership campaign organizations are firmly established and will not fade away. Journalists, their editors, and their producers will not readily downplay the horse-race framework in their coverage of election and legislative campaigns. Good or bad, that is reality. As Charles O. Jones suggests, it is a reality Americans need to recognize, and politicians need to accommodate, so that they can channel the phenomena that reinforce the permanent campaign to best advantage in their desire to govern.

Certainly, it would be a mistake to lionize the politics of the prepermanent campaign era or to demonize excessively the political dynamics of today. Politics in an earlier era insulated policymakers from campaign pressures—even as it insulated voters from the decisionmaking process. If voters largely remain uninvolved today, they at least have access to vastly more information than did voters in earlier periods. "Smoke-filled rooms" let politicians wheel and deal, logroll, and bargain without facing a barrage of television ads demanding action or threatening retribution—but also allowed a small group of elites to exclude others, including not just poor people but other competing interests, while they cut deals in their own interest outside public view. Corruption of different varieties was often tolerated or at least occurred with little opportunity for investigative reporters or independent legal authorities to root it out and deal with it.

Some changes that brought about the permanent campaign were reformist reactions to corruption and insulation, with both positive effects and unintended consequences. For all its problems, the era of the permanent campaign has not kept Americans from throwing incumbent administrations out of office, showing their displeasure with policy directions, or signaling their desire for change. The era of the permanent campaign has opened a window onto the operations of parties and policymaking, provided an unprecedented cornucopia of information and insight into politics, politicians, and policy processes, and created a huge number of avenues for participation by Americans of all stripes—even if most people have not followed them and even if much of the participation has been dominated by smaller numbers of ideological activists. New avenues for participation, including the Internet's capacity for instant and costless communication between voters and their representatives, offer great promise for broadened public participation.

The Costs of the Permanent Campaign

But the increase in openness and the opportunities for accountability that accompanied the ascendance of campaigning over governing have come at a substantial price. One part of the price, ironically, has been paid in public cynicism and disengagement. Opportunities for public participation in politics abound—but less than half the voting-age population cast a ballot in the last presidential election, almost fourteen percentage points below the turnout in 1960.[1] Moreover, the youngest cohorts' striking disengagement from politics promises even lower turnout rates in the future.[2]

Contemporary election campaign practices, including attack ads with nasty, inaccurate, and unfair charges, have left millions of Americans manifestly dissatisfied with the electoral process and disposed to assume the worst about those who compete for their attention and votes. The same style of attack ads, applied in policy wars in Washington and in sham "issue-advocacy" barrages against candidates, has added to the cynicism about the legitimacy of policy decisions. Media coverage of presidential campaigns, especially on local television news programs, has shrunk in recent cycles, and much of what is provided does little to engage or inform ordinary citizens. Coverage of other races is minuscule compared with the presidential ones![3] As Stephen Hess notes in his chapter, the dramatic consolidation in media, with major new entrants like Loews and General Electric having no experience in news, has contributed to the declining news hole.

Most important, campaigning has become increasingly antithetical to governing. Candidates decreasingly use campaigns to build public support for governing decisions or to forge public consensus before making policy and decreasingly look for ways to insulate controversial or difficult policy decisions from the vulnerability of campaigns to demagoguery and oversimplicity. Legislative leaders no longer apply rules or norms to make votes and policy decisions less open to campaign manipulation. Instead, parties and individual officeholders have fallen into patterns where they routinely manipulate the policy process to gain tactical advantage in the next election. Candidates often frame campaign themes and take positions in ways that frustrate rather than facilitate the task of governing after the election.

Campaigning intrinsically is a zero-sum game with a winner and a loser. Governing, ideally, is an additive game that tries to avoid pointing fingers or creating winners and losers in the policy battles. Campaigning and campaigners use the language of war—opponents are enemies to be vanquished. Policymakers use the language of negotiation—today's adversaries may be tomorrow's allies. The more campaigning absorbs governing, the more difficult it becomes to facilitate coalition building and the more strained are intraparty relations. Modern polling, as Karlyn Bowman notes, exacerbates those problems as pollsters "chart the performance of elected office holders the same way they cover the fortunes of candidates."

We can decry those developments as long and as intensely as we want. But as Charles O. Jones emphasizes, we cannot wish them away. The question is what can be done to enhance the positive developments, like improved communications and information, and the opportunities for greater accountability, while ameliorating the negative ones. Can issues of governing be injected into campaigns? Can a meaningful transition be created, one that creates a real separation from the campaign to the period of governing and that facilitates a smooth and expeditious entry into policymaking? Can the corrosively cynical political climate that has flowed from the dynamics of the permanent campaign be altered? Can the use of extrainstitutional mechanisms like lawsuits and the discovery process or accusations of ethics violations to further political goals be reduced or discouraged?

Both small and large steps might be able to tilt the American political system a bit away from the obsession with campaigns and campaign tactics and a bit toward a focus on governing and coalition building. If changing political culture is extraordinarily difficult, it is not impossible. Several years ago, some distinguished political scientists devised the "broken windows" thesis to reduce urban crime. Their belief was that crime had been encouraged by a crime culture that signaled that anything was allowable and infractions would likely go unpunished. The indicators of this culture included things like out-of-control graffiti, buildings with large numbers of broken windows, and toleration of turnstile violators on subways and of "squeegee operators" shaking down motorists at stop signs. Small steps taken to end those practices and punish violators would have larger impact: they would signal the end of the "anything goes" culture.[4]

The broken windows thesis has apparently worked, as evidenced by the dramatic declines in urban crime in cities across America. It is quite plausible that small but significant steps taken to challenge today's corrosive political culture, such as reforming the appointment and confirmation process of executive appointees, would have a positive impact on that broader culture.

It would be a mistake, however, just to focus on the obvious problems of today's politics. One of the most important factors underlying the rise of the permanent campaign has been change in telecommunications. As change in telecommunications continues and accelerates, contemporary politics will be transformed even more. Cyberdemocracy will bring its own consequences that will further challenge the governing process and deliberative democracy generally. Those intent on moving American politics more toward a focus on governing must anticipate what future deleterious developments may emerge.

Coping with the Present

During this time of extraordinary economic prosperity and encouraging improvements in a wide range of social indicators, the public is inclined toward the view that "the country works, but Washington doesn't."[5] That view may be a bit unfair, given the positive contributions of policy decisions in turning budget deficits into surpluses and the restraint exercised by policymakers in avoiding actions that might well have frustrated constructive steps taken in the private and nonprofit sectors. But the strength of Senator John McCain's insurgent candidacy for the Republican presidential nomination underscores the extent to which the features of contemporary politics that Americans find distasteful are associated with nonstop year-round campaigning for election and for policy. The ubiquitous political consultants, pollsters, fund-raisers, public relations specialists, talk news entertainers, and pundits create an impression that politics and governance are bereft of principles, hopelessly rigged by special interests, and manipulated and gamed by politicians consumed by their own reelection. Money fuels the permanent campaign in ways that distort how politicians spend their time and the process of gaining advantage in national policymaking.

The intensely competitive position of the political parties and the high political and policy stakes of the 2000 elections exacerbate those features and complicate efforts to mitigate the harmful effects of the permanent campaign. In the short term, the best one can hope for is a "broken windows" strategy for the political system. That would entail a series of modest steps—by politicians, journalists, activists, and citizens, in formal rules and informal practices—to articulate serious differences rather than to generate artificial conflict, to engage in genuine deliberation rather than crude manipulation, to accept the legitimacy of one's political adversaries rather than to attempt to destroy them, and to search for reasonable accommodation of policy differences rather than to wage unyielding war.

Pious exhortation is unlikely to sway politicians, the press, or the public to take the initial steps that might eventually accumulate to noticeable change in the political culture. Proposals for improving the practice and coverage of campaigning and governing must serve the interests of the key actors if those proposals are to have any chance of being adopted and sustained. There is no denying the reality that, as the Task Force on Campaign Reform put it recently, "candidates want to win elections, journalists want to exercise their craft, media executives want to earn profits, and citizens want to be informed and entertained and see the 'right' candidates win."[6] But self-interest, rightly understood, need not be devoid of all considerations of the health and vitality of the broader political community. The challenge is to appeal to those larger values without threatening the proximate goals of candidates, journalists, and citizens.

One place to begin is to inject realistic questions about governing into election campaigns. Now they tend to be at most an afterthought, relegated by candidates and the media far behind the campaign narrative, character, and issues. Yet those governing questions become absolutely central the day after the election—to the president-elect and his key advisers, to the new Congress, to the pool of candidates for high-level political appointments, and to the same journalists who largely avoid those questions during the campaign—not to mention to the citizens waiting to see how the election now concluded will influence their lives.[7]

In a general sense, those questions of governance touch on a presidential candidate's conception of the presidency in the American system of separated institutions; his recognition of the contextual dimensions of leadership (the nature of the times; public needs, wants, and engagement; the balance of party and ideology in Congress; the structure, resources, and strategies of those outside government seeking to influence policy); his executive temperament (organizing the White House, picking trusted advisers, staffing the administration, plugging into the permanent government, using information, and making decisions); and his appreciation of the need to think seriously about governing and the transition before the election. Routinely posing questions during the campaign about transition planning, recruiting and confirming political executives, developing a realistic legislative agenda, building majority and supermajority coalitions in Congress, and forging domestic political support for foreign policy leadership might modestly improve the climate for governing after the election. At the very least, presidents-elect will be forced to think about those matters before it is too late and possibly take steps to avoid a slow and ineffectual launch of their administration.

Small but significant steps might also be taken in Congress to try to deescalate the permanent campaign. While both parties, with justification, have their sights set on the majority in the next Congress, neither has any chance of achieving anything approaching working control, even if the election brings an end to divided government. Cross-party coalitions will be essential for the enactment of any positive policy agenda. After years of growing ideological polarization between the parties in Congress, signs of new life in the political center are beginning to appear. Those stirrings, more apparent in the Senate than in the House, ought to be encouraged by the new leadership and reinforced with steps to clear the air of the fumes that have poisoned the atmosphere in Congress in recent years. That is partly a matter of the tone set by the president and majority and minority leadership at the beginning of the new administration and Congress. But two areas merit more concerted attention.

First, something more should be done to discourage the abuse of criminal investigations, civil lawsuits, and congressional investigations for transparently political purposes. The demise of the independent counsel statute in June 2000 was a useful first step. Instead of removing sensitive matters of potential misbehavior by public officials from the cloud of conflict of interest, the statute served as a magnet for politically inspired demands by both parties and their allies for ever more special investigations. Let the Justice Department take responsibility and be held accountable for handling such matters.

But that is only a first step. Restraint at both ends of Pennsylvania Avenue is needed to reestablish some modicum of trust between the branches. The new president has to set a tenor of ethical behavior and forthrightness in responding to legitimate requests for information. The majority in Congress, especially if divided government continues, must resist the temptation to destroy the president politically by misusing its power to investigate and to impeach. And both should work together to find appropriate ways of limiting the abuse of the discovery process by ideological groups using civil litigation to advance their political agenda. That will also require more responsible behavior by federal judges overseeing such lawsuits and less sensational and more nuanced coverage of scandal allegations by the media. The latter, given recent experience and competitive pressures, will require a sharp change in press culture that seems unlikely now.

Second, it is hard to see how the permanent campaign can be contained in Congress without reducing the role of congressional party leaders in campaign fund-raising. The Corrado chapter shows how in the past several election cycles the congressional campaign committees have become major players in congressional election financing, especially in the soft-money market. Raising funds in soft-money multiples (five-, six-, or even seven-digit amounts) requires the personal involvement of congressional leaders—those who can speak authoritatively about agendas, schedules, and rules. The more the congressional party leaders involve themselves in high-stakes fund-raising and national campaign strategy, the more difficult it is for them to separate their governing responsibilities from the imperatives of campaigning.

While the broad topic of campaign finance reform is exceedingly complex and beyond the scope of this chapter, two steps seem particularly promising. The abolition of party soft money would lessen the pressure on congressional party leaders to spend so much of their time fund-raising. Much smaller hard-money contributions, even with limits raised to account for inflation, would not require the same level of personal involvement by congressional leaders. In addition, curbing the abuses of nonprofit political organizations, which exploit ambiguities in the law to avoid disclosure and limits on contributions, would remove a powerful mechanism for congressional party leaders to build off-the-book campaign organizations that inevitably link policy and fund-raising.

Back to the Future

Coping with the contemporary manifestations of the permanent campaign, in part by encouraging a series of small steps that might limit some of its harmful effects on our democracy, is itself a tall order. The challenge becomes even more daunting when we contemplate the rapid pace of change in modes of communication and the nature of politics and governance lying ahead.

We have barely reached the most primitive stages of e-democracy and e-government. Initial research findings that the use of the Internet in campaigns and elections largely reinforces the current structure of American politics—by producing greater polarization of political discourse and enlarging the gap between information haves and have-nots—are specific to this early period. As the forms, uses, and reach of digital technology multiply, so too will the technology newly shape public life in a myriad of ways. The attraction of "Third Wave Utopianism" has spawned a cottage industry of futurists opining on the possibilities of a more robust participatory democracy in the information age. The Internet and its successors will surely transform the way campaigns are waged, elections are conducted, public officials are contacted, citizens organize and cooperate, and the policy process operates. But it is by no means clear that the net impact of new communication technologies on politics and governance will be beneficial—or even benign.

Various forms of cyberdemocracy could well intensify the permanent campaign. Recent experience suggests that making government more open and inclusive and giving citizens unprecedented access to information about public affairs is not inconsistent with increasing public cynicism and disengagement from politics. An irony of this era is that plebiscitary politics is on the rise at a time when the public is turning off politics. A greater burden is being placed on a citizenry that is largely disconnected from the world of public affairs. Widespread public disengagement from politics elevates the importance of money and the influence of those highly motivated to participate. That admixture makes the political system especially vulnerable (in Heclo's words) to the professionally managed efforts of elites to orchestrate and amplify the supposed voices of the people to serve their own interests. That, of course, is the essence of the permanent campaign. And it is not difficult to imagine how a networked society could reinforce that pattern.

The central questions are whether and how the new technologies might be harnessed to reinvigorate citizen engagement in public affairs without further weakening the institutions of representative (and deliberative) democracy. Can the possibilities of the digital world be exploited creatively to improve the quality of campaigning and of governing in a way that at least partially recovers the distinctive elements of each? To imagine how that question might be answered in the future, we may go back to the animating principles and the debates at the founding of the American republic. The principles are embedded in the Constitution and *The Federalist Papers,* but they have been subject to recurrent challenge beginning with the Anti-Federalist opposition during the ratification debates over 200 years ago.

The Federalist case was built upon a belief that the self-interested ambitions of representatives must be channeled to serve the larger public purposes of government—namely, securing the rights of life, liberty, and the pursuit of happiness. That required an extended republic, a multiplicity of factions, an institutional separation and sharing of powers, and a deliberative assembly, featuring informed direct discussion among elected members who do not simply reflect the opinions and factions that exist in the general public but instead "refine and enlarge the public views."[8] Terms longer than one year were essential to give members time to live near, talk to, and work with their colleagues and thus broaden the perspectives they brought with them from home.[9] Also essential was explicit rejection of instruction, recall, and rotation.

The Anti-Federalists favored vigilant watch and zealous control over the actions of their representatives. In the words of the Federal Farmer:

> A full and equal representation is that which possesses the same interests, feelings, opinions, and views the people themselves would were they all assembled—a fair representation, therefore, should be so regulated that every order of men in the community, according to the common course of elections, can have a share in it.[10]

They favored small legislative districts, frequent elections, the ability of citizens to instruct representatives on specific issues, the power to recall representatives in midterm, and mandatory rotation.

The objective was for Congress to mirror the electorate and for the political system to get as close to direct democracy as possible.

While the Anti-Federalists lost the immediate battle when the Constitution was ratified, the democratic values they championed soon challenged the republican cautions of many of the Founding Fathers. Their arguments and the public sentiment they spoke for have exerted a powerful force on American politics throughout our history. Today, with the rapidly developing information superhighway, they seem once again poised to take the ascendant position in the debate over how we govern ourselves.

Can the republican form of government imagined by Madison be adapted for the digital age? The complexity of public problems, the rich diversity of our nation, and the personal preoccupations of its citizens make most conceptions of electronically facilitated direct democracy infeasible if not dangerous. At the same time, it is wildly unrealistic to imagine wholesale delegation of responsibility to elected representatives that flies in the face of the democratic wish. The trick is to rehabilitate both democratic and republican instruments of governance. In the first instance, as Heclo puts it, "organizing the talk of democracy in ways that make it better—more honest, more deliberative . . . [thereby] engaging the informed and active consent of a much broader public."[11] In the second, it means creating incentives and structures for elected officials to take seriously their responsibility to help create that more informed public, which in turn can nurture and support genuine discussion, bargaining, and compromise in legislative bodies.

Notes

1. Committee for the Study of the American Electorate, *Early Summer Report 1998.*
2. Richard Kimball, Lance LeLoup, Nicholas Lovrich, Brent Steel, and Robert Sahr, *Project Vote Smart/Pew Charitable Trusts General Population and Youth Survey on Civic Engagement Summer 1999* (Philipsburg, Mont.: Project Vote Smart, 1999).
3. See, for example, Barbara Bliss Osborn, "Election Neglected on L.A.'s Local TV," *EXTRA!* (July/August 1997).
4. James Q. Wilson and George L. Kelling, "Broken Windows: The Police and Neighborhood Safety," *Atlantic Monthly* 249, no. 3 (March 1982): 29–38.

5. This formulation was suggested by *Los Angeles Times* political reporter Ronald Brownstein.

6. *Campaign Reform Insights and Evidence: Report of the Task Force on Campaign Reform* (Princeton: Woodrow Wilson School of Public and International Affairs, 1998).

7. Thomas E. Mann and Norman J. Ornstein, "After the Campaign, What? Governance Questions for the 2000 Election," *Brookings Review* 18, no. 1 (Winter 2000): 44–48.

8. *The Federalist Papers* No. 10.

9. See, for example, *The Federalist Papers* No. 53.

10. Federal Farmer, "Letter of October 9, 1787," in *The Anti-Federalist: Writings by Opponents of the Constitution,* edited by Herbert J. Storing (Chicago: University of Chicago Press, 1985), 39.

11. Hugh Heclo, "Hyperdemocracy," *Wilson Quarterly* (Winter 1999): 71.

Index

About the Editors and the Contributors

Norman J. Ornstein is a resident scholar at the American Enterprise Institute for Public Policy Research and cochair of the President's Advisory Committee on Public Interest Obligations of Digital Television Broadcasters. His books include *Renewing Congress* (with Thomas E. Mann), *Debt and Taxes* (with John H. Makin), *Intensive Care: How Congress Shapes Health Policy* (with Thomas E. Mann), and *Vital Statistics on Congress 1999–2000* (with Thomas E. Mann and Michael J. Malbin).

Thomas E. Mann is the W. Averell Harriman Senior Fellow in American Governance at the Brookings Institution, where he was previously director of the Governmental Studies Program. With Norman J. Ornstein he codirected the AEI-Brookings Renewing Congress Project, which produced *Congress, the Press, and the Public* and *Intensive Care: How Congress Shapes Health Policy*. He is the author of *Vital Statistics on Congress 1999–2000* (with Thomas E. Mann and Michael J. Malbin). He coedited *Campaign Finance Reform: A Sourcebook* with Anthony Corrado, Daniel Ortiz, Trevor Potter, and Frank Sorauf.

Karlyn Bowman is a resident fellow at the American Enterprise Institute, where she edits the public opinion section of *The American Enterprise*. She is the author of numerous books, including *The 1993–1994 Debate on Health Care Reform: Did the Polls Mislead the*

Policy Makers?, *Attitudes toward the Environment: Twenty-Five Years after Earth Day* (with Everett Carll Ladd), *Public Opinion in America and Japan: How We See Each Other and Ourselves* (with Everett Carll Ladd), and *What's Wrong: A Survey of American Satisfaction and Complaint*.

David Brady is the McCoy Professor of Political Science at the Graduate School of Business and the Department of Political Science at Stanford University. He is a member of the American Academy of Arts and Sciences.

Anthony Corrado is associate professor of government at Colby College. He currently serves as cochair of the Campaign Finance Institute and as chair of the American Bar Association Advisory Commission on Election Law. He is the author of *Campaign Finance Reform: Beyond the Basics* and coauthor of *Campaign Finance Reform: A Sourcebook*.

Morris Fiorina is professor of political science and a senior fellow of the Hoover Institution at Stanford University. Previously, he taught at the California Institute of Technology and at Harvard University. He is the author of many books, including *Representatives, Roll Calls, and Constituencies, Congress—Keystone of the Washington Establishment*, and *Divided Government*. On the editorial boards of numerous journals, he is a member of the American Academy of Arts and Sciences and the National Academy of Sciences.

Hugh Heclo is the Clarence J. Robinson Professor at George Mason University and former professor of government at Harvard University. He has served as a consultant to the Office of Personnel Management, the National Research Council, the Office of Management and Budget, the General Accounting Office, and the British Department of Health and Social Security. He is the author of such prize-winning books as *Modern Social Politics* and *A Government of Strangers* and is a member of the American Academy of Arts and Sciences and the National Academy of Public Administration.

Stephen Hess is a senior fellow in the Governmental Studies Program at the Brookings Institution. He served on the presidential staffs of Dwight D. Eisenhower and Richard M. Nixon. He is the author of many books, including *International News and Foreign Correspondents, Drawn and Quartered: The History of American Political Cartoons, Live from Capitol Hill: Studies of Congress and the Media, The Presidential Campaign* (3d edition), and *The Little Book of Campaign Etiquette.*

Charles O. Jones is the Hawkins Professor of Political Science Emeritus at the University of Wisconsin Madison and a nonresident senior fellow at the Brookings Institution. He is a former president of the American Political Science Association and editor of the *American Political Science Review.* His recent books include *The Presidency in a Separated System, Passages to the Presidency: From Campaigning to Governing,* and *Clinton and Congress, 1993–1996: Risk, Restoration, and Reelection.*

Burdett A. Loomis is professor of political science at the University of Kansas, where he is program coordinator at the Robert J. Dole Institute for Public Service and Public Policy. His publications include *The New American Politician, The Sound of Money* (with Darrell West), and the edited volume *Esteemed Colleagues: Civility and Deliberation in the U.S. Senate.*

Kathryn Dunn Tenpas is associate director of the University of Pennsylvania's Washington Semester Program. Her research centers on American government, particularly the presidency, presidential campaigns and elections, and public opinion. She is the author of *Presidents as Candidates: Inside the White House for the Presidential Campaign* and has published articles in such journals as *Political Science Quarterly,* the *American Review of Politics, Presidential Studies Quarterly,* and the *Journal of Law and Politics.*